Evolutionary History

Uniting History and Biology to Understand Life on Earth

We tend to see history and evolution springing from separate roots, one grounded in the human world and the other in the natural world. Human beings have become, however, probably the most powerful species shaping evolution today, and human-caused evolution in populations of other species has probably been the most important force shaping human history. This book introduces readers to evolutionary history, a new field that unites history and biology to create a fuller understanding of the past than either field of study can produce on its own. Evolutionary history can stimulate surprising new hypotheses for any field of history and evolutionary biology. How many art historians would have guessed that sculpture encouraged the evolution of tuskless elephants? How many biologists would have predicted that human poverty would accelerate animal evolution? How many military historians would have suspected that plant evolution would convert a counterinsurgency strategy into a rebel subsidy? How many historians of technology would have credited evolution in the New World with sparking the Industrial Revolution? With examples from around the globe, this book will help readers see the broadest patterns of history and the details of their own lives in a new light.

Edmund Russell is Associate Professor in the Department of Science, Technology, and Society and the Department of History at the University of Virginia. He has won several awards for his work, including the Leopold-Hidy Prize for the best article published in *Environmental History* in 2003; the Edelstein Prize in 2003 for an outstanding book in the history of technology published in the preceding three years; and the Forum for the History of Science in America Prize in 2001 for the best article on the history of science in America published in the previous three years by a scholar within ten years of his or her PhD. His previous books include *Natural Enemy, Natural Ally: Toward an Environmental History of War* (coedited with Richard P. Tucker, 2004) and *War and Nature: Fighting Humans and Insects with Chemicals from World War I to* Silent Spring (Cambridge University Press, 2001). He has published articles in the *Journal of American History, Environmental History, Technology and Culture,* and the *Washington Post.*

Studies in Environment and History

Editors

Donald Worster, *University of Kansas*
J. R. McNeill, *Georgetown University*

Other Books in the Series

Donald Worster   *Nature's Economy: A History of Ecological Ideas*, second edition

Kenneth F. Kiple   *The Caribbean Slave: A Biological History*

Alfred W. Crosby   *Ecological Imperialism: The Biological Expansion of Europe, 900–1900*, second edition

Arthur F. McEvoy   *The Fisherman's Problem: Ecology and Law in the California Fisheries, 1850–1980*

Robert Harms   *Games against Nature: An Eco-Cultural History of the Nunu of Equatorial Africa*

Warren Dean   *Brazil and the Struggle for Rubber: A Study in Environmental History*

Samuel P. Hays   *Beauty, Health, and Permanence: Environmental Politics in the United States, 1955–1985*

Donald Worster   *The Ends of the Earth: Perspectives on Modern Environmental History*

Michael Williams   *Americans and Their Forests: A Historical Geography*

Timothy Silver   *A New Face on the Countryside: Indians, Colonists, and Slaves in the South Atlantic Forests, 1500–1800*

Theodore Steinberg   *Nature Incorporated: Industrialization and the Waters of New England*

J. R. McNeill   *The Mountains of the Mediterranean World: An Environmental History*

Elinor G. K. Melville   *A Plague of Sheep: Environmental Consequences of the Conquest of Mexico*

Richard H. Grove   *Green Imperialism: Colonial Expansion, Tropical Island Edens, and the Origins of Environmentalism, 1600–1860*

Mark Elvin and Tsui'jung Liu   *Sediments of Time: Environment and Society in Chinese History*

Robert B. Marks   *Tigers, Rice, Silk, and Silt: Environment and Economy in Late Imperial South China*

Thomas Dunlap   *Nature and the English Diaspora*

Andrew C. Isenberg   *The Destruction of the Bison: An Environmental History*

Edmund Russell   *War and Nature: Fighting Humans and Insects with Chemicals from World War I to Silent Spring*

Judith Shapiro   *Mao's War against Nature: Politics and the Environment in Revolutionary China*

Adam Rome   *The Bulldozer in the Countryside: Suburban Sprawl and the Rise of American Environmentalism*

Nancy J. Jacobs   *Environment, Power, and Injustice: A South African History*

Matthew D. Evenden   *Fish versus Power: An Environmental History of the Fraser River*

Myrna I. Santiago   *The Ecology of Oil: Environment, Labor, and the Mexican Revolution, 1900–1938*

Frank Uekoetter   *The Green and the Brown: A History of Conservation in Nazi Germany*

James L. A. Webb Jr.   *Humanity's Burden: A Global History of Malaria*

Richard W. Judd   *The Untilled Garden: Natural History and the Spirit of Conservation in America, 1740–1840*

Evolutionary History

Uniting History and Biology to Understand Life on Earth

EDMUND RUSSELL

University of Virginia

CAMBRIDGE
UNIVERSITY PRESS

Vincennes University
Shake Learning Resources Center
Vincennes, In 47591-9986

CAMBRIDGE UNIVERSITY PRESS
Cambridge, New York, Melbourne, Madrid, Cape Town, Singapore,
São Paulo, Delhi, Dubai, Tokyo, Mexico City

Cambridge University Press
32 Avenue of the Americas, New York, NY 10013-2473, USA

www.cambridge.org
Information on this title: www.cambridge.org/9780521745093

First published 2011

Printed in the United States of America

A catalog record for this publication is available from the British Library.

Library of Congress Cataloging in Publication data
Russell, Edmund, 1957–
Evolutionary history : uniting history and biology to understand
life on Earth / Edmund Russell.
p.   cm. – (Studies in environment and history)
Includes bibliographical references and index.
ISBN 978-0-521-76211-3 (hardback)
1. Evolution (Biology)   2. Evolution – History.   I. Title.
QH366.2.R88   2011
576.8–dc22   2010037126

ISBN 978-0-521-76211-3 Hardback
ISBN 978-0-521-74509-3 Paperback

This book is about continuity and change over generations,
so it is for the generation before me,
Anne Caldwell Russell (1934–1992) and Edmund Paul Russell Jr.,
and the generation after,
Anna Sankey Russell and Margaret Sankey Russell

Contents

Figures		*page* xi
Tables		xiii
Preface		xv
Acknowledgments		xix
1.	Matters of Life and Death	1
2.	Evolution's Visible Hands	6
3.	Hunting and Fishing	17
4.	Eradication	31
5.	Altering Environments	42
6.	Evolution Revolution	54
7.	Intentional Evolution	71
8.	Coevolution	85
9.	Evolution of the Industrial Revolution	103
10.	History of Technology	132
11.	Environmental History	145
12.	Conclusion	151
Note on Sources		167
Glossary		171
Notes		177
Index		211

Figures

2.1. Darwin's branching bush of evolution.   *page* 7
3.1. Hunting was an evolutionary force for elephants.   18
6.1. Domestication in action.   62
8.1. Rickets may be the reason for light skin.   88
9.1. Products of different evolutionary histories.   112
9.2. New cottons, then new machines.   115
9.3. Inventors capitalized on New World cotton.   116
9.4. Industry relied on New World fiber.   117
9.5. Paying a premium for New World traits.   118
9.6. Different genomes, different odds.   123
9.7. Old World cottons were superior in India.   126

Tables

2.1. Understanding of Evolution   *page* 9
9.1. Alternative Explanations for Industrialization of Cotton   130
12.1. Social Forces Have Shaped Evolution   154
12.2. Evolution Has Shaped Human History   162

Preface

Beverly Rathcke planted the seed of this book in a lecture she gave in an ecology class during my first semester in graduate school. She told us about cotton farmers who tried to control an insect pest by spraying an insecticide. This strategy worked for a while, but then a couple of puzzling things happened. The first was that farmers found themselves battling more and more **species**[1] of insect pests as the years went by. The second was that their insecticide lost its ability to kill insect species that it once had clobbered. Farmers substituted a new type of insecticide, which worked for a while, and then it, too, failed. They kept replacing insecticides, and increasing the frequency of spraying, until they had no poisons left. With no way of halting crop destruction by insects, farmers had no choice but to abandon growing cotton on thousands of acres.

To understand why farmers battled ever more species of pests over time, Beverly explained, one had to bring ecology to bear. One of the central concerns of this discipline is explaining the abundance of organisms. In farm fields, one finds many species of insects. Some species live in such large populations, and eat so much of a farmer's crops, that we call them pests. Populations of dozens of other insect species also live in farm fields, but most pass without notice because they cause no measurable damage to crops. In some cases, they are not pests because they eat something other than the crop. In other cases, they do feast on the crop, but their populations are too small to cause measurable losses. Several factors keep populations of insect species small, including predation by other species of insects. (Picture ladybugs preying on aphids.) This means that from the farmer's point of view, some insect species in fields are harmful (because they gobble up crops), but other insect species are beneficial (because they kill the insects that eat the crops).

A children's rhyme supplies an analogy. In the house that Jack built, Jack was like a farmer. The malt in the house that Jack built was like a crop. The rats that ate the malt in the house that Jack built resembled crop-eating insects. (Because we are talking about populations of animals rather than single individuals, we will make some species in the story plural.) The cats that ate the rats that ate the malt in the house that Jack built were predators akin to insects that prey on other insects. Now let us modify the story and add another species: the mouse. Mice lived in the house and ate the malt, but the cats killed them so efficiently that losses to mice were trivial. Mice resembled insect species living in farm fields in very small populations.

Now we have three species of mammals in Jack's house (not counting Jack) and a pair of predator-prey relations. One species, the rat, was numerous enough, and fond enough of malt, to qualify as a pest. A second malt-eating species, the mouse, inhabited the house in such low numbers one rarely noticed it and so it did not rise to pest status. A third species, the cat, benefited Jack by killing rats and mice. A similar cast of insect characters inhabited cotton fields – a large population of a crop-eating species (a pest), small populations of other crop-eating species, and populations of varying sizes of insect-eating (predatory) species.

Next imagine that Jack decided his losses to rats were unacceptably high. How might he respond? One way would be to import more cats. Another would be to poison the rats. Let us say Jack chose the latter route and scattered poison about the house. And let us say he chose a poison lethal to many mammalian species, including cats and mice, and these two species succumbed along with the rats. Furthermore, let us say other rats and mice lived in surrounding fields and migrated quickly into the house once the poison decayed. Cats, on the other hand, migrated in more slowly because they lived in the barns of distant neighbors. It would not be hard for populations of rats and mice to explode and for the mice to cause enough damage to join the rats as full-fledged pests. Now Jack lived in the house with lots of rats and mice but no cats. Ironically, in trying to kill one species, Jack accidentally helped a second species become a pest.

Insecticides had similar effects on insects in cotton fields. Many insecticides kill a wide range of insect species, beneficial as well as harmful. When spraying for one species of insect pest, farmers accidentally killed off populations of beneficial species of predatory insects, too. Freed from predation, populations of formerly rare plant-eating insect species blossomed into full-blown pests. Spraying thus had the ironic effect of increasing rather than decreasing the number of pest species. (Enough insect species have become pests as a by-product of spraying that entomologists have a term for them: *secondary pests*.) Spraying did not create new species, but it helped populations of several species become plentiful enough to cause economic problems. This explained why the number of pest species attacking cotton fields increased over time despite regular doses of insecticides.

To solve the second puzzle – the failure of insecticides to kill species they formerly controlled – Beverly turned to evolutionary theory. Unwittingly, cotton farmers had been carrying out experiments in **Darwinian evolution** by **natural selection**. In *On the Origin of Species*, **Charles Darwin** summed up his theory this way: if "variations useful to any organic being ever do occur, assuredly individuals thus characterized will have the best chance of being preserved in the struggle for life; and from the strong principle of inheritance, these will tend to produce offspring similarly characterized. This principle of preservation, or the survival of the fittest, I have called Natural Selection."[2]

Darwin would have little trouble applying his theory to insects in cotton fields. First, he would note that "variations useful" to individuals did occur. When spraying began, most individual insects of a given species in a given field (that is, a population) were susceptible to a given insecticide. A few individuals, however, were resistant to the insecticide because they happened to possess some biochemical machinery that detoxified the poison. So individuals varied in a "useful" **trait**. Second, Darwin would observe that this difference in traits influenced the "chance of being preserved in the struggle for life." Resistant individuals *survived* spraying more often than susceptible individuals. In Darwinian terms, spraying *selected* for one trait (**resistance**) and against another (**susceptibility**). Third, because of "the strong principle of inheritance," individual insects "produced offspring similarly characterized." Susceptible parents produced susceptible offspring, and resistant parents produced resistant offspring. Today we attribute "the strong principle of inheritance" to the passing of **genes** (strings of DNA with instructions for how cells should operate) for traits from parents to offspring.

Puzzle solved. Insecticides did not lose their ability to kill insects because the poisons changed; they lost their ability because the target insect populations changed. When spraying began, susceptible individuals outnumbered resistant individuals in a cotton field by far, which made the insecticide effective. But each round of spraying acted as a selective force, favoring the survival and reproduction of the resistant over the susceptible. Repeating this process over many insect generations increased the proportion of resistant individuals in the population until the insecticides failed to kill enough pests in the population to make it worth spraying. The insect population had evolved.

The encouragement of secondary pests and the evolution of resistance launched farmers onto something called the pesticide treadmill. In the short run, a pesticide worked, but in the long run, it failed. Farmers substituted a new insecticide, and the process repeated itself, ad infinitum. Beverly described this process as a **coevolutionary** arms race: insects evolved resistance, which led to a technological change by people, which led to more evolution for resistance, which led to more technological change, and so on. Farmers mimicked the Red Queen in *Alice in Wonderland*, running ever faster on the treadmill just to stay where they were.[3]

That evening, I gushed about Beverly's lecture to my wife as she was preparing dinner. (I think we were having burritos, but it could have been spaghetti. On our budget, we had one or the other most nights.) I have a feeling that even now, I have not identified all the reasons the story seemed so compelling, but I can point to some. It occupied the middle ground between the human and the natural. It showed reciprocal effects over time. It required the linking of tools from science (evolutionary ecology) and humanities (history) to understand events. You will see those same ideas in this book.

Acknowledgments

I owe many people debts for making this book possible. Beverly Rathcke and John Vandermeer, cochairs of my PhD committee at the University of Michigan, taught me about the role of human beings in ecology and evolution. I will always be grateful to them and to Earl Werner for encouraging me to write a history-oriented dissertation in a biology department as well as to three historians at Michigan (Richard Tucker, Gerald Linderman, and Susan Wright) for their support and advice as committee members. I wrote my dissertation while a predoctoral Fellow at the Smithsonian Institution's National Museum of American History, where curators and Fellows created a community that functioned much like a graduate program in history. Pete Daniel and Jeffrey Stine played especially important roles in helping a biologist become a historian. All these people helped me write my PhD dissertation, which used the history of chemical weapons and insecticides to examine the relationship between war and environmental change. The dissertation discussed the coevolution of insects and insecticides (among other things), and this book generalizes on that theme.

I was fortunate to publish my revised dissertation with Cambridge University Press (*War and Nature: Fighting Humans and Insects with Chemicals from World War I to* Silent Spring, 2001), which enabled me to work with Frank Smith and Donald Worster. They were model editors, patient and insightful in their advice. That experience led me to return to Cambridge with a proposal for a book on evolutionary history (defined in Chapter 1) using dogs as a case study. Frank advised splitting the book in two, with one book making a big argument about evolutionary history and the other focusing on the canine case study.

It was excellent advice and made me grateful, once again, to be working with such an astute and helpful editor. You have the first of those books in your hands, and I hope you will look for the dog book when it appears (also from Cambridge).

Frank Smith, Donald Worster, John McNeill (who now coedits the Cambridge series), Michael Grant, Brian Balogh, and Lucy Russell commented helpfully on the entire manuscript. Jonathan Wendel and Guy Ortolano offered excellent advice on Chapter 9. Brian Balogh also served as an important sounding board on our weekly walks. The book incorporates these people's suggestions about matters large and small. Tom Finger and Jennifer Kane have been model research assistants. Heather Norton and Jonathan Wendel responded with extraordinary care to queries about their work. Thank you all so much.

As editor of the journal *Environmental History*, Adam Rome played a key role in advancing the ideas in this book. I presented a conference paper with some rudimentary notions about evolution and history, and Adam suggested I turn the paper into an article. He did me a big favor by sending back the first two versions of the manuscript. The third, and much improved, version appeared as "Evolutionary History: Prospectus for a New Field," *Environmental History* 8 (April 2003): 204–228. *Environmental History* is a publication of the American Society for Environmental History and the Forest History Society, and I thank them for permission to reprint material from that essay in the chapter on environmental history (Chapter 11) and elsewhere in this book.

I owe a similar debt to the organizers of the 2002 Industrializing Organisms conference at Rutgers University: Philip Scranton, Susan Schrepfer, and Paul Israel. Philip and Susan edited a collection of essays growing out of the conference, which they subtitled "Introducing Evolutionary History." Introductory comments I made at the conference became a chapter in that volume (Edmund Russell, "Introduction: The Garden in the Machine: Toward an Evolutionary History of Technology," in *Industrializing Organisms: Introducing Evolutionary History*, ed. Susan R. Schrepfer and Philip Scranton [New York: Routledge, 2004], 1–16). I thank Taylor and Francis Group LLC for permission to reprint material from that essay in the chapter on history of technology (Chapter 10).

Figure 9.1, a photo of cotton bolls, appears here after a good-faith effort to find the rights holder. The photo appears without attribution in Arthur W. Silver, *Manchester Men and Indian Cotton 1847–1872* (Manchester University Press, 1966), 293. Manchester University Press has no record of the photo's source and claims no rights. The press and the history department at Temple University (the affiliation listed in the book for Mr. Silver) have no contact information. I was unable to find him in a Google search.

I have appreciated the support and advice of colleagues in the Department of Science, Technology, and Society and the Department of History at the University of Virginia. A sabbatical leave from the University of Virginia and a grant from the National Science Foundation (SES-0220764) supported research for this book. Any opinions, findings, and conclusions or recommendations expressed in this material are those of the author and do not necessarily reflect the views of the National Science Foundation. I thank those institutions and individuals for their support.

Audiences at Cambridge University, Massachusetts Institute of Technology, University of British Columbia, Juniata College, Virginia Tech, University of Kansas, University of Oklahoma, University of Virginia, the American Society for Environmental History annual meeting, the Society for the History of Technology annual meeting, and the Rutgers University conference on Industrializing Organisms commented helpfully on ideas.

Thanks go to my wife, Lucy, and our daughters Anna and Margaret for tolerating this project with good cheer. I could not live without you.

Charlottesville, Virginia
April 14, 2010

I

Matters of Life and Death

When I was thirteen, my grandfather died of a heart attack. He had entered the hospital for treatment of a prostate problem. Once there, he picked up an infection that led to heart failure. His death saddened me, of course, but it also puzzled me. I had seen wonder drugs such as penicillin cure ailments plaguing members of my family, so I could not understand why similar drugs would not have controlled my grandfather's infection. It seemed especially odd that he died in a hospital, where he should have benefited from the best treatment available. But the shelf of memory devoted to unsolved mysteries is long and dark, and I stored my grandfather's death there for decades.

Recently, I realized that a potential solution to the puzzle glowed on the computer screen in front of me. My grandfather's death might have been an example of this book's argument: people have encouraged evolution in populations of other species, which in turn has shaped human experience. I had known for decades that pathogens evolved resistance to antibiotics, but I had never applied that idea to the death of a loved one. The realization sent my heart racing and my fingers trembling so much I could not type for an hour.

Here is what might have happened. Before my grandfather arrived, doctors at a hospital in Omaha used a certain antibiotic (such as penicillin or a newer drug) after surgery to prevent and treat infections. It worked effectively. However, with time, a population of pathogenic bacteria living in the hospital evolved resistance to the drug. Alternatively, this strain may have evolved elsewhere and arrived at my grandfather's hospital in the body of a patient. (If evolution of resistance sounds mysterious, Chapter 2 is for you. For now, please take my word that populations of pathogens can evolve resistance to antibiotics.) Because this population differed in a trait (drug resistance) from other populations of the same species, we call it a **strain**.

Initially, doctors did not realize that a new, resistant strain had infected their patients, so they continued prescribing the same antibiotic that had worked in the past. Bacteria belonging to that strain traveled from one patient to the next on equipment and the hands of hospital personnel. Some rode a catheter into my grandfather's urinary tract, thrived despite antibiotic treatment, challenged a weakened body, sparked a fever (which stressed his heart), and contributed to my grandfather's death.

We can predict the fate of the pathogenic strain with some confidence because the pattern has repeated itself in hospitals around the world. After enough failures, doctors realized that the drug had lost potency against the pathogen in their hospital. They substituted a second antibiotic drug, the hospital's population of bacteria evolved resistance to it, doctors substituted a third antibiotic, and so on up to the present.

As for my grandfather and pathogens, so for the world. This book makes four arguments that help us understand events ranging in scale from the personal to the global:

1. People have shaped evolution in populations of human and non-human species.
2. Human-induced evolution has shaped human history.
3. Human and nonhuman populations have coevolved, or continually changed in response to each other.
4. A young, synthetic field called *evolutionary history* can help us understand the past and present better than history or biology alone.

We shall see evidence for these arguments and their implications throughout the book. Here let me list some examples to illustrate their significance:

1. Human beings shape evolution today more powerfully than any other species. We have encouraged game animals and fish to shrink in size, pathogens and pests to evolve resistance to poisons, and domestic plants and animals to display traits we value. Organisms evolve in specific **environments**. We have modified terrestrial and marine environments over vast areas. Today our (probable) effect on climate is influencing the evolution of populations of species around the globe.

2. **Anthropogenic** (human-caused) evolution made possible the most important transition in human history, the agricultural revolution of about twelve thousand years ago, which was essential for nearly everything historians traditionally have studied. The agricultural revolution was an evolutionary revolution. It led to settled societies, which produced writing, class conflict, classical Greek philosophy, capitalism, nation-states, complex technologies, Kabuki theater, the Federal Reserve System, and management by objectives.

3. Anthropogenic evolution sparked the second most important transition in human history, the Industrial Revolution of the late eighteenth and early nineteenth centuries. One of the leading edges of the Industrial Revolution was mechanization of cotton textile manufacturing, which depended on the long, strong cotton fibers that Amerindians (peoples who inhabited the Americas before Europeans) had encouraged to evolve.

4. Coevolution between people and populations of agricultural species may have been responsible for the evolution of light skin, the trait that racists and segregationists used to divide social groups.

5. Linking history and biology in the new field of evolutionary history enables us to understand events more fully than either discipline can achieve in isolation. History may explain why my grandfather entered a hospital, but traditional historical approaches would have little to say about why an antibiotic would fail. Biology can explain the antibiotic failure, but it would have little to say about the rise of the organizations and technologies that brought antibiotics and pathogens together in the first place.

6. Social forces have been evolutionary forces. Historians usually study the impact of human beings on each other, but nearly all fields of history could widen their understanding of impact to include the evolution of populations of other species. Few political historians, to pick one example, have written about state building as an evolutionary force, but we shall see that the strengths and weaknesses of states have influenced the evolution of populations of elephants and mountain goats. Similarly, biologists could include state capacity as one of the variables in evolutionary models.

7. Anthropogenic evolution has been a social force. The previous point emphasized that historians can extend their understanding of impact beyond the human realm to include evolution in nonhuman species. Similarly, we can extend our understanding of causation

beyond the human realm to include evolution. Manipulating the traits of populations of agricultural species has enabled states to conquer other states.

Subsequent chapters develop these arguments in stages. Chapters 2–8 explore the first argument, that *people have shaped the evolution of other species.* Chapter 2 defines evolution, explains how it works, clarifies the ability of human beings to influence it, and defines key terms (which also appear in the glossary). Chapters 3–8 provide examples of anthropogenic evolution, organized by types of human activity. We will look at hunting and fishing, eradication of organisms, environmental modification, domestication, intentional evolution, and coevolution.

Chapters 3–8 also develop the second argument, that *anthropogenic evolution has shaped human history.* We will see how changes we have wrought in populations of other species have circled back to shape human experience. Anthropogenic evolution has boosted and reduced our food supply, helped and harmed our health, added to and cut the cost of agriculture and medicine, perhaps helped rebels and cocaine producers circumvent government control, and expanded the gross national product of nations.

Chapter 8 explores the third argument: *people and populations of other species have coevolved.* This argument looks beyond one-way impacts to trace ways in which populations of people and other species have repeatedly evolved in response to each other.

Chapter 9 applies the ideas from previous chapters to show how evolutionary history can change our understanding of well-studied historical episodes. I will use one of the most important transitions in history, the Industrial Revolution, to make this argument. Scholars usually credit the English, their inventions, and their organizations with creating the Industrial Revolution. Using the history of the cotton industry as a case study, Chapter 9 suggests that anthropogenic evolution made the Industrial Revolution possible. The introduction of extra long cotton fiber from the New World, I suggest, enabled inventors to develop machines to spin and weave cotton. Extralong fiber evolved in the New World as a result of selection by Amerindians, so the Industrial Revolution in cotton was a response to anthropogenic evolution in the New World.

I hope these chapters will convince you that a synthetic field called **evolutionary history** *can help us understand the past better than history or biology alone.* Biologists already use *evolutionary history* to refer to the ancestry of species (as in the evolutionary history of elephants).

I propose broadening the term to mean the field (or research program) that studies the ways populations of human beings and other species have shaped each other's traits over time and the significance of those changes for all those populations.

Evolutionary history has the potential to expand the scope of many fields. As examples, I spell out implications for two fields – environmental history and history of technology – in Chapters 10 and 11. These chapters aim not to provide exhaustive reviews of the literature but rather to show how these fields lay the foundation for evolutionary history and could benefit from it. I envision evolutionary history as a crosscutting approach to scholarship rather than as a stand-alone field. In the concluding chapter, I suggest ways that evolutionary history might shape other fields of history as well.

One of the central goals of this book is to contradict the sense many of us have that evolution is something that happens "out there" – well away from us in time, well away from us in space, well away from us as a species, and certainly well away from us as individuals.[1] My grandfather's experience with evolution took place in an ordinary hospital in an ordinary city as a result of ordinary actions by ordinary people performing ordinary jobs with ordinary patients from ordinary families living ordinary lives.

Evolution is ordinary, not exceptional. It happens all around (and inside) every one of us – you, me, and the dog next door – every day. We rarely notice it, but it shapes our lives continually.

2

Evolution's Visible Hands

When discussing the ideas in this book with others, I have come to recognize a certain puzzled look. It usually involves a knitted brow and occasionally a sideways tilt of the head. Then a hand rises and objections follow. One of the most common objections has to do with the definition of evolution: "I think of evolution as **speciation**," people have said. "Are you saying people create new species? Didn't speciation take millions of years to accomplish, and didn't it finish a long time ago?" Another common protest has to do with the mechanism of evolution: "Darwin showed that evolution happens because of natural selection. What you are describing is artificial selection, so it does not qualify as the same thing Darwin described at all. That is not real evolution." If you have similar questions or objections, this chapter is for you.

The goals of this chapter are (1) to explain why processes described in this book qualify as evolution, (2) to provide a primer (or refresher) on ideas about evolution that will be essential for understanding the rest of this book, and (3) to clarify terminology. We will look at current concepts of evolution, list essential elements, and watch those elements at work in the wild and in everyday life. We will clarify the meanings of terms such as *natural selection, artificial selection, anthropogenic evolution, drift, sampling effect,* and *extinction.* If all these ideas are familiar to you, please feel free to skip to the next chapter.

It is not hard to see why many of us would equate evolution with speciation. The latter is the evolutionary outcome that has grabbed most of the headlines and sparked most of the controversy. Charles Darwin focused attention on speciation in the title of his landmark book *On the Origin of Species* (Figure 2.1), and for 150 years, religious fundamentalists

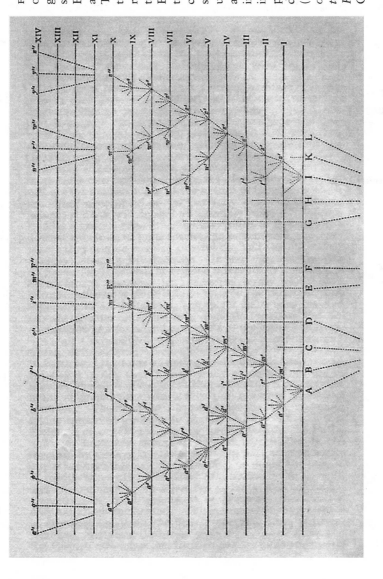

FIGURE 2.1. Darwin's branching bush of evolution. Darwin used this diagram to illustrate the idea that new species evolved from older species. Each branch (A–L) represents an ancestral species and its descendants. The diagram shows change through time, with the top horizontal line representing the present day and the bottom line representing an earlier era. Branches that end before reaching the top line represent extinct species. One can use the same diagram to represent the evolution of varieties and populations, although it would be more accurate to include horizontal lines to indicate that populations and varieties interbreed with each other. Darwin pointed out that there was no clear division between varieties and species. (From Charles Darwin, *On the Origin of Species by Means of Natural Selection; or The Preservation of Favoured Races in the Struggle for Life* [London: Odhams Press, [1859] 1872], 127.)

have challenged the idea that human beings evolved from other species rather than arriving on earth wholly formed on the sixth day of God's creation. They have sought to ban the teaching of evolution in public schools because of this aspect of evolutionary theory.

Biologists think of evolution as a broader process than speciation alone. To understand why, let us look at an example from the islands that Charles Darwin helped make famous: the Galapagos. Peter and Rosemary Grant of Princeton University began studying birds there in 1973. They and their collaborators have shown that the traits of finch populations change rapidly. During a drought in 1977, for example, the supply of small seeds on one of the islands plummeted, forcing finches to rely on big, tough seeds for food. Finches with bigger beaks opened these seeds more easily than finches with smaller beaks, and bigger-beaked individuals survived more often than their smaller-beaked relatives. Offspring resemble their parents when it comes to beak size, and the average size of beaks increased in the next generation.[1]

The increase in beak size fits the definition of **evolution** that is common among biologists: *change in inherited traits of populations over generations.*[2] This definition requires several things, some explicit and others implicit, that we can illustrate with the finches:

1. A **population**, which we can describe roughly as *a group of individuals of a given species living in a certain place.* The population we mentioned consists of members of a species of ground finch (*Geospiza fortis*) living on one island (Daphne Major) in the Galapagos.
2. **Variation** among individuals in **heritable** traits. Within the ground finch population on Daphne Major, individuals grow beaks of various sizes. Big-beaked finches have big-beaked offspring, and small-beaked finches have small-beaked offspring.
3. **Reproduction**, which is essential to pass traits to future generations.
4. **Change in inherited traits of a population over generations.** The average size of beaks in this population increased from one generation to the next.

Note that this definition does not require several things that many of us associate with evolution. It does not limit evolution to speciation because any change in traits in a population qualifies. It does not require millions of years because a population can evolve in just one generation. It does not require natural selection because the mechanism for change in traits goes unspecified. (The finch population did change as a result of natural selection, but the definition allows other mechanisms as well. We will see

TABLE 2.1. *Understanding of Evolution*

Criterion	Popular Ideas	Evolutionary Biology
Definition of evolution	Speciation	Change in traits of populations over generations
Most common form of evolution	Speciation	Changes in populations short of speciation
Reason for speciation	Goal of evolution	One outcome of evolution, which has no goal
Direction of evolution	Toward speciation	Multiple, changing directions
Time required for evolution	Long (thousands or millions of years)	Long or short (hours for bacteria)
Cause of evolution	Natural selection only	Anything that influences traits of populations over generations, including natural selection, sexual selection, methodical selection, unconscious selection, sampling effects, genetic engineering
Role of people in evolution	None – we cause artificial selection, not natural selection	Important because we affect traits of many populations over generations
Composition of species	Unitary	Made up of populations with overlapping genes and traits
Options people create for species	Survive in same form or go extinct	Survive in same form, evolve, or go extinct
Extinction	Only species can go extinct	Any population can go extinct
Status of evolution today	Largely complete	Continuing (no more complete or incomplete than other periods)

Note: Not everyone thinks of evolution the same way as evolutionary biologists. This table highlights some of the most common differences. This book builds its arguments on the ideas in the evolutionary biology column.

examples later.) The definition does not require that we exclude human beings as evolutionary forces because it does not limit evolutionary forces to so-called nature. Finally, it does not require that evolution be random because the definition is silent on intentionality (Table 2.1).

Those who believe evolution happens only as a result of natural selection might be shocked to learn that Charles Darwin identified not one but four types of **selection**. Two of them occur in the wild. The first and most famous is *natural selection*, which Darwin defined as "the preservation of favourable individual differences and variations, and the destruction of those which are injurious."[3] Darwin considered natural selection to be the most important force driving evolution. The second is *sexual selection*, which Darwin described as "a struggle between the individuals of one sex, generally the males, for the possession of the other sex. The result is not death to the unsuccessful competitor, but few or no offspring."[4]

The other two occur under domestication. One is *methodical selection*. Darwin wrote, "Nature gives successive variations; man adds them up in certain directions useful to him." Darwin thought this process helps create breeds of animals and plants that are well adapted to human desires.[5] The other is *unconscious selection*. Darwin believed that this process "results from every one trying to possess and breed from the best individual animals.... [The owner] has no wish or expectation of permanently altering the breed.... This process, continued during centuries, would improve and modify any breed."[6]

The striking fact about this list is that Charles Darwin included things that many of us believe Darwinian evolution excludes. Changes short of speciation? Check. Mechanisms other than natural selection? Check. Human beings as evolutionary actors? Check. Domestic plants and animals? Check. Human intentionality? Check. It is not Darwin's fault if, in popular retelling, people have confined his ideas to natural selection.

These clarifications make it easier to see why events in my grandfather's hospital (see Chapter 1) qualify as evolution. We saw four elements coincide to shape evolution among finches in the distant and exotic Galapagos. The same four elements shaped evolution among pathogens in the more familiar setting of a hospital room in the United States:

1. *A* **population** *of a pathogenic species lived in a hospital* (more specifically, in the hospital's patients). We do not know the name of the species, but we know it existed because it caused infections.
2. *There was* **variation** *in a* **heritable** *trait.* In one or more patients, some individual members of the pathogen population survived treatment with an antibiotic, and some did not. We call the individual pathogens that survived treatment **resistant** and those that did not **susceptible**. Individual pathogens inherited resistance or susceptibility from the previous generation.

3. **Reproduction** *occurred*. Members of the pathogen population reproduced themselves in patients. Hospital equipment and personnel helped the population survive by carrying its members (germs) from one patient to the next.

4. **Change in inherited traits of a population over generations** *occurred*. Before doctors used an antibiotic on patients in the hospital, most individual pathogens in the population were susceptible (otherwise, doctors would have abandoned the drug immediately). One or more generations later, resistant individuals made up a higher percentage of the pathogen population than they did before the antibiotic arrived.

Our understanding of the second element, inheritance of traits, has changed over the past 150 years. Darwin's study of breeding convinced him that parents passed traits to their offspring, but the mechanism stumped him (a fact he freely admitted). It was hard to fathom, for example, how a trait might appear in one generation, disappear in the next, and reappear in the following.

Darwin made a game effort by hypothesizing a mechanism he called *pangenesis*, in which individual parts of the body throw off *gemmules* that concentrate in sperm and egg. As an offspring develops from the fertilized ovum, the parents' gemmules travel to the appropriate body parts in the offspring. If external conditions alter a part of the parent's body, that part throws off modified gemmules and the offspring inherits modified traits.[7] Darwin's hypothesis might come as a surprise. Many of us learned to contrast Darwinian evolution with **Lamarckian evolution**, the key difference being that Darwinian evolution rejects the idea of inheritance of acquired traits, whereas the latter embraces it. In fact, Darwin and Lamarck both believed in inheritance of acquired traits.

The development of the field of genetics supplied a more durable mechanism than Darwin's gemmules. Gregor Mendel and others documented predictable patterns of inheritance that involved, among other things, dominant and recessive traits. Biologists dubbed the hypothesized units that controlled traits *genes*. Over the twentieth century, scientists figured out that genes were stretches of DNA that carried instructions for cell functioning. Some geneticists broadened their perspective from genes as traits of individuals or families to genes as traits of populations, giving rise to the field called population genetics.

In the mid-twentieth century, evolutionary biologists and population geneticists merged their insights in the modern (or neo-Darwinian) synthesis. The synthesizers held that the laws of genetics and evolutionary biology were compatible. Though this idea may seem obvious today, it was not so clear early in the twentieth century. In the synthesis, genes explained inheritance of traits, genetic variation explained variation in traits, and mutations explained the generation of new traits. The synthesizers placed populations at the center of evolutionary processes, and they credited natural selection with the biggest role in driving evolution. The neo-Darwinian synthesis remains the dominant model in evolutionary biology today.[8]

The synthesis led to a new definition of **evolution** as *changes in the genetic makeup of populations of organisms over generations.*[9] This definition is common among biologists but unfamiliar to many members of the public. The key idea is that genetic change is the measure of evolution. If even a single gene becomes more or less common in a population over generations, evolution has occurred. One of the most important benefits of this definition is that it helps us understand evolution across all scales, from individual populations to species and on up to kingdoms. There is no difference in mechanism between what some call microevolution and macroevolution. The degree of change differs across scales, but the process does not.

Recent discoveries in a field known as **epigenetics** have challenged the dogmas that limit evolution to genetic inheritance and exclude the inheritance of acquired traits. It appears that the addition or removal of a certain chemical structure (methyl) on DNA can turn genes on or off, which in turn can influence the traits of organisms. It also appears that offspring can inherit methylation from their parents. Methyl groups are not genes, so they do not qualify as genetic inheritance, but they do provide a nongenetic means of inheriting acquired traits. Epigenetics is a young, fast-changing field that might lead to revisions in the neo-Darwinian synthesis.[10]

Readers familiar with the term **artificial selection** may wonder why it rarely appears in this work. It is, after all, a popular term. A Google search for it turned up 311,000 hits. Biologists have applied it to processes described in this book such as the development of resistance and breeding. It is a legitimate term but one I avoid because it obscures more than it clarifies.

One source of confusion is disagreement over the meaning of *artificial selection.* Some authors, especially in textbooks, have more or less equated the term with breeding. Following are a couple of examples:

- Douglas Futuyma's evolutionary biology textbook defines *artificial selection* as "selection by humans of a consciously chosen trait or combination of traits in a (usually captive) population; differing from natural selection in that the criterion of survival and reproduction is the trait chosen, rather than fitness as determined by the entire genotype."[11]
- Helena Curtis's introductory biology textbook defines *artificial selection* as "the breeding of selected organisms for the purpose of producing descendants with desired traits."[12]

Both definitions highlight a conscious desire to shape future generations, human control of reproduction, and the development of desirable traits.

Other biologists have used *artificial selection* to refer to processes with opposite features – accidental effects on future generations, no human control of reproduction, and the development of undesirable traits. Following are examples from the peer-reviewed literature:

- Stephanie Carlson et al. describe trait-selective harvesting (catching big fish, in this case), which accidentally leads wild fish populations to become smaller, as *artificial selection*.[13]
- Jean-Marc Rolain et al. describe the evolution of pathogens resistant to multiple antibiotics as *artificial selection*.[14]

Biologists use *artificial selection* in contradictory ways, but they agree on one thing: artificial selection is something people do. In practice, if not in theory, then, the major job of *artificial selection* is to separate human beings from all other actors (which we usually call *nature*). The first definition of *artificial* in the *Oxford English Dictionary* is "opposed to natural." Every time we use *artificial selection*, we confirm our self-image. If we are fundamentally different from nature, then our actions and their effects are also fundamentally different. Once *artificial* slips its nose into the evolutionary tent as a synonym for *human-influenced*, it wastes little time dragging in other meanings. Two of the most insidious are *false* and *feigned*. Familiar with artificial flowers and artificial fruit, we might easily conclude that artificial selection is an imitation of real selection. This conclusion would, quite logically, lead us to see the effect of artificial selection as imitation evolution. But this idea is mistaken. Changes in traits of populations are just as real whether they take place on a remote island or in a barnyard.

To head off the confusion created by *artificial*, this book relies on terms such as *human-induced*, *human-shaped*, and **anthropogenic**. These terms (which I use interchangeably) identify human beings as evolutionary actors without implying that the effects of our own species are any less real or important than those of other species. My preferred terms also enable us to sidestep the confusion over whether *artificial selection* includes accidental impacts. When intentionality or its absence matters, I rely on Darwin's adjectives *methodical* and *unconscious*.

Given that authors attribute the term *artificial selection* to Darwin, it is worth clarifying that the evolutionist did not push the term very hard. He did use it in contrast with *natural selection*, but he never defined it or listed it in his taxonomy of selection. *Artificial selection* appears twice in *On the Origin of Species* and once in *Variation of Animals and Plants under Domestication*. The latter is a detailed, two-volume study of plant and animal breeding, so the term's lone appearance is striking. *Artificial selection* does not appear in the indexes to *Origin* or *Variation*. As we saw earlier, Darwin did highlight two other terms for human actions: *methodical selection* appears seven times in *Origin*, twenty-three times in *Variation*, and in the indexes of both books; *unconscious selection* appears seven times in *Origin*, forty-three times in *Variation*, and in the indexes of both books.[15]

Darwin may have used *artificial* sparingly because he ranged types of selection along a continuum rather than assigning them to separate boxes. Methodical selection anchors one end. It shades into unconscious selection, which shades into natural selection at the other end.[16] In a passage worth quoting at length, Darwin took to task authors who cleaved the continuum into the artificial and the natural:

Some authors have drawn a wide distinction between artificial and natural breeds; although in extreme cases the distinction is plain, in many other cases it is arbitrary; the difference depending chiefly on the kind of selection which has been applied. Artificial breeds are those which have been intentionally improved by man.... The so-called natural breeds, on the other hand,... have been rarely acted on by man's intentional selection; more frequently by unconscious selection, and partly by natural selection.[17]

We owe Darwin's most famous term, *natural selection*, to his desire to emphasize commonalities rather than contrasts between human and natural selection. In the nineteenth century, *selection* referred to what we call *breeding* today. Darwin's readers knew that *selection* involved human actions, so he had no need to add *artificial* to imply human action.

Quite the opposite: he had to add *natural* to give the term a new twist. It was a risky move. As he noted, "the term 'natural selection' is in some respects a bad one, as it seems to imply conscious choice."[18] But Darwin thought the risk was worthwhile because he wanted to blow down the walls separating the human from the natural. He wrote, "The term [*natural selection*] is so far a good one as it brings into connection the production of domestic races by man's power of selection, and the natural preservation of **varieties** and species in a state of nature."[19]

Another term that can spark confusion is *extinction*. Consistent with the idea that evolution equals the birth of a species, many of us have the idea that extinction equals the death of a species. This belief has led to objections when other taxonomic units, such as varieties of plants or breeds of animals, are described as going extinct. The broader view of evolution developed in this chapter points a way out of this confusion. Populations stand at the center of evolution. In some cases, we aggregate populations into entities we call *varieties* and *species*. The extinction of a variety or species happens when all its populations disappear, that is, go extinct. Extinction, like evolution, is a population process. All disappearances of species are extinctions, but not all extinctions are disappearances of species.

Darwin held much the same view. He emphasized that species assignments reflect a scientist's judgment and that no clear line demarcates varieties from species. "I look at the term species as one arbitrarily given, for the sake of convenience," he wrote, "to a set of individuals closely resembling each other, and that it does not essentially differ from the term variety, which is given to less distinct and more fluctuating forms. The term variety, again, in comparison with more individual differences, is also applied arbitrarily, for convenience sake."[20] Out of this idea flowed Darwin's conclusion that varieties (as well as species) "may become extinct, or they may endure as varieties for very long periods."[21]

Darwin's ideas have proved so powerful that many people equate evolution with evolution by natural selection. We have already seen one flaw in this equation, which is that Darwin thought evolution proceeded by sexual, unconscious, and methodical selection as well as by natural selection. Here we turn to another flaw, which is to limit evolution to the effects of selection of any stripe.

Evolution can occur without selection, especially in small populations, as a result of **sampling effects**. If **chance** limits reproduction to an unrepresentative subset of individuals in a population (e.g., only members of professional basketball teams rather than all Americans), the traits of the population will change over generations (individuals in the next generation will be taller, on average, than individuals in the previous generation). Selection also limits reproduction to an unrepresentative subset of individuals, so the distinction between selection and sampling effects is subtle. The key lies in the role of variation in traits. In selection, a subset of individuals reproduces because of advantageous traits. In sampling effects, a subset of individuals reproduces by chance, independent of traits. (Selection and sampling effects can also operate at the same time in a population.) Chapter 3 provides examples of sampling effects, so here our purpose is to flag the process.

Knowing about sampling effects helps us nail down the difference between evolution and selection. Evolution involves changes in inherited traits or genes of populations over generations. It can result from any mechanism, including selection and sampling effects. The key idea in selection is that an individual's traits affect its reproduction. Selection includes natural, sexual, methodical, and unconscious selection. The key idea in sampling effects is that they affect all individuals in a population with equal likelihood. If variation in traits has no impact on reproduction, selection is not at work. All cases in which selection affects the genetic makeup of populations over generations is evolution, but not all cases of evolution happen because of selection.

I like to think of this book as following in the Darwinian tradition, which partly explains my fondness for appealing to Darwin's ideas. Although we associate him with natural selection, Darwin believed one of the best ways to understand this process was to study selection in domestic plants and animals. He was glad he did. When puzzled, he wrote, "I have invariably found that our knowledge, imperfect though it be, of variation under domestication, afforded the best and safest clue. I may venture to express my conviction for the high value of such studies, although they have been very commonly neglected by naturalists."[22] I am not a Darwin, but I take inspiration from his belief that one of the best ways to understand evolution is to look at what we ourselves have wrought.

3

Hunting and Fishing

If you and I were to travel to the South Luangwa National Park and the adjacent Lupande Game Management Area in Zambia, we would likely keep our eyes peeled for elephants. For every ten elephants, we would expect to see six with tusks and four without (Figure 3.1). Those of us familiar with Asian elephants, but not African, might come up with a reasonable explanation: the park harbors a few more male elephants than females. And indeed, in Asian elephants, males bear tusks and females do not. But those of us familiar with African elephants will reject that hypothesis, for both males and females grow tusks in Africa. Historically, almost all adult elephants bore tusks. Tusklessness is an inherited genetic trait, and it has become more common, so elephants in Zambia fit our definition of an evolving population of a species.[1]

Tuskless elephants illustrate one argument of this chapter: by selectively harvesting animals, human beings have altered the traits of populations of wild species; that is, we have pushed their evolution in certain directions. We will see similar processes affecting other animals in mountains, plains, and seas. In most of these examples, people have altered the traits of populations without encouraging new species to arise. The modern plains bison of North America, on the other hand, might be an example of changing a population's traits so radically we consider it to have become a new species.

These examples illustrate an important way in which we need to broaden our concept of **unconscious selection**. As we noted in Chapter 2, Darwin used the term to refer to the impact of **culling** on the traits of domestic animals. Because people kept the animals they most valued, this process usually led to the enhancement of traits people found

FIGURE 3.1. Hunting was an evolutionary force for elephants. Hunting and fishing have altered the traits of populations of wild animals by selecting for and against certain traits. Traditionally, adult African elephants of both sexes bore tusks. Ivory hunting inflicted high mortality on tusked elephants. Once-rare tuskless elephants like this one became common because they survived hunting. Tusklessness is a genetic trait, so the offspring of tuskless parents are usually tuskless. The proportion of tuskless elephants in one African national park reached 38 percent. This photo is from Kruger National Park, South Africa. (Photo copyright © Scotch Macaskill. Reprinted by permission of Wildlife-StockPictures.com.)

desirable. This chapter shows that culling (in the form of selective hunting and fishing) has affected traits of populations of wild animals in ways that people find undesirable.

This chapter makes a second argument that links human history with evolution: the state has been an evolutionary force. By requiring hunters to harvest larger bighorn sheep, the government of Canada created selection for smaller animals. We extend our understanding of the state as an evolutionary force by drawing on the concept of state capacity (the ability of a state to control behavior). Governments with high capacity, such as Canada, affected evolution by controlling the behavior of big game hunters. A government with lower capacity, Zambia, affected evolution by failing to control the behavior of poachers who killed elephants for their tusks.

The evolution of tuskless elephants in Zambia is striking but not unique. It is striking because African elephants (*Loxodonta africana*) benefit from tusks. They use them to dig for water and salt, move objects, and mark territory by stripping bark from trees. Natural selection favored tusk bearing. But Zambia's elephants are not alone in evolving higher rates of tusklessness. In 1920, hunters in Uganda's Queen Elizabeth National Park killed two thousand elephants. Only one was tuskless, or 0.05 percent of the population. The feature seemed so odd that the specimen was sent to the British Museum to check for diseases. By 1988, tuskless elephants made up about 10 percent of the overall population. The proportion grew to two-thirds for those over forty years old.[2]

A likely reason these populations evolved tusklessness was selective hunting. People have killed African elephants for various reasons, including to use them as food and to protect farm fields from destruction, but the primary motive over the past couple centuries has been ivory harvesting. Ivory has found its way into sculptures, billiard balls, cutlery handles, and piano keys. A trade in African ivory grew up alongside its sibling, the slave trade, and sent mind-boggling numbers of elephant tusks onto the world market. The name of one of Africa's nations, Côte d'Ivoire (Ivory Coast), testifies to the historical demand for this product.

Selective hunting converted a liability into an asset and vice versa. Absent human hunting, tusk bearing was an asset and tusklessness a liability. Heavy ivory hunting reversed their roles. Cutting a tusk off a live, wild elephant is a task recommended only for the suicidal, so ivory hunters killed elephants to get at the tusks safely. Numbers of elephants plummeted so low that, in the twentieth century, conservationists launched efforts to save the species through the creation of national parks and bans on hunting. But a flammable brew of poverty, lax enforcement, and global demand fueled poaching in Africa, even in protected areas. Poachers wanted nothing from elephants except tusks (they usually left the rest of the carcass to rot or be eaten by scavengers). A once-rare genetic trait, tusklessness, grew far more common as poachers made its advantages outweigh its disadvantages. Tuskless elephants usually lived to reproduce; tusked elephants often did not.[3]

Hunting and government also played important roles in evolution on Ram Mountain in Alberta, Canada. As you would guess from the mountain's name, bighorn sheep rams (and ewes) inhabit this peak. It is a popular place for hunters. The demand for trophy bighorn rams has grown so enormous that hunters have paid hundreds of thousands of dollars for auctioned permits. One ponied up more than one million Canadian dollars for special permits in 1998 and 1999.

Hunter preferences have paired with government regulations to encourage selective hunting of rams based on horn size. Trophy hunters prize rams with large horns, and hunting regulations limited hunters to rams with horns above a minimum size. On Ram Mountain, hunters harvested an average of 40 percent of the trophy rams in the area between 1975 and 2002. This 40 percent fatality rate created a strong selective force. Rams with large horns often died, whereas those with small horns tended to survive. Rams inherit horn size from their sire, so we can predict the result: the size of ram horns declined as rams with small horns gained a selective advantage. And because big horns grew on rams with big bodies, the bodies of rams shrank as well.[4]

We can tease out several lessons from evolution by bighorn sheep and elephants. The first is the irony of hunting: hunters have reduced the production of the very things they want, such as elephant tusks or rams with large horns, by selectively hunting the individuals with those traits. The traditional way of thinking about hunting's negative effects on target species gravitated toward ecological impact – that is, the effect on population size – thus the government's imposition of bag limits for hunters and fishers. Limiting one hunter's take enabled more hunters to bag a ram. But these examples from Africa and Canada show that hunting affected the evolution of game species along with their ecology. On a mountain where hunters harvested 40 percent of big rams, adult rams with small horns stood a better chance of surviving and passing their genes along to the next generation than did the more hulking members of their generation.

Second, these examples illustrate the impact of states and their strength on evolution. By influencing the behavior of individual human beings, the state indirectly reshaped the gene pools of other species. Canada illustrated the impact of state strength. Government regulations forced hunters to kill sheep with big horns rather than small ones. Absent enforcement of these rules, hunters probably would have shot rams of all sizes (thus the rationale for regulations), which would have reduced selection for small horns. (Hunting still would have been an ecological force because it would have affected population size.) In contrast, Zambia showed the impact of state weakness. By failing to control poaching, the government allowed hunters to hunt tusked elephants selectively. A state with the power and will to enforce game laws would have reduced poaching to a low level and reduced its selective impact.

Third, the sheep example showed the importance of correlation among traits and indirect evolutionary impact. Trophy hunters wanted ram necks, heads, and horns to mount on the walls of their cabins, not ram bodies. But big horns grow on rams with big bodies, so selecting against big horns also selected against big bodies. Rams became smaller on average on Ram Mountain. So even when people consciously sought certain traits in organisms, they unconsciously selected for other traits because selection acts on whole organisms, and traits (such as size of body and size of horns) are often correlated.

If we travel south from Canada along the spine of the Rocky Mountains to the first national park in the world, Yellowstone, we will see one of the most dramatic examples of anthropogenic evolution. The emblem of the U.S. National Park Service, which manages the park, brings together two key elements of our story. One is the shape of the emblem, which traces the outline of a stone arrowhead or spear tip that implies a human presence. The second is bison, a silhouette of which rests near the bottom.

When human beings wandered from Asia into North America, they found an enormous, now extinct creature known as the giant long-horned bison (*Bison priscus*). We know that early Americans hunted these beasts because excavated skeletons of the bison bear stone spear tips. The style of the points dates them to twelve to thirteen thousand years ago, not long after the first wave of human immigrants washed south and east across the continent. These early Americans ate a variety of plants and animals, but judging from campsite remains, they had a special taste for giant long-horned bison. It was their favorite prey, perhaps because one animal filled so many bellies.[5]

The giant horns that gave *Bison priscus* its common name tell us some important things about its lifestyle. Animals with gigantic weapons on their heads usually live alone or in small groups. Animals that live in herds usually have small horns.[6] Horns and antlers help males in several ways. Animals use these daggers to fight with other members of the same species, to increase their appeal to potential mates, and to protect themselves from predators. Fossil bones suggest that giant bison used their long, outward-facing horns to impale their opponents. An individual with longer horns had a better chance of circumventing its opponents' sabers and burying a fatal jab than one with shorter horns. Females probably preferred to mate with winners of these contests rather than with losers, either because they liked what they saw in the male or because they liked the territory that the male could defend from competitors.[7]

The giant bison's architecture served it well for thousands of years, but its body shrank and changed shape starting about twelve thousand years ago. The timing gives us an important clue about the cause. Only two major predators, wolves and lions, had hunted giant bison for tens of thousands of years. If they caused the change, it would have happened much earlier. The big change in the bison's environment twelve to thirteen thousand years ago was the arrival of a new predator. This one walked on two feet, hunted in cooperative bands, and carried spears with well-designed stone points. Its remarkable efficiency at hunting seems to have caused a reduction in the body size of other large mammals, too. Over the past ten thousand years, North American sheep, elk, moose, musk ox, bears, antelope, and wolves have all shrunk.[8]

Scholars have offered various explanations for these changes, but it seems likely that these new hunters converted the giant bison's shape and habits from virtues into liabilities. Hunters who needed to get close to their prey, such as wolves and human beings armed with spears, preferred to attack lone individuals rather than many victims at once. Hunting punished solitary, territorial giant bison and rewarded those that stayed close together. Clumps of bison became more common and grew into herds.

Herding is a classic response to heavy predation. It brings a statistical advantage to herd members because the odds that a predator will hone in on any one individual will decrease with the size of the herd. Herds further improved odds for members through cooperative behavior. Members warned each other of danger, and they fought off predators by joining forces (e.g., by forming a circle with vulnerable rumps to the center and dangerous horns facing the periphery).

But bison paid a price for herding. In a given area, the supply of food per individual declined along with the chances of being attacked. Smaller bodies probably resulted from a decline in food availability as bison crowded together. Herding changed the bison's shape as well as size. Now survival depended on the ability to crop grass, bison's main food, quickly. Shifting the head closer to the ground, reducing horn size, and growing a hump to cantilever the head's weight enabled bison to graze for long periods without strain. Giant horns, which enabled males to defend territory, may also have become a liability as being able to stay close together became more valuable.[9]

In sum, human hunting may have created a new species. By selecting for clumping and against traveling alone, hunters could have created the short-horned, humpbacked bison (*Bison bison*) from the giant long-horned bison (*Bison priscus*). Most of this book focuses on ways in which human beings have affected the evolution of traits within species, but here we have an example of human beings who seem to have pushed the traits of one species so much that its descendents became known as a separate species.

So far we have stressed **unconscious selection**. But people also may have shaped bison by encouraging another type of selection. Male bison grow dramatic, hairy pantaloons on their forequarters. Great-horned bison did not. Pantaloons do not seem to increase survival, so it is not clear how natural selection would have encouraged their evolution. The trait may have developed and spread by chance. Or, some researchers have suggested, they may have evolved because of mate choice.

Female bison may have chosen to mate with pantaloon-bearing males more often than with duller males. If so, it would be an example of **sexual selection**. Natural selection acts by increasing or reducing survival (and thus reproduction). Sexual selection acts by increasing or decreasing the ability to find mates (and thus reproduction). Why would females prefer pantaloons? Females of a number of animal species also prefer males with showy displays. Biologists have offered various hypotheses to explain this pattern, including the *good genes hypothesis*, which holds that showy displays cost the male a lot of calories, so only strong, fit males can afford them. Sick, parasite-filled animals have a hard time keeping up appearances. When bison began clumping in herds, they made it easier for pathogens and parasites to jump from one individual to the next. So pantaloons may have been visible signs of strong immune systems. Females that mated with showy males may have given birth to offspring that survived and reproduced more often than offspring of females that mated with duller males, encouraging the trait to spread as a by-product of herding, which might in turn have been a by-product of human hunting.[10]

Bison and other animals adapted to hunting by shrinking or herding, but other species met a different evolutionary fate: **extinction**. A number of large mammals disappeared from North America at the end of the last Ice Age, or roughly twelve thousand years ago, including the wooly mammoth and the mastodon. Two main explanations have emerged for these extinctions. One blames climate change, and there is no doubt that the climate warmed a great deal at the time. The other blames human hunting. One name given to this argument is the *Pleistocene overkill*. Another is the *black hole hypothesis* because it holds that animals disappeared into the black hole between the jaws of human beings.[11]

I find the black hole hypothesis more likely than the climate change hypothesis for three reasons. First, these species survived earlier periods of warming and cooling, which encourages us to look for a factor unique to this episode. The most striking change was the immigration of human beings from Asia. Second, mass die-offs did not take place at the same time in other regions of the world, which also would have undergone climate shifts. And third, mass extinctions occurred, in other periods and on other continents, shortly after human beings first arrived.[12]

Bison survived the Pleistocene epoch by evolving into a new species with different traits, but the arrival of a new brand of human being in the nineteenth century almost sent the species to the same graveyard as the mammoth and mastodon. These new people converted herding from an asset back into a liability. In less than a hundred years, hunters slaughtered bison so efficiently that they reduced herds of twenty-eight to thirty million on the Great Plains to about a thousand individuals by 1890.[13] They achieved such ruthless efficiency by harnessing two technologies. One was the rifle, which made herding (an adaptation to an earlier mode of hunting) into a liability. Buffalo hunters, such as the famous Buffalo Bill Cody, fired shot after shot into herds of bison, which collapsed and died on the spot. Solitary individuals would have been harder to track and kill.

The other technology was the railroad. It enabled people to reach bison more quickly and in larger numbers. Some hunters did not bother leaving the comfort of railroad cars as they shot bison through the window for sport. But the railroad played a more important role by providing a way to ship a few valued buffalo products, such as hides (for use as robes) and tongue (a delicacy), to markets in the East. It also facilitated the replacement of the bison's habitat, grasslands, with farms because it enabled the transport of farm produce to eastern markets. The relative contribution of hunting and habitat destruction is hard to gauge, but hunting clearly had an impact.[14]

Collapsing giant herds into a handful of marooned individuals opened the door for **sampling effects** to walk into bison lives. One type of sampling effect is known as the **founder effect**, which I like to picture as a genetic bottleneck. The estimated twenty-eight to thirty million bison that roamed the Great Plains would have carried a lot of variation in genes and **genetic traits**. But when one plucks a thousand individual bison out of twenty-eight to thirty million, the sample (about 0.003% of the parent population) would not have all the genes carried by the twenty-eighty to thirty million. Only the genes of those thousand would survive. So their descendents – the founders of today's herds of bison in Yellowstone – inherited only a subset of the genes available to their ancestors. Some genes disappeared, which means the traits of today's herd are not identical to those of the ancestral herd, which means the herd evolved. So the founder effect refers to differences in traits between ancestral and descendent populations because of a small, unrepresentative sample of individuals from the ancestral population surviving to found the descendent population. This can lead to rapid evolution over just a few generations.

The founder effect has also been at work in African elephants. In 1931, South Africa set up the Addo Elephant National Park to protect eleven elephants that managed to survive hunting in the Eastern Cape Province. Since then, no elephants have migrated into the park, creating a genetic island as effectively as if the park had been plunked onto an atoll far out to sea. The herd numbered 324 in 2000, all descended from those 11 elephants.

We can see the founder effect in the rate of tusklessness. Of the eight founding females, four or five were tuskless (selective ivory hunting probably created this high rate), so the founder effect alone would likely produce a 50 percent tuskless rate today – higher even than the 38 percent rate at an African national park with a recent poaching problem. And indeed, the rate of tusklessness in Addo is high. The park has protected the herd from hunting and poaching for the past quarter century, so selection via ivory harvesting appears to have played little role.[15]

But something else has also been at work, for the proportion of tuskless females is 98 percent rather than 50 percent. That factor is probably another sampling effect known as **genetic drift**. It refers to the tendency, in the absence of selection, for the frequency of genes and traits to change randomly through time. Drift is strongest in small populations because random events affecting a small number of individuals have a big effect on the population as a whole. In this case, if just two of the three or four tusked female ancestors happened not to produce offspring, and if that same thing happened several years running, the proportion of tuskless elephants would quickly grow. By creating a genetic island with a few founders, South Africans appear to have set in motion genetic drift that created a population of almost tuskless female elephants.[16]

One of the major problems facing a growing world population is the collapse of fisheries. Common explanations for the collapse of live natural resources (fish, birds, and trees) are anthropogenic mortality and habitat destruction. A 1996 report from the United Nations Food and Agriculture Organization on worldwide fisheries concluded that 35 percent of the world's fisheries were declining. Another 25 percent were "mature," meaning that catches had leveled and probably would drop. The report blamed overfishing and damage to breeding grounds. Its policy recommendations, mainly limits on the numbers of boats and tonnage, grew out of this emphasis on ecological impacts (i.e., on population size and habitat).[17]

Evolutionary history can revise this interpretation by demonstrating the effect of humans on fish evolution as well as ecology. In his study of salmon in the American Pacific Northwest, environmental historian Joseph Taylor argues that fish hatcheries pushed salmon populations into "new evolutionary paths." Hatchery fish clumped together, carried less genetic variation, and were smaller than wild fish. These factors combined to increase mortality. Fishways in dams reinforced these trends. By causing more damage to large salmon than small, fishways selected for smaller and faster-maturing fish.[18]

Taylor's study emphasizes the impact of human beings on fish populations in streams and rivers. We can push his analysis further by drawing on fishery biologists to show that anthropogenic selection at sea also reduced catches. Between 1950 and 1990, the size of spawning salmon declined 30 percent. Absent people, natural selection favored big fish. Salmon hatched, went to sea, returned to their natal stream, and either laid or fertilized eggs. Big fish were better than small fish at fighting their way upstream and at competing for spawning sites, resulting in their selective advantage. Ocean nets changed the odds. By snaring up to 80 percent of returning fish, the nets selected against large fish and for those small enough to slip through. Small fish produced fewer and smaller offspring than large fish, reducing the number and size of salmon in the next generation even more. Smaller fish meant lower tonnage (the usual measure of commercial fishery harvests) even if the number of fish caught remained the same.[19]

Size selection drove catches down in another way: by selecting for and against certain behaviors. Traditionally, going to sea for eighteen months was a good strategy because it made salmon bigger than if they were to stay home. A few salmon (called jack) came back a year earlier than normal, and some (called parr) never went to sea at all. Jack and parr competed poorly against big fish for spawning sites and mates. By catching oceangoing salmon, however, fishers altered the odds. Ocean nets selected against fish that went to sea and grew large. Now jack and parr had as much chance at reproducing as the traditionalists who ventured out to sea, although they produced fewer and smaller offspring than did large fish. The number and size of oceangoing salmon declined.[20]

This revision of the received view becomes more persuasive when we find similar patterns elsewhere. Whitefish in North American freshwater lakes once supported commercial fishing. The average size of whitefish declined between 1941 and 1965, when the fishery collapsed. In the 1940s, the average nine-year-old whitefish weighed two kilograms. By the 1970s, the average had declined to one kilogram. Observers blamed the size reduction on removal of older, bigger fish, but it also resulted from changing whitefish genetics. Young fish grew as rapidly in 1970 as they did in 1940, but adults grew more slowly. In the 1950s, nets caught fish aged two years and up. In the 1970s, nets caught fish aged seven years and up. The 5.5-inch holes in nets had created a size threshold beyond which fish grew at their peril. Similarly, the average size of fish in populations of Atlantic cod (*Gadus morhua*) declined under heavy fishing pressure.[21]

After hastening decline, adaptations to heavy fishing may have slowed the recovery of fish stocks as well. Once relieved of heavy harvesting, some commercial fisheries have rebounded more slowly than fishery managers expected. Evolution might be at least part of the explanation. One reason is the time lag built into adaptation. Natural selection acts over generations, and many commercial fish species have long generation times, so populations may adapt slowly to new environments. In this case, it appears that natural selection for larger fish requires years to reverse the effects of heavy selection for smaller fish.[22]

Another evolutionary factor is the impact of size selection on other traits that dampen population growth. Although selection may favor an individual because of a single trait, it acts on the whole organism. Traits correlated with the selected trait get pulled along with it into the next generation. Experiments with the Atlantic silverside (*Menidia menidia*) found that populations subjected to heavy harvesting of large fish displayed reductions in "fecundity, egg volume, larval size at hatch, larval viability, larval growth rates, food consumption rate and conversion efficiency, vertebral number, and willingness to forage." All these traits lower the ability of a population to rebound rapidly from low numbers.[23]

Fisheries offer us a chance to see how anthropogenic evolution in populations of other species can circle back to affect human experience. The cod of the North Atlantic have been famous for centuries for their productivity, and heavily fished as a result, but a spike in harvests came with the arrival of larger trawlers after World War II. The average size of cod populations near the Canadian coast decreased, probably because of a combination of evolution and removal of older fish. In the 1980s, fishers responded by illegally lining their nets with smaller-mesh nets. This response hastened the collapse of the fishery, and the Canadian government had little choice but to declare a moratorium on fishing in 1992. But the stocks did not rebound as hoped, and the government closed the fishery in 2003.[24]

Plummeting catches in the late 1980s set in motion, and the 1992 moratorium accelerated, a variety of social effects in Newfoundland fishing villages. Unemployment rose, reaching 43 percent in one headland, and brought stress in its wake. Young adults moved away from their villages more often, leaving smaller and older populations behind, and the remaining young people stayed in school longer than their parents. Fishers turned their attention to catching a more diverse range of species, especially invertebrates (shrimp and scallop). But technology-intensive invertebrate fishing created fewer jobs than cod fishing, so the outlook for full employment remained dim.[25]

Some biologists have suggested that fishery policies informed by evolutionary thinking might reduce the chances of collapse in the future. Instead of selecting *against* the traits we want (such as big fish), what if we selected *for* those traits? A study of Atlantic silverside put this idea to the test. Researchers took a population of silverside and divided it into six smaller populations in tanks. They subjected two populations to selection against large size by harvesting the largest 90 percent of individuals. (This mimicked the usual direction of selection exerted by fishers.) They subjected two other populations to selection for large size by harvesting the smallest 90 percent of individuals. In the remaining two populations, they harvested 90 percent of the fish randomly with respect to size. They repeated this protocol for four generations.[26]

The results were both predictable and dramatic. Predictable, because fish evolved in the directions we would expect. In populations where selection worked against large size (by harvesting larger fish), the average size of harvested individuals and their aggregate weight declined over generations. In populations where selection favored large size (by harvesting smaller fish), the fish became larger. In populations subjected to no size selection, sizes stayed the same. These results were dramatic because of the speed and degree of the divergence. In just four generations, harvested individuals from populations under selection for large size became twice as large as fish in populations under selection against large size.

The reason was not that the larger fish produced more offspring but that their offspring grew faster.[27]

Many of us might find these results surprising. It seems logical that catching bigger fish would lead to bigger catches, and in the first generation, that was true. But in the longer run, catching bigger fish led to smaller catches. The practical import of this idea is easier to see if we translate the terms into commercial language. Imagine the experimenters were fishers, harvests were their catches, and the experimental populations were fish in the sea (in this case, silverside, which have a generation time of one year). If the same pattern were to hold at sea as in the experimental tanks, fishers who caught the smallest 90 percent of fish in one population would, after just four years, bring home twice as much fish as fishers who consistently caught the largest 90 percent of fish in a different population.

Salmon, cod, and silverside are hardly alone. A 2007 study of fish, invertebrates, and terrestrial vertebrates found that human hunting and fishing have created size-dependent selection in populations of 108 to 136 wild species. In most cases, these practices select against the traits people want (usually, bigger animals). A strategy informed by evolutionary ideas might reverse this effect by forcing hunters and fishers to catch only small or mid-sized individuals and leave the largest behind to reproduce.[28]

We can draw several lessons from bison, mastodons, elephants, and fish. First, human beings seem to have changed some populations of organisms so radically that today, we consider them to be different species from their ancestors. With bison, the selection came in the form of hunting. Second, we have done the converse – eliminated species by driving them extinct. So human beings have played the role of the alpha and omega of evolutionary forces.

Third, people have been evolutionary forces for a long time. We probably have been shaping bison (as well as North American sheep, elk, moose, musk ox, bears, antelope, and wolves) for as long as twelve thousand years. Fourth, technology is an important variable in anthropogenic evolution because it can affect survival so dramatically. The introduction of the rifle and the railroad accelerated the devastation of millions of bison on the Great Plains. Fifth, reducing populations to small sizes has encouraged evolution via the founder effect and genetic drift. Sixth, intensive selection may have played a role in the collapse of fisheries, an important source of food for a growing world population, and slowed their recovery once fishing pressure lifted.

But seventh, evolutionary history offers lessons useful to policy makers. We make choices that influence evolution in populations of other species. Evolutionary history can help us understand why people made some choices in the past and see the impact of those choices. By linking the social and biological, it can help make clear to policy makers the value of making different choices in the future. In the case of fishery management, evidence suggests that current policies have the opposite effect of that intended. Taking evolution into account, as some biologists have suggested, might lead to a reversal of policies that encourage depletion of the traits we most desire in other species.

Hunters and fishers were not alone in encouraging undesired traits in populations of species they killed. So did eradicators, as we shall see in the next chapter.

4

Eradication

I run most mornings with a dog named Riley. We have worked out a clear division of labor: he defecates, and I clean up. Riley takes his role very seriously. Picking the location to make his deposit seems to be the most important decision of his day, for he takes great care to sniff out precisely the spot he thinks best, does his business, and draws attention to his feat by scratching up big wads of grass. Then I ruin his achievement by slipping a plastic bag over my hand, picking up the deposit, tying the bag, and tossing this canine gold into a trash bin. I try to minimize hand-feces contact, but tears in the bags (they previously held newspapers or groceries) lead to failures. Dogs can transmit some nasty germs in their feces, such as *Salmonella* bacteria that cause human gastroenteritis. So when I get home, I wash my hands with soap and water, and perhaps I cause some evolution by selecting for strains of bacteria resistant to a chemical called triclosan in antibacterial soap.[1]

My hand washing is one example of a larger human enterprise that has driven evolution: efforts to eradicate organisms. Although hunters and fishers kill animals, they like having the species they target around – the more abundant the better. Eradicators bring the opposite sentiment to their task. *Eradication* has various meanings. Here I use it to mean the elimination of a species from a certain place. The scale has varied from the individual (trying to rid my hands of a pathogen) to the local (trying to free a house from rats) to the regional (trying to exterminate the cotton boll weevil from the American South) to the global (trying to eradicate malaria from the earth).

This chapter argues that eradication efforts have driven evolutionary change in populations of target species. It identifies social forces that have acted as evolutionary forces, including advertising, profit making, repression of political insurgents and drug trafficking, and war. It steps back from specific examples to draw some broader lessons about adaptability of species to human actions. The key idea is that some species stand a better chance of surviving human impact than others because their traits enable them to evolve more quickly. As it happens, people tend to like the species that have the hardest time adapting to our world, and we tend to dislike the species that adapt most easily. So in remaking the world as we wish, we are favoring companions that we might not wish to have with us in the future.

For many years, the soap in our house contained an antibacterial ingredient called triclosan. We started using antibacterial soaps when we were changing diapers on our infant daughters, and we continued after our children grew older because it became hard to find liquid soaps without such ingredients. When we got a dog and resumed our feces handling, antibacterial soap seemed like a good idea again. The Web site of the manufacturer of the brand we used said its soap was "clinically proven to eliminate ninety-nine percent of the germs your family encounters. Offers antibacterial protection."[2]

Sounds great, right? But notice that pesky 1 percent that survives. That is one bacterial cell in a hundred. I must encounter one-in-a-hundred individuals all day long because colonies of bacteria host thousands and millions of individuals. Bacterial populations found anywhere carry variation, but I like to think my hands harbor supersized variation. Students from most states and over a hundred countries study at my university. When they arrive in August and return from break in January, so do germs from their hometowns and vacation sites. Students leave germs on doorknobs, handrails, coins, and computer terminals. I use all those things, too. I must have picked up germs from every state in the union, plus Asia, Africa, South America, Australia, and Europe. (We get few students from Antarctica.) To be fair, this is a two-way street. When I travel, I leave germs in the places I visit.

All the elements for evolution of resistance to triclosan came together on my hands. My hands provided a welcoming environment for bacteria because I used them to pick up dog feces and handle objects other people touched. The bacteria surely varied in inherited traits. Frequent washing may have selected for triclosan-resistant strains, which multiplied over time. I do not know this occurred, but experiments suggest it could have. Many germs have evolved resistance to triclosan in the laboratory, including populations of *Escherichia coli* (strains of which cause severe intestinal illness), *Salmonella enterica* (strains of which cause salmonella poisoning and typhoid fever), *Pseudomonas aeruginosa* (which causes gastroenteritis and urinary tract infections), and *Staphylococcus aureus* (the most common cause of staph infections).[3]

When we were still using antibacterial soap, I expected it was losing its punch over time because of resistance. But I saw no great harm – the soap still functioned as soap and helped wash off germs. It turns out, though, that I may have been playing for higher stakes. Making germs resistant to triclosan could also have made them resistant to antibiotics. In the same way that trenches protect soldiers against bullets and bombs, bacterial methods of defense can work against more than one weapon. The traits that protect bacteria against triclosan – such as impermeability, pumps to get rid of noxious compounds, and enzymes that disable poisons – also work against antibiotics. Triclosan-resistant bacterial strains survive some of the most valuable antibiotics we have – tetracycline, chloramphenicol, erythromycin, amoxicillin, ciprofloxacin, and ampicillin.[4]

Inadvertently, I could have been encouraging antibiotic-resistant bacteria on my hands. I could have passed these strains to my daughters while preparing dinner, and they could have grown ill. When their pediatrician prescribed an antibiotic, she might have chosen ampicillin. Because triclosan resistance can also confer resistance to ampicillin, the antibiotic may have been useless. So my daughters might have suffered longer than necessary until the pediatrician tried an antibiotic to which the pathogen had not evolved resistance.

You might be performing a similar experiment. Seventy-five percent of Americans show triclosan in their urine. (Not all of it need come from soap. Manufacturers put triclosan in toothpaste, mouthwash, deodorants, toys, and plastic kitchenware.) The concentration people carry in their bodies increases with income, possibly because wealthier people consume more – and more expensive – products. There are also age differences. Concentration accelerates from ages six to twenty-nine and then declines among older people. Our bodies are environments for the bacteria that live in and on them, and the products we use affect that environment, so each one of us is a little evolutionary laboratory. And odds are, the wealthier you are, the more likely you are selecting for triclosan-resistant bacteria.[5]

At our house, we have tried to end our little evolutionary experiment by changing to soap without antibacterial ingredients. A peer-reviewed study showed antibacterial soaps to be no more effective than ordinary soaps at removing bacteria from hands. Even in septic cities in the third world, washing with triclosan prevents no more diseases than regular soap. So far as I can tell, then, triclosan soap offers us no benefits, and it does create risks. It was hard to find liquid soap without triclosan, but a diligent search by my wife finally located some. I like to think we may have done our tiny share to improve public health by slowing the evolution of resistance to antibiotics.[6]

This example shows the power of the profit motive and advertising to drive evolution. It is no surprise that manufacturers advertise products to increase sales and thereby profits – the profit motive is supposed to drive our economy. But advertising can spur consumers to act in ways that otherwise we would not, which can in turn affect evolution. In this case, the company created the impression that antibacterial soap offered protection above that provided by regular soap. Otherwise, there would be no point in adding (and paying for) antibacterial ingredients.

The advertising also created the impression that clinical tests (i.e., research involving patients) had proven that the soap protected family members from almost all germs and, one would conclude, infections. Without those expectations, we would not have bought the soap. A close reading of the label reveals that the company raised these expectations without precisely claiming its soap would prevent infections, a feat I can only attribute to astute lawyers and an advertising genius.

To isolate advertising as an evolutionary force, we need to show that its effects differed from other ways of conveying information. It is easy to do so here because advertising convinced us to use the soap, and knowledge of resistance (derived ultimately from peer-reviewed scientific publications) convinced us to stop. It is possible, though, that my search missed the research that proved a benefit to family health, in which case, peer-reviewed research might also have convinced us to use the soap. So I wrote to the company and asked for the research behind its claims. The company replied with a message listing five pathogens the soap killed – but no references or explanation of the research. A second request produced the same result.[7] A good faith effort thus produced a divergence between the information conveyed in advertising and that conveyed through other media, and the difference affected behavior in a way with potential evolutionary implications.

Now let us widen the scope a bit while staying on the personal scale. The manufacturer of our soap guided our attention to five disease-causing germs. But those are not the only species on my hands. When researchers sampled the hands of fifty-one college students, they found that the average hand harbored 150 species of bacteria. So when I washed my left hand, I may have been selecting for triclosan resistance in 145 bacterial populations in addition to the five the company mentioned. Washing my right hand at the same time drove the total higher. The species on the left and right hands of the same person vary – only 17 percent of those on one usually appear on the other. That is about twenty-five species in common, so washing my right hand might have selected for triclosan resistance in an additional 125 populations, or populations of 275 species of bacteria on my two hands alone.[8]

The number of simultaneous evolutionary experiments soars as we bring more people into our circle. The hands of the fifty-one college students in the study hosted 4,742 species of bacteria, with only 5 percent of the species appearing on all the hands. So each hand of each person was a petri dish of bacteria living in a unique environment that probably selected for some traits over others. Although the researchers did not compare strains of bacteria within species, they did find differences in the patterns of species that seem to result from environmental differences. Women's hands harbored more bacteria than men's hands, perhaps because men had more acidic skin than women. The sexes also differed in sweat and oil production, use of moisturizers and cosmetics, skin thickness, and hormone levels, and any of these might have played a role.[9]

We can measure the significance of anthropogenic evolution by pathogens in deaths. A study in the United States estimated that 6 percent of hospital-acquired infections were drug resistant in 1999–2002. In China, 41 percent of infections picked up in hospitals in 1999–2001 were resistant to drugs,[10] and in Vietnam, antibiotic-resistant germs infected 74 percent of children with respiratory infections in 1999.[11] When coupled with the ecology of hospitals, which encouraged the spread of infections, these strains became grimly efficient reapers. A study estimated that in 2002 alone, American hospitals gave patients 1.7 million infections, 98,787 of which resulted in death; that is, almost one hundred thousand people entered the hospital for one problem, contracted a new infection in the hospital, and died of the latter.[12]

Malaria has killed millions of people each year thanks to a similar process. After World War II, a worldwide effort to eradicate malaria relied on insecticides (such as DDT, which killed the mosquitoes that carried the malaria plasmodium) and antimalarial drugs (such as atabrine and quinine, which stopped the malaria plasmodium from reproducing inside human bodies). The project saved an estimated fifteen to twenty-five million lives but foundered when, among other things, mosquito and plasmodium populations evolved resistance to their respective poisons. Unable to reach its goal, the World Health Organization halted the program in the early 1970s. By 2000, malaria was killing roughly two million people each year.[13]

We can also measure the impact of anthropogenic evolution in pathogens by tallying treasure lost. By 2000, tuberculosis infected one-third of humanity and caused three million deaths each year. Strains of tuberculosis resistant to the major drugs infected 11 percent of the new cases. Fallback medicines cost more than the drugs of first choice. Similar patterns hold for other pathogens. Overall, resistance to antibiotics costs Americans thirty billion dollars each year.[14]

Now let us board a plane to Colombia to see what has happened in efforts to eradicate plants. As we cruise over remote mountainsides, we might spy the effects of U.S. and Colombian efforts to fight a pair of foes. One is the coca industry, which supplies the raw ingredient for the cocaine that finds its way into American noses, lungs, and veins. The United States has aimed for years to eradicate the coca crop by funding the Colombian National Police, who go into the field to kill plants. The other foe is political insurgents. Coca thrives in areas controlled by guerrillas, making it hard for government forces to eradicate the crop. National Police aircraft flying over these areas face ground fire. Guerrillas (rightist and leftist) finance their activities with profits from the drug trade.[15] In their struggles against the United States and the Colombian government, then, coca and insurgents form a strategic alliance. Insurgents help coca by planting and protecting coca, and coca helps insurgents by generating income.

The United States has spared little expense in this two-front war, spending more than five billion dollars in hopes of victory. The coca eradication effort has relied on two weapons. One is manual eradication, or tearing up plants by hand. In 2007, Colombia's drug police used this method on sixty-five thousand hectares of coca fields. The method has disadvantages. It is labor intensive, and it requires that government agents walk into fields, a dangerous proposition in areas controlled by insurgents. The other and more important weapon is glyphosate, the herbicide better known by its trade name Roundup. Although dangerous, aerial spraying risks fewer lives and takes less time than manual eradication. Colombian police sprayed herbicide on 153,000 hectares in 2007, more than twice the area attacked manually.[16]

In the early 2000s, rumors began circulating that coca farmers were planting coca resistant to glyphosate. A reporter for *Wired* magazine learned from the head of a Colombian farmers union (himself a former coca grower) that farmers called the new strain *Boliviana negra*. The union leader guided the reporter to fields to see the result. The pair first hiked through a field of coca plants devastated by herbicide spraying. The leader identified the (dead) coca plants as *Peruviana blanca*. Then they topped a hill and came on healthy, neck-high coca plants stretching as far as the eye could see – *Boliviana negra*. Herbicides had rained down on both sides of the hill, but one variety perished while the other survived.[17]

How did the glyphosate-resistant *Boliviana negra* strain of coca evolve? One possibility was that drug traffickers hired scientists to insert a gene for resistance to glyphosate. The manufacturer of Roundup, Monsanto, had already demonstrated proof of concept by inserting such a gene in cotton. A Colombian geneticist told *Wired* that traffickers had offered him about ten million dollars to do the same thing with coca, but he had declined. The scientist did, however, test samples of *Boliviana negra* and found no evidence of genetic engineering. A second possibility was that coca plants generated the new trait themselves via mutation. Plants with the trait would have stood out like green lighthouses in brown seas of devastation after spraying, so it took no great skill for farmers to notice them. Growers propagated the new variety, which replaced older varieties in their fields.[18]

A third possibility is that growers switched species. There are two cultivated species of coca (*Erythroxylum novogranatense* and *E. coca*). I was unable to find a peer-reviewed study of the susceptibility of the two species to glyphosate, though one study mentions that *E. novogranatense* is more susceptible than *E. coca*. *E. novogranatense* is from Peru, and *E. coca* is from Bolivia. It is possible that *Peruviana blanca* is *E. novogranatense* and *Boliviana negra* is *E. coca*. If the resistance of *E. coca* is strong enough to survive glyphosate, growers may have altered the genetic composition of their plants by replacing one species with another.[19]

Resistance to glyphosate converted eradication programs into allies of coca plants and their human comrades. Glyphosate normally kills all plants it encounters, which makes it useful for clearing fields but not for killing weeds among crops. Monsanto inserted a gene for glyphosate resistance into cotton because it opened up a huge market for its herbicide. Roundup increased yields from glyphosate-resistant cotton by eliminating competition from weeds. Now it did the same for coca. Yields jumped as spraying wiped out weeds but not the coca crop. Thanks to a little bit of evolution, the millions of dollars spent on the eradication program amounted to government subsidies for coca production. The U.S. and

Colombian eradication program became a free aerial weed-killing service for coca farmers.[20]

Now let us sail to Europe during World War II to see how little six-legged creatures fared against total war. The desire to protect soldiers from insect-borne diseases, especially typhus (carried by lice) and malaria (transmitted by mosquitoes), led belligerent nations to launch crash programs to find effective insecticides. Paul Müller, a chemist at the Swiss chemical company Geigy, had recently discovered a long-lasting, synthetic insecticide known as DDT (for dichlorodiphenyltrichloroethane). Geigy shipped a sample to the United States for testing. It seemed miraculous. Small concentrations killed many species of insects for long periods of time, and the chemical had low acute toxicity to human beings. The United States launched a crash production program, modified chemical warfare gear to disperse the chemical from the air, and sprayed DDT over vast areas to protect soldiers from malaria. The United States had brought the malaria rate down to low levels through other means before DDT, but publicity credited DDT with victory.

Wartime success sent hopes for eradicating insect-borne diseases over the moon. Müller won the Nobel Prize for Medicine or Physiology in 1948. Governments, foundations, and international organizations launched ever-larger efforts to eradicate malaria until they reached the apex of ambition – to wipe malaria from the earth. But as we saw, these efforts foundered when mosquitoes evolved resistance to insecticides and malaria plasmodia evolved resistance to drugs. Evolution enabled insects and simple, one-celled creatures to defy the most powerful weapons fired at them.

The list of species that have evolved resistance to pesticides is a long one, and the economic cost is high. By 1986, populations of some 450 species of insects and mites, 100 species of plant pathogens (largely fungi), and 48 species of weeds had evolved resistance to their respective poisons.[21] By 1991, pesticide resistance led American farmers alone to spend $1.4 billion per year to apply extra insecticide. This cost has risen each year as the number of resistant species has grown. In some cases, resistance has forced the abandonment of enterprises altogether. In the 1960s, farmers in the American Southwest and northern Mexico had to stop growing cotton on seven hundred thousand acres because insecticides no longer controlled major pests.[22]

We can learn many things about anthropogenic evolution from eradication efforts, but let us focus here on four ideas. The first deepens our understanding of the role of states: governments and international organizations have often driven rapid evolution because they mobilized large-scale eradication efforts. A homeowner might hope to eradicate mosquitoes from her home, but she alone has little power over large areas. A mosquito with a DDT-resistant mutation might happen to fly into her home, starting a new variety, but odds are small. But the odds that a mosquito somewhere in the world will evolve a helpful mutation are high. Government has the power to mobilize large amounts of resources, override property rights, and spray pesticides over thousands of square miles. So the more government involves itself in eradication efforts, the more likely it is that the target of eradication efforts will evolve resistance.

The second idea also adds to our thinking about states: war has driven evolutionary change. One of the central responsibilities of any state has been national defense. Usually we think of human enemies as threatening national security, but natural enemies threatened security, too. The United States poured so much effort into developing insecticides during World War II because it knew malaria and typhus posed bigger threats to its military than enemy soldiers did. Early in the Pacific war, malaria caused eight times more casualties than battle. So the ability to defeat human foes rested on the ability to defeat natural foes. The chemicals, dispersal technology (planes, spray tanks, fogging machines), personnel, and organizational models of World War II flowed right into postwar malaria control efforts and quickly prompted evolution in mosquitoes. In South America, efforts by the United States and Colombia to battle political insurgents produced evolution in coca plants.

The third highlights the role of economic scale: the larger the reach of a corporation, the likelier it is to cause evolution. If a company markets only locally, its effects parallel those of the homeowner encountering a mosquito. Its drug might encounter a pathogen with a mutation for resistance in one town, but the odds increase dramatically with market area. When gigantic companies sell identical antibiotics around the globe, their drugs almost inevitably chance on a resistant individual somewhere.

The fourth idea predicts the kinds of species our eradication efforts tend to favor: those we like the least. By accident and intent, people have managed to eradicate (globally, regionally, or locally) a number of species of large mammals. These include, in North America, wolves and cougars (also known as mountain lions or pumas) as well as perhaps mammoths and mastodons. Against little critters, they have usually failed.

An evolutionary thought experiment reveals why small-bodied species have adapted more quickly to eradication efforts than have large-bodied species. If we were to invent two species, one designed to evolve slowly and the other quickly, what traits would we give them? My slow-evolving species would have (1) little variation in traits among individuals, reducing the options for adapting to a threat; (2) long generation time, slowing the rate at which populations could change; and (3) few offspring per individual, slowing the rate at which a trait could spread. My fast-evolving species would have (1) great variation among individuals, increasing the chance that some individuals bear traits that enable them to survive any given threat; (2) short generation time, accelerating the rate at which a population can change; and (3) large numbers of offspring per individual, accelerating the rate at which traits can spread.

Next let us do an ecological thought experiment. If we were to invent one species designed to go extinct quickly and another to persist, what would they look like? My fast-faltering species would have (1) a small population size, so killing an individual would have a measurable impact; (2) a long generation time, preventing populations from rebounding quickly; (3) few offspring per individual, also preventing populations from rebounding quickly; (4) large territories, making it easier to eradicate all individuals in a given area; and (5) the ability to live in only a narrow range of environmental conditions, so eliminating one habitat would kill off the species. My persistent species would have (1) a large population; (2) a short generation time; (3) many offspring per individual; and (4) the ability to survive in a variety of habitats.

Now let us apply the results of our thought experiment to eradication. Wolves, cougars, and other predators fit the bill for slow-adapting, easily extinguished species. They have long generation times (a year or more), few offspring per individual (we could count the pups in a litter on one or two hands), and large territories (measured in square miles) that keep population density low.[23] They could not evolve or reproduce rapidly enough to find a way around well-organized eradication efforts by U.S. federal and state agencies. Insects, viruses, bacteria, and fungi are the opposite. They live in large populations (billions and trillions of individuals), have short generations (measured in hours or days for some bacteria and viruses), and produce huge numbers of offspring per individual (hundreds or thousands). It is easy for many of them to evolve and reproduce rapidly enough to survive conscious or unconscious actions that could wipe them out.

That big-bodied species tend to evolve more slowly than small-bodied species is no accident. Species with large bodies usually have long generation times and produce few offspring per individual. It takes time to grow from infant to adult wolf or whale, postponing the arrival of sexual maturity. Big-bodied animals bear relatively big offspring, limiting the number a female can carry at one time. The offspring require a lot of help from parents until they mature, which also lengthens generation time and limits the number of offspring. Species with small bodies, on the other hand, reach sexual maturity more quickly. They produce tiny offspring (in the form of cells for bacteria and eggs for insects) that require no parental care to mature, which aids in keeping generation times short and numbers of offspring large.

Evolutionarily, both types of organisms are betting that their offspring will survive to the next generation, but they go about it in opposite ways. Big-bodied animals often take the quality approach: by investing large resources in a few offspring, they bank on bringing a high percentage to maturity. Small-bodied organisms generally take the quantity approach: by investing little in each offspring, they can produce so many offspring that a few survive even though most die young.[24] This brings us to our general conclusion: among the species that have grabbed human attention, small-bodied creatures have generally adapted to threats more quickly than large-bodied organisms. The small-bodied organisms that live in large populations, and spread over wide areas and habitats, have met with the most success.

The implications for the kind of world we might expect in the future are profound – and opposite of what most people would like to see. People tend to like big, showy birds and mammals. Conservationists call them *charismatic megafauna* and highlight them in publicity campaigns. Even the people who shoot megafauna want to have them around. But megafauna adapt slowly to a changing world, and it is not hard to drive them extinct by hunting and habitat destruction. In contrast, people tend to dislike little creepy things and germs. But many little species have the traits that enable them to adapt quickly to threats. The faster we change the environment, the more likely we are to drive specialized large mammals extinct while keeping small generalist organisms, some of whom do not have our best interests at heart, around for company.

Hunting, fishing, and eradicating resemble each other in that all involve intentional efforts by people to interact with specific species. In the next chapter, we turn our focus to the evolutionary impact of environmental change, which changes species without most of us noticing.

5

Altering Environments

I hope your walking shoes and Mackintosh are at hand, for we are off on a ramble through the English countryside. We have jumped back to the nineteenth century, and as we head out, we see green hues burst forth from crops and weeds, grasses and shrubs, and trees and marsh. Birds and insects seem to be flying, buzzing, or crawling most places we look. We can even see a tall, tweedy fellow with a net chasing butterflies at the edge of the woods. Generations of farmers have encouraged this diversity of plants by dividing fields, plowing some and leaving others fallow, growing several types of crops, and planting hedgerows.

Now let us jump forward to today. The landscape looks very different. Large fields have replaced small fields, hedgerows and woods have disappeared to make tractor plowing easier, manufactured fertilizers have substituted for plant and animal manures and fallowing, single crops grow over large areas, grasslands are closely cropped, herbicides have annihilated weeds, and combine harvesting has left few seeds behind for avian gleaning. Monotony has squeezed out diversity.[1] Mostly these changes have been ecological, altering the distribution and abundance of organisms, but some of the changes have been evolutionary, changing the traits of organisms.

We know about some of the evolutionary changes. The farmer plants crops bred for high yield and likes to hunt with a retrieving dog, both of which have been inbred to reduce variation of genes and traits. The insects and diseases infesting the crops probably evolved resistance to an earlier generation of pesticides. Crops, pets, and pests – these are the types of species we notice because they affect our lives. And these have been the types of species on which we have focused so far in this book. This chapter shifts our focus from the species we notice to those we usually do not. We change the evolution of unobserved species, too.

This chapter argues that we have accidentally shaped the evolution of populations by altering environments. We have no idea how many species we have changed in this way, or how radically, or how quickly. The reason is that most of the species in the world are tiny little things that pass beneath our gaze. Many of them, such as bacteria, become visible only under a microscope. Others are big enough to see but seem trivial. Hundreds of species of insects live in farm fields, but farmers usually notice only those that become numerous enough to cause economic damage. What is true of farm fields is true of the globe. Scientists have named 1.75 million species, and they estimate that 5 to 100 million more remain to be classified.[2] Insects account for perhaps half this diversity. The range of the estimates, spanning orders of magnitude, provides a clue to our ignorance. We know so little that we cannot confidently predict how much we do not know.

This chapter explores accidental selection via environmental change on three scales. The first section looks at the personal scale, using bacteria as an example. The second looks at the regional scale, using peppered moths as a case study. And the third looks at the global scale, looking at several species of plants and animals that have altered their traits in response to climate change. A variety of human activities have affected environments on all these scales. We have been changing sea levels, increasing ultraviolet radiation, transferring species across continents, contributing pollutants to air and water, and changing the pH of rain through additions of sulfur dioxide and nitrogen oxides.[3]

If you dislike the idea of bacteria in your body, I have some bad news. Our bodies teem with bacteria. Inside your gut alone, so many bacteria live that the number of their cells is ten times higher than the number of human-derived cells in your entire body. So 90 percent or more of the cells in and on our bodies belong to other species hitching a ride. This is a good thing, too. We depend on these bacteria to survive. The bacteria in our intestines, for example, digest our food.[4]

Given that we harbor so many bacteria, we can safely predict that each of us is managing thousands of evolutionary experiments even when we are not thinking about bacteria at all. Take the impact of weight loss. Thousands of species of bacteria live inside each of us, and they differ dramatically from person to person, but most (92.6%) belong to two major divisions: the bacteriodetes and the firmicutes. The ratio of bacteriodetes to firmicutes is smaller in obese than in lean people, but when obese people lose weight, the ratio increases significantly.[5] These data are ecological – they describe differences in species abundance. But environmental changes large enough to alter species composition probably alter selection for varieties within species as well.

This leads me to propose a testable hypothesis: changes in diet affect the evolution of human gut bacteria. I would venture that populations of bacteria in the gut of an alcoholic, for example, might have evolved traits different from populations in the gut of a teetotaler. This is an example of using evolutionary history to generate hypotheses that future research can test and support or refute. At the moment, we have little grasp on how selection has shaped the genomes and functions of human gut bacteria at all, much less the role of diet, though the recently launched Human Microbiome Project should lay the groundwork for deeper understanding.[6]

What social factors have driven evolutionary change on the personal scale? The most obvious factors are personal decisions – the soaps we use to wash our hands or the food we eat and thus how much we weigh. But we can push the historical side much harder. In the case of gut bacteria, obesity is not just a function of personal choice. It is also grows out of broad social choices that shape personal decisions. A variety of institutions shape those choices.

Let us return to the role of the U.S. federal government and highlight just two ways it has contributed to obesity and thus to the types of bacteria favored in American guts. One is by subsidizing the production of corn. The cost of producing a bushel of corn often exceeds the price it would command on the market. The only reason farmers can afford to raise an uneconomical crop is government crop subsidies.

Those subsidies result from many factors, but one is the constitutional distribution of power. Every state, no matter how small the population, has two senators. So sparsely populated agricultural states have enormous clout in Congress, which enables senators to channel billions of dollars to farmers. The subsidies reward farmers who produce the most bushels per acre. The result is predictable – huge mountains of cheap corn at harvest time. Processors realized that cheap corn enabled them to make a cheap sweetener, high fructose corn syrup, which replaced more expensive crystalline sugar (sucrose) in hundreds of products, from soft drinks to spaghetti sauce. Cheap sweeteners mean cheap calories for consumers, so caloric consumption has risen steadily in the United States.[7]

Now let us turn from the energy we put into our bodies to the energy we burn up. Once again, we will look at the role of the state. Eating more calories increases our body weight only if we eat more than we use carrying out daily activities. Unfortunately, calorie consumption rose at the same time that physical activity declined. The biggest factor was a shift in the labor market, with service jobs at desks replacing labor-intensive jobs involving constant motion. But activity outside work also declined, and two of the biggest reasons were the automobile and television. People who commuted by car walked a few feet from house to car, drove to work, walked a few feet from parking lot to desk, walked the same few feet back to the parking lot, drove home, walked a few feet to the house, and sat on a couch to watch television all evening.[8]

The growth of automobile-dependent suburbs encouraged this pattern of behavior, and government policies encouraged the growth of suburbs through permissive zoning, road building, mortgage subsidies, and tax breaks. Suburban living almost always forced a person to drive to work and shopping. State actions thus modulated the amount of physical activity Americans got, which influenced their weight, which influenced their gut bacteria, which probably encouraged the evolution of some strains over others without anyone ever thinking about this effect.[9]

The growth of suburbs provides a nice transition from the personal to the regional scale of evolution-inducing environmental change. Here I cannot resist looking at one of the classic stories of human-induced evolution involving peppered moths (*Biston betularia* Linn.). Remember the tweedy fellow at the edge of the woods we saw at the beginning of this chapter? He is important to our story, for his hobby led him to skewer butterflies and moths on pins and store them in special boxes that we can examine today. He, his predecessors, and his successors created the physical record we need to chart changes in peppered moths over time.

Let us begin with colors. The first transition in coloring of peppered moths is better known, though the second part is equally important. In the first part, the frequency of dark wings increased in certain populations over time. In the eighteenth century, the species looked the way its common name suggests – mottled, with black spots on white wings. In the nineteenth and early twentieth centuries, dark wings became more common over much of England. The second transition is less famous. Beginning around 1970, the traditional mottled coloring became more common once again. Understanding the reasons for the seesaw pattern requires that we bring together biology (moth genetics and bird predation) with history (economics and politics).[10]

When English lepidopterists of the eighteenth century sent their nets
swooping, the peppered moths they caught were almost always light
colored. Collectors did capture a few with dark wings, but the scientific
community remained ignorant of their existence until the second half of
the nineteenth century. In the years 1848 to 1860, collectors in Lancashire
and Yorkshire noticed a surge in the frequency of dark individuals. This
pattern radiated north and south from there over the following decades,
until dark moths turned up in London in 1897. By the 1950s, 90 percent
of the peppered moths over a large swath of England flitted around on
dark wings.[11]

Continental Europe and North America saw similar patterns. Dark
peppered moths appeared in Breda, the Netherlands, in 1867. They spread
to Germany by 1880; to the Ruhr by 1882; and to Berlin, Prague, northern Bohemia, the Baltic coasts, and Copenhagen by the early twentieth
century. Once they arrived, they became increasingly common. In Berlin,
records show dark moths present in 1903. They made up 25 percent of
the population in 1933, 50 percent in 1939, and 85 percent by 1955.
In North America, the first reports came from southeastern Pennsylvania in 1906. Dark moths appeared in Pittsburgh in 1910 and Detroit in
1929, and from there, they spread up the east coast to New England. By
1960, the frequency reached 80 to 97 percent in Michigan, 36 percent in
Ontario, and 3 to 11 percent in Massachusetts.[12]

The percentage of dark moths soared because birds preyed on light-
colored individuals more heavily. At least nine bird species feasted on
peppered moths in England, and a similar variety probably did so elsewhere. Light-colored moths stood out against dark trees and buildings,
which made it easier for birds to find them than the dark moths that
blended in with the background. Light individuals probably suffered
25 to 50 percent more predation than dark individuals during the century
or so when the dark color came to predominate.[13]

Then the pattern reversed itself. In the last third of the twentieth century, the frequency of dark moths plummeted from over 90 percent to
about 50 percent in northeast England and from 90 percent to 10 percent in Michigan and Pennsylvania. Again birds shifted the proportion
by playing a biased grim reaper. They gobbled up dark individuals 5 to
20 percent more often than light moths during this period, and they did
so for the same reason as before – they could see the dark moths more
easily against the light backgrounds that dominated the landscape.[14]

The main force darkening the environment in which moths lived
was coal burning. Early research in peppered moth coloration credited

(or blamed) coal soot for the change. All the places where peppered moth populations evolved dark wings – England, the upper Midwest of the United States, and northern continental Europe (especially the Ruhr Valley) – saw an increase in coal usage in the nineteenth and early twentieth centuries and then a decline late in the twentieth. More recent research has supported the idea that coal use darkened the landscape but suggested that sulfur dioxide bore more responsibility than soot. Sulfur dioxide contributed to acid rain, which killed plants, including the light-colored lichen that used to grow on tree trunks. The switch from coal to cleaner fuels dramatically lowered the amount of soot and sulfur dioxide in the air, which enabled trees and lichen to regrow in lighter colors and urbanites to wash away the grime that had hidden light-colored walls from view.

The rise and fall of coal as fuel tells us why the environment changed color, but it does not explain why coal rose and fell in popularity. For that, we have to turn to history. The usual, quick explanation is industrialization. The Industrial Revolution created an enormous appetite for energy, both in factories and in the homes of workers, and coal fed the maws of steam engines and fireplaces. But coal was not the inevitable fuel of the Industrial Revolution. Water powered the English Industrial Revolution at first, which explains why the vanguard of change – the textile industry – grew up in the northwest part of the country. That mountainous region received steady rainfall, so it could pour plenty of water over steep drops to power water mills. Had the Industrial Revolution continued to rely on water, peppered moth populations would have retained their traditional mottled colors.

As industry and cities expanded, though, demand for power exceeded water's reach. Before the invention of hydroelectric dams and power grids, water offered nothing to homeowners wanting to drive the chill out of their bones and homes. Factory owners found that water lacked reliability (when it froze or dried up) and constrained their choice of factory locations (next to rivers with steep drops in elevation). Firewood could have fueled homes and factories, but England would have had to rely on imports because it had already leveled its forests.

England happened to sit over large coal deposits near rivers and canals, making this black rock a cost-effective replacement for wood and water. And as it happened, the coal deposits also lay in northern England, enabling industry to continue to grow there. Factories and power plants in the blackened regions of the United States and Germany turned to coal because of the same price advantages growing out of location. In other regions, such as the Northwest of the United States, hydroelectricity powered factories without churning out soot and sulfur dioxide. It was not industrialization per se that caused coal use to increase but rather a price advantage over other fuels in regions that happened to lie near deposits.[15]

Similarly, deindustrialization offers a too-quick explanation for plummeting coal use. It played an important role, especially in the past few decades, but the decline began before industry left these regions. Politics, more than economics, drove the initial drop. England saw bouts of horrendous urban air pollution in 1952, and Manchester (one of the centers of industry, coal burning, and dark moths) established smoke control zones the same year. Four years later, Britain's Clean Air Acts required the use of smokeless fuels over more of the country and dispersed power plants to rural areas. The 1960s saw a big shift from coal to oil and electricity, which further reduced air pollution. In the United States, the Clean Air Act (especially the Extension of 1981) slashed urban air pollution and helped drive the shift to less-polluting types of coal.[16]

We can draw several lessons from this case study. First, human beings have changed environments over large areas by accident. People burned coal to power factories and heat homes, not with the goal of darkening the countryside. Second, human impact on other species via environmental change has been neither unidirectional nor final – it has changed and continued over time. The frequency of dark peppered moths rose and then fell again because human beings alternately darkened and lightened the landscape.

Third, economics, technological choice, and politics all have influenced the way people have shaped environments and thus evolution. Economics played a key role in technological choice: people used coal where it was cheap and abundant, and that drove parallel evolution in England, continental Europe, and the United States. Moths in other regions, where dams provided a cheap and abundant source of power, did not face the same selective pressures, but politics intervened in the economy to prompt a shift from coal to cleaner fuels, which ushered in a different selective regime for moths in places where coal could have continued to pollute the landscape.

Fourth, we change populations of species without knowing it. When English laborers decided to light the coal in a grate, they had no thought of peppered moths. Few could have recognized or named the species. But striking the match contributed in a small way to evolution within this species. And fifth, we have no way to track the evolution we cause in most species. We know people changed the peppered moth because we happen to have records in the form of moths on pins. But human beings do not keep records on the vast majority of species on earth. The peppered moth is the tip of an iceberg of inadvertent evolution.

Although estimates vary, serious efforts to quantify our environmental impact have produced some impressive numbers. One dimension is spatial. Human beings now affect, at least moderately, 60 percent of the world's land surface area. We shape 41 percent of the world's marine environments. In a given year, roughly 40 percent of all the world's plant growth goes to human uses, and we almost certainly have been altering climate around the globe. Another dimension is temporal. In wild populations that human beings harvest (such as fish), evolution occurs at a pace as much as three times faster than that observed in natural systems.[17] Small wonder that some scientists and historians believe we have entered a new geological epoch dubbed the Anthropocene.[18] By altering most of the world's environments, we are altering most of the crucibles in which populations evolve.

How have we managed to do this? Key enterprises include agriculture, industry, commerce, and recreation. These endeavors have visibly altered the face of the earth by clearing land and cutting trees. Less obviously, at least to the casual visitor, is the extent to which we affect ecosystems through grazing, hunting, fishing, species introductions, extinctions, and nutrient use. One study estimated that human beings have depleted, fully exploited, or overexploited 66 percent of the world's fisheries, increased atmospheric carbon dioxide by 30 percent, commandeered over half the accessible surface water, doubled nitrogen fixation, introduced new species almost everywhere, and driven up to 25 percent of bird species extinct.[19]

Our impact extends beyond those species we affect directly. Plants and animals live in ecological webs, and plucking one strand often twangs others as well. Yellowstone National Park provides a dramatic example. Government programs drove many large predators almost extinct in the lower forty-eight states by the 1920s. Over the next sixty or seventy years, almost no new cottonwood trees (*Populus* spp.) established themselves along the Lamar River. The population of beaver (*Castor canadensis*) also plummeted.

The Lamar River's ecology changed after the reintroduction of wolves to the park in 1995 and 1996. Young cottonwoods shot up in some places. Beaver returned to areas in which they had become rare. The best explanation appears to be that wolves indirectly affected cottonwoods and beaver via their effect on elk. With no fear of predators, elk had browsed wherever they pleased for six or seven decades. Once wolves returned, elk changed their behavior. Wolves find it easier to kill elk in some terrain than others (e.g., depending on whether elk have an escape route). Elk began avoiding areas with a high risk of predation, including certain stretches along the Lamar River, and concentrating in other, lower-risk areas. Freed from heavy browsing, young cottonwoods thrived in the higher-risk areas, and they in turn attracted beaver.[20] This is an example of ways in which a keystone predator (an animal at the top of the food chain) affects the ecology of other species below it in the chain. By affecting wolf populations, people indirectly altered environments for cottonwoods and beaver as well.

We do not have enough evolutionary biologists to track any but the tiniest fraction of the ways in which populations have adapted (or gone extinct) as a result of human actions. We do know, however, that changing environments around the globe potentially affect every species on earth, and the scale of our impact appears to have become global. As coal plants and fireplaces spewed soot and sulfur dioxide into the air, they also churned out an invisible gas, carbon dioxide. Carbon dioxide (along with methane and a few other gases) rose into the sky and erected a gaseous roof around the world. Like glass roofs in greenhouses, this gaseous roof allowed sunlight to shine through to warm earth and water. But again like glass roofs, greenhouse gases trapped heat when earth and water exhaled their warm breath. Our planet has warmed, almost surely because of anthropogenic greenhouse gases, and it will continue to do so in the foreseeable future.

We hear most about how global warming shapes geography and ecology, but it also has affected evolution. Geographical and ecological effects include melting glaciers, rising sea levels, spreading deserts, and shifting animal and plant ranges, to name just a few. But changes in climate affect the environments in which populations evolve, so climate change has made human beings a selective force around the globe. When the laborer struck the match to light the coal in a nineteenth-century English terrace house, the evolutionary impact extended beyond the peppered moths fluttering in the countryside downwind. That fire also pushed the temperature of the entire earth the tiniest bit higher and pushed the traits of species in a different direction. We are only just beginning to get data on the evolutionary impact of climate change.

The species with the best chance of navigating the storm of climate change are those with the capacity for fast evolution. As we saw in Chapter 3, they tend to reproduce in large numbers, live in a variety of habitats, have short generation times, and carry great genetic variability. We have already seen that many species of bacteria and insects fit the bill (though other species in these groups are quite specialized). Now let us look at the plants we call weeds. Technically, a weed is a plant growing anywhere people do not want it, so trees can be weeds. But most plants we call weeds are annuals growing in disturbed soil such as farm fields. With plows churning up their homes every year, these species have to live in rapidly changing habitats (in fact, many live only in disturbed areas). As a result, they arrive at the evolutionary dance dressed to the nines.

So let us take a twirl on the evolutionary dance floor with a common weed, wild mustard (*Brassica rapa*). Global warming has been predicted to bring, among other things, drought. In 2000 to 2004, a drought that struck southern California gave researchers a chance to see whether mustard populations could adapt genetically to this type of change over a short period. By a stroke of luck, the researchers had happened to collect wild mustard seeds in 1997. They collected more seeds in 2004, grew seeds from both years under wet and dry conditions, and found that offspring of the 2004 population flowered 1.9 or 8.6 days sooner (depending on moisture) than offspring of the 1997 population. The population had evolved genetically in just seven years.[21]

Insects are champion evolvers, so it is no surprise that they have been dancing to the new tune. On O Pedroso Mountain in northwest Spain, a population of fruit fly (*Drosophila subobscura*) faced rising temperatures between 1976 and 1991. One *Drosophila* chromosome (called O) carries genes responsible for enabling flies to tolerate heat. The chromosome comes in fifteen versions. As temperatures rose, the frequency of one version declined 47 percent in the population while the frequency of another rose. The version that declined was originally common in northern parts of the fly's range and more rare in the south, and the one that rose was originally more common in the south and more rare in the north. Because southern areas are warmer than northern areas, the shift in gene frequency is consistent with adaptation to rising temperatures.[22] Mosquitoes have also adapted to global warming. Between 1972 and 1996, populations of pitcher-plant mosquitoes across a broad swath of North America shifted their hibernation (more precisely, entered diapause) later in the year as temperatures warmed.[23]

Now let us switch dance partners to a mammal. Between 1989 and 2002, the environment near Kluane Lake, Yukon, Canada, changed rapidly. The average spring temperature rose two degrees Celsius, less rain fell, and white spruce cones became more abundant. At the end of the period, local red squirrels (which fed on spruce cones) gave birth to young eighteen days earlier than at the beginning. The habitat might have encouraged earlier births in two ways – by affecting physiology or evolution. By comparing the dates on which individual females gave birth to each of their litters, researchers concluded that individual (physiological) responses were responsible for 62 percent of the change. Physiological changes advanced the date 3.7 days per generation. (We will not go into the mathematics behind these calculations.) Evolution accounted for 13 percent, or 0.8 days per generation. Unknown causes accounted for another 25 percent.[24]

These examples might tempt us to conclude that adaptation will enable other species to keep time with global warming no matter how fast the music plays, and to some extent, it will. But we have to remember that species vary widely in their ability to adapt quickly. Species with long generations, specific habitat requirements, and little genetic diversity will have a much harder time. Some of the species we like best – such as trees and large mammals – fall into this category. A 2004 study estimated that climate change will drive 15 to 37 percent of species to extinction by 2050.[25]

And unfortunately, our main strategy for saving the most threatened of these – nature preserves – will begin to fail. We create preserves where species live now. As the earth warms, those species will have to migrate toward the poles (or up mountains) to stay within the temperature range they need. But we have no plans to move preserves with them, so they will have to enter unprotected land. Unless we create long, protected north-south corridors (which some have proposed), plants and animals will have to leave national parks and face the very dangers that parks now keep at bay.[26]

So far we have focused on species that adapted to environmental change. But not all species adapt to change in time, and the long-term fate of most species in the history of the world has been extinction. Some have disappeared from the ranks of the living with a big splash, as when dinosaurs expired en masse. Others have limped to the boneyard one by one. Most extinct species disappeared with no help from human beings, but we have also tipped some into their grave. One famous example is the disappearance of the passenger pigeon from North America. Hunting contributed, but habitat destruction played the most important role.[27] As the scale on which we have changed the earth has increased, so, too, has the scale on which we have driven species extinct.

Human beings have threatened the survival of the largest number of species through the same enterprise that changed the largest terrestrial area of the globe: habitat destruction, especially for agriculture. A 1997 study found that the single best predictor of the location of endangered plants, mammals, and reptiles in the United States was the presence of agriculture.[28] Cutting of tropical rainforests is perhaps the quickest way we drive species extinct today. An estimated two-thirds of terrestrial species live in tropical humid forests, so eliminating these biodiversity hot spots (or replacing them with less diverse assemblages of plants and animals, as agriculture does) is an efficient way to send species to their graves.[29]

The motives for environmental change range as widely as the human spirit. They have included economic, political, social, cultural, and military goals. Because environmental change causes evolutionary change, economic forces have been evolutionary forces. Social forces have been evolutionary forces. Cultural forces have been evolutionary forces. Military forces have been evolutionary forces. Anthropogenic evolution, thy forces are legion.

6

Evolution Revolution

As I write this chapter in a third-floor garret, my family's dog Riley naps on a rug in front of a fireplace on the first floor. We enjoy having him in our lives because he bubbles with affection, cheers us when we are low, and enlivens our walks and runs. We love him, even though he is undistinguished by the usual measures of canine fame. He carries no proud pedigree and has won no shows. He came to us not from an elite kennel but from a shelter, and his ancestry remains a mystery. He might be a flat-coated retriever, he might have sprung from a Labrador retriever that coupled with another breed, or he might belong to some other clan. He is the most ordinary of dogs.

He is also extraordinary, for he belongs to one of the first species of domesticated animal. **Domestication** refers to the *process through which species adapt other species to live and reproduce in captivity.* In the domestication hall of fame, the plaque for dogs greets us as soon as we enter. Dogs hold pride of place because in addition to being one of the first domestic species, they experienced two dramatic transformations. One transformation saw one or more populations of wolves evolve into dogs. It is remarkable that descendents of wolves could become companions we trust around our babies, especially since the first domesticators had no example of other domestic animals to inspire them. The second transformation fashioned dogs into breeds that looked and behaved in very different ways. It is hard to believe that dachshunds and St. Bernards descend from the same ancestors, but they do. Riley, like all dogs, is a testament to the extraordinary power of human beings to shape the evolution of other species.

The key argument of this chapter is that the most momentous transition in human history was an evolutionary revolution. The agricultural revolution was that momentous transition, for it gave rise to settled societies, advanced technology, nation-states, and nearly everything historians study. The agricultural revolution was an evolutionary revolution because it depended on domestication, which altered inherited traits and genes of populations of organisms over generations. So most of recorded history is a by-product of anthropogenic evolution.

Making the case for what happened requires little space, so most of the chapter will focus on a secondary argument about how this evolutionary revolution happened. I will compare the traditional explanation for domestication, methodical selection, with a challenger, unconscious selection. I favor the latter, which can be unsettling for those of us who like to attribute historical events to human intentionality. The debate over mechanisms is important and interesting, but it is secondary because either mechanism (methodical or unconscious selection) could have produced the evolutionary revolution.

Anthropogenic evolution has shaped human history, and thus the events historians study, more powerfully than any other human force. The reason is simple. To have human history, one has to have human beings. Without anthropogenic evolution, the great majority of people historians study would not have lived. Our ancestral way of obtaining food, hunting and gathering, supported only small populations of mobile bands. Large populations became possible only once agriculture boosted the output of usable food per hectare and per worker. And agriculture depended in turn on altering traits of wild plants and animals to make them more productive. Archaeological and genetic evidence suggests that humans began farming roughly ten thousand years ago. Intentionally and unintentionally, humans selected for sweeter fruit, nonshattering seedpods, less aggressive animals, and fatter cows. Today, all but a tiny fraction of the world's 6.4 billion people rely on agricultural products for survival.[1]

Now comes my trump card: without anthropogenic evolution, you would not be reading this book. Historians have long suggested that history began with the invention of writing. (They assigned earlier events to prehistory.) Writing is a by-product of anthropogenic evolution. When farmers churned out more food than their families needed, other members of their societies lived off the surplus and turned their attention to other tasks. They created social hierarchies, bureaucracies, armies, complicated technology, international conquest, and writing – which led to this book. More seriously, the point is not whether this book would exist; it is that nearly everything we consider part of civilization (including this book), and most of the topics historians study, developed because of domestication.[2]

We rely just as much on the products of the evolutionary revolution today as in the past. In 2006, agriculture employed about 39 percent of the world's workers. The proportion was higher in the third world, reaching 63 percent in sub-Saharan Africa.[3] Like individual workers, nations relied on agricultural income to stay afloat. In 2002, agriculture contributed about 30 percent of the gross domestic product in sub-Saharan Africa and South Asia, about 20 percent in East and Southeast Asia, and about 7 percent in Latin America and the Caribbean.[4] Plus, almost all of the world's people rely primarily on domestic plants and animals for their food.

The number of species involved, and the range of taxonomic groups to which they belong, suggests the enormous effort humans have poured into domestication for thousands of years. Domesticated animals have included mammals (dog, ass, horse, cow, sheep, goat, reindeer, camel, buffalo, rabbit, elephant, ferret, mongoose, yak), birds (chicken, turkey, pheasant, quail, pigeon, falcon, goose, duck, pelican, cormorant, crane, canary, ostrich), insects (silkworm, honeybee), and fish (eel, carp, goldfish, paradise fish).[5]

The list of domesticated plants is even longer. The plants thought to have originated in Southwest Asia alone include cereals (oats, barley, rye, wheat), pulses (chickpea, lentil, fava), tubers (beet, turnip, carrot, radish), oil crops (rapeseed, mustard, safflower, olive, flax), fruits and nuts (hazelnut, melon, fig, walnut, palm, almond, apricot, cherry, pear, apple, grape), vegetables and spices (onion, garlic, leek, cabbage, coriander, cucumber, cumin, anise, purslane), fiber plants (hemp, flax), forage crops (bentgrass, rye, clover, vetch), and drug sources (belladonna, digitalis, coca). Making use of some of these animals and plants has depended in turn on domesticating microorganisms. Bacteria turn milk into yogurt, and yeast is essential for making leavened bread, wine, and beer.[6]

Domestic plants and animals are so common that their state can seem inevitable. We eat food and wear clothes from domestic plants and animals, drink beer and wine made with domestic fungi, walk on domestic grass, fuel our cars with domestic corn, and share our homes with domestic flowers, cats, and dogs. At least in countries with plentiful food, it all seems to work quite well. The Bible can reinforce a sense of inevitability by describing domestication as divine will. Genesis tells us that God put other species on earth for our use and gave us dominion over them. Our original home, in this account, was a garden. What could be more normal than domestication?

A sense of inevitability and ordinariness can create a sense that domestication requires no explanation. Even when we remember that the process took some human effort, we often see it as simple. People spied a plant or animal with useful traits, bred it in captivity, and voila – we had dogs and cats underfoot, cattle in the barn, apples and cherries in pies, oranges and grapefruit on the breakfast table, and lilacs and begonias in the garden. This explanation can seem intuitive because we are all so familiar today with plant and animal breeding. Plus, we expect people to accomplish important things through intentional actions rather than dumb luck.

If we equate normality with commonness, however, domestication is abnormal. The first humans (genus *Homo*) evolved about seven million years ago, and our species (*Homo sapiens*) walked onto the scene about 250,000 years ago. We have lived with domestic species for about fifteen thousand years, or about 6 percent of our species' history (and well less than 1 percent of our genus's history). In light of its brevity and rarity, domestication looks more than a bit curious and is certainly in need of explanation.

The classic explanation for domestication, methodical selection, highlights traits in which human beings take a great deal of pride – foresight, planning, and control. As the British naturalist Thomas Bell put it in 1837, domestication showed the "triumph of human art and reason over the natural instincts of the inferior animals."[7] Under this hypothesis, people believed they could transform wild animals into creatures with traits the wild species did not have, and they used **breeding** – selectively mating males and females – to develop these new beings.

This explanation bears more than a passing resemblance to the Genesis story. Although it shifts the credit from God to human beings, the **master breeder narrative** posits a Godlike degree of omniscience and omnipotence. Crediting people with these traits might seem intuitive today because breeding is so common and, at first blush, simple. What could be more obvious than mating a champion mare to a champion stallion to breed fast racehorses? But breeding looks simple only in retrospect – that is, only after people have worked out the methods and produced a given result. In prospect, it can look daunting.

We may need to credit the agricultural revolution to unconscious selection. People may have domesticated plants and animals as the accidental by-product of actions taken for other, short-term reasons. They did not glimpse the long-term outcome of their efforts (Westminster Dog Show, Levi's, double cheeseburgers with fries, high school football, cattle dowries, the Parthenon, the Bhagavad-Gita, and the Crusades) when they killed off the hellions among the wolves lurking about camp or pinched longer-fibered cottonseeds more often than short-fibered ones (two examples we will explore in more detail). Yet actions like these added up to a revolution.

Unifying these actions was their effect on selection. By increasing the odds of survival for tamer animals, people set in motion a cascade of effects on appearance and behavior such as year-round reproduction, piebald coats, and responsiveness to human commands. And by altering the odds of survival for easily harvested plants, people created domestic populations with large seeds, simultaneous ripening, and nonshattering pods. People did become breeders eventually, but I doubt they were at the outset.

To see why, let us don parkas and travel to the steppes of East Asia and the lands of the Middle East about fifteen thousand years ago. Biologists believe people domesticated wolves (*Canis lupus*) and developed them into dogs (*Canis familiaris*) in one or both those places about that time.[8] There we will expect to find bands of human hunter-gatherers roaming the landscape, shifting their campsites to follow migrating animals and ripening plants. And we will expect to see bands of wolves hunting some of the same game. According to the master breeder hypothesis, the hunter-gatherers realized that they could tame wolves to help them create a better life. Some brave soul burrowed into a wolf den, captured cubs, brought the cubs back to camp, and trained them to hunt by command. This worked well. People realized that tame wolves (dogs) could perform other tasks, too, so they created breeds tailored to a variety of job descriptions. Breeders manufactured each variety by imagining the traits required, picking males and females with those traits, and mating them.[9]

This scenario places some big demands on early domesticators. Among other things, it requires that they

1. believed that current methods of survival, which their ancestors had used for hundreds of thousands of years, were so inadequate that they needed a new strategy

2. imagined they could domesticate a wild species, though they had never done so before
3. imagined traits in wolves (such as responsiveness to human commands and willingness to share a kill) that they had never seen
4. believed they could tame wolves by raising cubs in captivity
5. believed that individual wolves varied because they inherited traits from their parents
6. believed that one could manipulate traits by mating specific males and females
7. believed wolves would breed in captivity
8. considered all this a better use of time than gathering plants and hunting animals for immediate benefit

In addition to calling for almost divine foresight and skill, the master breeder narrative makes dicey assumptions about wolf biology. One assumption is that people created tame adults from wild cubs. Wolf cubs do behave a lot like dogs, but even human-raised pups turn so fierce as adults that a false move can incite a bloody, even lethal, attack. Another assumption is that one can turn wolves, a fierce animal, into a command-obeying ally in one generation. Wolves do not obey human commands, and it is hard to imagine that people persisted in raising dangerous animals for uncertain benefits far in the future. Another assumption is that wolves will mate with whichever animal people select. In fact, female wolves select the males with which they will couple rather than leaving the decision up to others.[10]

Now imagine we gather around a campfire with the hunter-gatherers of East Asia fifteen thousand years ago and present the master breeder scenario. To make this conversation realistic, we could not offer any information from the future (that is, no data that any of this worked). The hunters and gatherers might sign up, but I suspect they would laugh, suggest that we try out the idea ourselves, and get back to making a living in a time-tested way. Responding in this way does not make them foolish or stupid; it makes them rational.

Rather than assuming that people fifteen thousand years ago used breeding techniques common today, let us see how domestication might have resulted from actions hunter-gatherers took for immediate gain. The following sequence seems plausible. Hunter-gatherers tossed waste, such as bones and carcasses of game animals, just outside their camps. Mammals lurked nearby to scavenge this waste, which reduced the stench of rotting meat and offal, so people tolerated the scavengers. When other food ran short, human hunters turned their gimlet eyes on nearby wolves and slaughtered a few. But they did not choose at random. Wolves varied in their temperaments, and it made life a little less stressful to kill off the most cantankerous wolves first.[11]

Now let us hide ourselves just outside the camp and watch this process from the wolf's perspective. Wolves varied in their response to human beings. The continuum ranged from staying near people all the time to staying away all the time. Both extremes, and points in between, worked. Wolves were pack animals, they followed the leads of high-ranking males and females in the pack, and cubs learned how to behave by watching their elders, so some packs grew ever more specialized in camp following. Within camp-following packs, individuals varied in their skittishness. The less fearful individuals crept closest to camp and got the most food, whereas the most fearful stayed farther away and got the least. The most fearful were also those most likely to respond aggressively if they felt threatened by people.

So calmer individuals gained two advantages over their skittish kin – more food and less chance of being killed when people decided which wolf to impale at dinnertime. Over time, unconscious selection produced tamer wolves until they behaved so calmly people tolerated them in camp. Some proved more adept at understanding human signals (verbal and physical) and soliciting human affection than others, and those individuals got more food and survived the spear more often than their duller brethren. Over time, wolves learned to obey commands, and people kept the most responsive around because they performed useful work. Eventually, the domestic version of the wolf became distinctive enough to be called the Paleolithic equivalent of "dog."

This scenario credits unconscious selection with driving domestication. The key idea is that both people and wolves took actions for their own short-term gain, not with the intent of molding future generations at all. But their actions accidentally selected for the traits that distinguished dogs from wolves. Did you feel the arrow into the heart of our self-image? We like to think of ourselves as a species that plans, and we historians almost always credit change to human intentionality. Yet I am arguing that the most radical transformation in human history, domestication and the agricultural revolution, began by accident. Fortunately, I need not rely on thought experiments alone to find support for this unsettling argument.

Leave your parka on, for now we embark to Siberia. In 1958, a geneticist named Dmitri Belyaev arrived to become director of the Institute of Cytology and Genetics in Novosibirsk.[12] Belyaev found himself intrigued by the ideas of Nikolai Vavilov, the botanist and geneticist best known for locating the geographic origins of domestic plants. Belyaev was more interested in Vavilov's ideas about domestic animals, especially his observation that domestic species showed similar traits despite budding off different branches of the animal family tree. Many wild animals reproduced once per year, for example, and during a specific season. Yet their domestic descendents reproduced multiple times in a year and during any season. Belyaev hypothesized that selecting for "the domesticated type of behavior" created this pattern. Any domestic animal, he reasoned, needed to tolerate human presence, obey, and reproduce in captivity. And he thought people selected for domesticated behavior without realizing it. With that in mind, he decided to see if he could create animals that behaved like dogs.[13]

Belyaev decided to test his idea using silver foxes. Like wolves and dogs, foxes belong to the family Canidae. Belyaev chose a population that had lived on a fur farm for about sixty years but that had continued to reproduce once a year during a specific season. Although their handlers had not consciously selected for behavior, the foxes varied in their reaction to people. About 30 percent acted very aggressively, 20 percent fearfully, and 40 percent aggressively and fearfully. The remaining 10 percent showed little fear or aggression but, when handled, would bite. The experimenters eliminated the foxes that behaved most defensively and bred from the 130 (100 females and 30 males) at the calmer end of the scale. Experimenters repeated the procedure with subsequent generations, keeping only the best performers each time (about the top 10 percent of females and 3 percent to 5 percent of males). Selection continued for about forty generations, during which time the experimenters tested more than forty-seven thousand foxes.[14]

Fox behavior changed rapidly. It took only two or three generations to weed out the foxes that reacted aggressively and fearfully. In the fourth generation, the first pups appeared that went beyond staying calm around people. These pups whined and wagged their tails when they saw people approach. In the sixth generation appeared a few pups (1.8 percent of the population) that experimenters dubbed the "domestication elites" because they so resembled dogs (Figure 6.1). Not only did they whine, yelp, and wag their tails around people, they also tried to lick the experimenters' hands and faces. Some followed experimenters around.

FIGURE 6.1. Domestication in action. Russian geneticist Dmitri K. Belyaev domesticated foxes in the twentieth century. Wild foxes are aggressive, solid colored, straight eared, and elusive. Experimenters selected for a single trait, comfort around human beings, for several generations. Soon the population produced calm, pied (A), floppy-eared animals that rushed to human beings and wagged their tails to solicit affection (B). These experiments demonstrated that domestication might have resulted from human behaviors, such as allowing scavengers to feed on camp trash, that accidentally domesticated animals. Many traits we associate with domestic animals might have been by-products of accidental domestication. (Image from D. K. Belyaev, "Destabilizing Selection as a Factor in Domestication," *Journal of Heredity* 70, no. 5 [1979]: 301–308, see 303. Reprinted by permission of Oxford University Press.)

These behaviors did not result from training; they started appearing when the pups were just three weeks of age. The experimenters stopped regular contact with the foxes after generation six, but the domestication elites continued to wax. These doglike foxes made up about 18 percent of the pups in generation 10, 35 percent in generation 20, 49 percent in generation 30, and almost 70 percent in generation 40. Many responded when called by name. And, as Belyaev, hypothesized, some females became fertile twice a year instead of once.[15]

A more recent study discovered another behavioral trait the domestic foxes shared with dogs. Dogs are good at reading human cues, and this ability is inborn. Experimenters compared young dogs and wolves on their ability to find food hidden under some cups but not others. When experimenters pointed at the cups with food under them, the dogs looked under those cups more often than one would predict by chance. The wolves did not. When experimenters tried the same thing with domesticated foxes, they performed more like dogs than wolves. Belyaev's experiments did not use cue reading as a criterion for selection, but for some reason, this behavior, too, resulted as a by-product of selection for tameness.[16]

What caused these changes? Belyaev and his colleagues noticed that domesticated foxes developed at a different pace from the control group (foxes raised on farms but not selected for behavior). Domesticates responded fearfully to events for the first time around ninety days of age, compared to forty-five days for the control group. They also explored their environment more than the controls did. Digging deeper, researchers discovered a couple biochemical bases for these differences. One was a difference in levels of alarm hormones. The pituitary and adrenal glands of domesticated foxes pumped out alarm hormones at about half the rate of the control group. The other factor was a difference in neurotransmitters (chemicals that influence brain functioning), especially those that regulated fear responses. So in selecting for calm behavior, the experimenters unwittingly selected for lower levels of the compounds (hormones and neurotransmitters) responsible for the fight-or-flight response to danger.[17]

Such dramatic changes in behavior in such a short time were surprising enough, but even more unexpected were changes in appearance. In generations 8 to 10, the coats of domesticated foxes developed yellow-brown mottling and piebaldness (white areas caused by lack of pigment) on the usual silver-black coat. The floppy ears of control pups perked upright at two or three weeks of age but not until three or four weeks of age for domesticates. The ears of some domesticates stayed floppy their whole lives. The tails of domesticates curled, in contrast to the straight tails of controls. The skulls of domesticates, especially males, grew shorter and wider compared to controls, and the bodies of males became smaller on average.[18]

Belyaev and his colleagues explained these results by hypothesizing that alarm hormones and neurotransmitters had more than one job. In addition to creating fierceness, these chemicals told ears to straighten, tails to wag, and fur to turn silver-black. This hypothesis made sense because many of these unexpected traits were symptoms of absence more than presence. Tameness resulted not from the production of tameness hormones but from the failure to produce alarm hormones. Droopy ears resulted not from the body's effort to produce droopiness but from its failure to produce ear-stiffening tissue. Short snouts resulted not from making long snouts shorter but from short snouts failing to grow longer. White coats resulted not from the production of white pigment but from the failure to produce any pigment. (Black and white coats resulted when pigment genes darkened some patches of fur but failed to finish the job elsewhere.) Reducing multipurpose hormones for one reason also reduced their ability to produce other traits.[19]

But why should alarm hormones and neurotransmitters also control physical traits such as ear shape and pigment production? The answer to that puzzle came in locating these traits in the sequence of development from juvenile to adult. Tameness, droopy ears, short snouts, and wagging tails were all traits of juvenile foxes. Fierceness, straight ears, long snouts, and still tails were all traits of adults. Alarm hormones and neurotransmitters, the experimenters decided, controlled the development of juvenile foxes into adults. Without intending to, the experimenters had arrested many traits in their juvenile stage even as traits under control of other hormones developed normally. The experimenters did not emphasize this last point, but it was critical to the result. If alarm hormones had also governed the development of sexual maturity, tame foxes would have been unable to reproduce, and the experiment would have ended.[20]

At a deeper level, selecting for low levels of alarm hormones and neurotransmitters meant selecting for genes that produced those low levels. How did domestication change the fox genome? Definitive answers await further tests, but we can identify at least two hypotheses. One we might call sleeping workers. Imagine that a fox's body is a factory that, at a certain age, normally produces adult traits. Certain genes act as workers, assembling alarm hormones at one step and passing them along. Arrival of the hormones at the next step tells the workers to produce straighter ears or some other adult trait, and so on down the line. Selecting for napping workers at the alarm hormone step halts the assembly line and prevents the later stations from doing their job. This is the hypothesis the experimenters favored.

We can imagine another hypothesis called the sleeping manager. Imagine fox bodies house a factory with parallel assembly lines that produce a variety of adult traits simultaneously. In each factory, managers control workers on the assembly lines. Managers work under a simple rule: either turn on all the assembly lines at once or keep them all off. Some managers work their factories long hours, while others allow workers to slack off while they nap. Experimenters favored those factories that produced less alarm hormone, which meant favoring snoozing managers, which meant inadvertently favoring factories that produced less of everything. Other hypotheses, including a combination of these two, are also plausible.

The important point is that the experimenters, and hunter-gatherers before them, could have created creatures that looked as well as behaved like dogs by selecting for only one behavioral trait, tameness, because the genes controlling that trait also controlled the development of a variety of other adult traits.

Taken together, these findings provide evidence that people could have created dogs from wolves by piling chance on unwitting chance. To make life better in the present, hunters and gatherers fed gentler wolves and eliminated the troublesome. These actions accidentally selected for increasing tameness in future generations. Tameness resulted from genes that failed to turn on the development of fierceness, an adult trait. The genes that controlled fierceness also happened to control the development of other adult traits, so halting one halted many. Wolves with shorter snouts, affectionate adult behavior, and black-and-white coats appeared. But other genes happened to control the development of sexual maturity, so wolves with juvenile traits could still reproduce themselves. These modified wolves eventually differed so much in appearance and behavior from their wild relatives that people considered them to be the separate beings that we call dogs.

These findings also help explain why many domestic animals bear similar traits. Domestic cows, sheep, pigs, and guinea pigs may have relatively short jaws, black-and-white coats, droopy ears, and a white patch on the forehead. These similarities may have resulted not from people intentionally producing each of these traits, as the methodical selection hypothesis holds, but from selecting for the one thing they all had in common: tameness. In these cases, too, we may well be able to credit unconscious selection or actions taken to get short-term benefits rather than intentional efforts to change plants and animals in the long run.

The unconscious selection scenario also helps explain the separation of dogs into breeds. Under the methodical selection hypothesis, as we have seen, people imagined jobs for dogs and then used selective mating to create breeds for each task. One problem with this explanation is the height of the imaginative leap. People might have imagined that wolfish dogs would herd rather than ravage sheep, just as they might have imagined that winged dogs would flit in the air with birds rather than walk the earth. But both skills probably seemed unlikely to develop. Another problem is that even if people imagined dogs with new traits, they could not create those traits from nothing. People could encourage the development of wings once dogs grew protowings, but they could not cause dogs to sprout wings in the first place.

Instead, mutations caused certain dogs to develop desirable traits that people then encouraged by accident or on purpose. As with domestication, unconscious selection probably played a more important role than methodical selection because it was simpler and brought benefits in the present. Dogs might well have aided in the hunt early in their evolution, for their lupine ancestors worked in packs to bring down game. If one dog then tried to scare the human hunter away from the kill while its sister did not, the hunter probably would have killed the aggressive individual before the cooperative one. Keeping the dogs best at a certain task in each generation would have steadily enhanced desired traits.

Agriculture depends on plants as well as animals. Here, too, domestication requires explanation. And here, too, the classic explanation for domestication has been methodical selection. You will not be surprised to learn that I find unconscious selection more likely for plants, too.

To see why, let us go to Peru five thousand years ago and watch the domestication of cotton. Human beings have domesticated four species of cotton around the world. The longest fibers come from *Gossypium barbadense*, better known today as Sea Island, Egyptian, or Pima cotton. An archaeological dig in Peru, where *G. barbadense* was domesticated, has turned up seeds whose fiber length varies depending on the layer in which they were found. In the deepest (thus probably the oldest) layers, *G. barbadense* seeds have short, fuzzy, chocolate-colored fibers. In more recent layers, seeds carry longer fibers. It is possible that *G. barbadense* evolved this way on its own, in which case, the layers simply record the result of natural selection. But it seems likely that people selected for seeds with longer fibers over time, and the layers reveal effects of human hands as well as natural selection.[22]

The methodical selection hypothesis calls for human beings to do much the same thing for cotton as for wolves, though with some differences driven by the plant's biology. The people living in what is now Peru would have

1. imagined a trait in a wild species (here much longer fibers) that they had never seen
2. believed they could create that trait by mating specific plants
3. believed that individual plants varied because they inherited traits from their parents
4. knew how to take pollen from one plant and fertilize another plant
5. knew how to prevent pollination by other plants (cotton plants readily fertilize each other, leading to constant gene mixing)
6. continued this breeding program, with little or no benefit, for years (probably decades or centuries)
7. considered all this a better use of time than gathering plants and hunting animals for immediate benefit

The unconscious selection hypothesis charts a different course. Instead of the seven ideas essential to the master breeder narrative, it requires that people had only one key idea: to use species for short-term benefit. Pre-Columbian Americans might have gathered seeds for fiber or food. It would have been easier to pick seeds with long fibers than those with short fibers because they gave the harvester something larger to grab. Longer fibers would also have been preferred for making thread, leading to selective harvesting. So the seeds coming into camp would have borne longer fibers, on average, than their brethren still in the field. After removing fiber, the early Americans probably dropped seeds (by accident or on purpose) near their camps, which would have produced plants near dwellings with slightly longer fibers than the average in the wild. It was easier to harvest near to home than far away, so people would have relied more heavily in future years on the closer, longer-fibered plants. Even when harvesting close to home, harvesters would have favored seeds with longer fiber, so fiber length increased a bit each year.

Over time, these short-term decisions could have produced seeds with fibers long enough to be useful in fishing nets and clothing. If we travel to Peru today, we see the results we would expect from this hypothesis. The *G. barbadense* varieties (both those now living and remains found by archeologists) range across a continuum from wild to highly bred. Moderately domesticated versions (called *dooryard cottons*) live near homes. Some farmers raise traditional, local strains (called *landraces*), whereas others rely on modern varieties produced by professional breeders.[23]

Unconscious selection can also explain convergent evolution of traits in the most important plants for human survival today: the cereals. Compared to their wild relatives, the domestic versions of these species have larger seeds, more simultaneous ripening, seed containers that shatter less, and shorter dormancy. The first three traits, in particular, would have appealed to human seed gatherers. These harvesters of wild seed would have been more likely to collect

1. the largest seeds because they were easier to pick and yielded more food
2. seeds from plants that ripened at the same time, leaving behind unripe seeds and those that ripened earlier and fell from the stalk
3. seeds still on the stalk versus those propelled through the air by shattering (the explosive opening of a seed container that enables plants to disperse seeds over a larger area than letting them fall beneath the parent).

After-harvest selection would have continued through a process similar to that of cotton. Gatherers would have carried seeds back to camp, where some kernels would have fallen to the ground by accident, some might have been buried in containers for future use, some would have been eaten whole, and some might have been processed (by grinding and cooking). Accidental dropping and intentional burying of seeds for future use in porous containers would have planted seeds near camp. Eating seeds whole would have, too, though through a less obvious route. Seeds of many species pass through bird and mammal digestive tracts unscathed, and some even require such passage to germinate. When human beings defecated, most likely near camp, they would have deposited seeds and fertilizer on the ground at the same time. When these seeds grew into plants, unconscious selection would have enhanced the same traits, and so on for generations, until the wild and domestic versions differed dramatically.

Most of the literature on domestication implies that humans have sat in the driver's seat while other species rode in the back of the truck. The first word in the title of anthropologist Yi Fu-Tuan's analysis of pets, *Dominance and Affection,* reflects this view. For John Perkins, who described the green revolution as one stage in a long evolutionary process, this unidirectional view is inadequate: "Wheat and people *coevolved* in ways that left neither much ability to prosper without the other."[24]

This bidirectional view opens the possibility that organisms domesticated humans as well as vice versa. Biologist Raymond P. Coppinger and English professor Charles Kay Smith have argued that since the last ice age some ten thousand years ago, much of the most important evolution has taken place within the arena of human activity. Becoming useful to human beings helped organisms adapt to a rapidly changing environment.[25] Popular writer Stephen Budiansky has made this argument in two books. In *Covenant of the Wild*, he suggests that domestic animals have "chosen" to become domesticates because this path offered more chances of survival than did living in the wild. The wolves that became dogs have thrived and now number in the millions in the United States. The wolves that remained wild found themselves all but exterminated in the lower forty-eight states. Budiansky expands on this theme in *The Truth about Dogs*.[26]

Another popular writer, Michael Pollan, has argued a similar thesis about plants. In *The Botany of Desire*, he points out that bees probably "see" plants as doing work for them by supplying pollen and nectar, just as Pollan had seen his plants as doing work for him by producing vegetables. But the plants could just as well "see" the bee *and* Pollan doing work for them. Wild varieties of plants had to compete for resources with other species, protect themselves against herbivores, and hope for rain. Their domesticated relatives got Pollan to do that work for them, which enabled their genes to become much more common than the genes of wild versions.[27]

I favor the coevolutionary view of domestication. The unconscious selection hypothesis is consistent with this view because it emphasizes that a series of actions taken for short-term gain eventually added up to dramatic changes. Many of those actions would have been taken in response to changes in other species. Because identifying either partner as the leader in a coevolutionary dance is arbitrary, it is best to think of domestication as a process of mutual change and adjustment rather than as one species simply imposing its will on another.

Viewing domestication as a changing relationship between two species contrasts with the usual view of domestication as a fixed state of a non-human species. Domestication places demands on human beings as well as on our partner species. If we stop doing certain things, intentionally or accidentally, the relationship breaks down and can disappear (breeds of domestic plants and animals have gone extinct once they fell out of favor). We might say that domestication depends as much on domesticating a population of human beings as on domesticating a population of a nonhuman species.

The main point of this chapter is not whether the agricultural revolution occurred because of methodical or accidental selection. It is that the agricultural revolution was an evolutionary revolution. It marked a turning point in the degree to which human beings affected the evolution of other species. (In Chapter 8, we will see how the agricultural revolution also affected our own evolution.) This evolutionary revolution enabled domestication partners – human beings and human-modified populations of plants and animals – to dominate ever-larger areas of the earth. An evolutionary revolution set in motion an ecological revolution.

7

Intentional Evolution

I awoke this morning enveloped by a cotton t-shirt, cotton shorts, and cotton sheets. Now cotton socks, cotton jeans, a cotton shirt, and cotton underclothes clad me. You might spend much of your life swaddled in cotton, too. As we saw, we owe this comfortable fiber to the domestication of cotton some five thousand years ago. But that was not the end of the process. We also owe our comfort to breeders, who more recently modified the plant on purpose. So in living with cotton, we are surrounding ourselves with a product of intentional evolution.

The thesis of this chapter is that people have used a variety of techniques to modify the traits of populations intentionally, and they continue to invent new ones. The term *intentional evolution* does not imply that people thought, "I intend to affect the evolution of a species." Few would have done so. Most have thought of themselves as doing something else such as breeding plants or animals. We will organize those actions by the evolutionary processes they affect. We will start with a pair of selective techniques: **culling** and **methodical selection (breeding)**. Then we will turn to efforts designed to increase or decrease variation. These include **hybridizing**, transporting, **acclimatizing**, promoting **mutations, genetic engineering, inbreeding**, and **cloning**. We will examine methods that affect inheritance. In addition to three ways of influencing variation (**cloning, genetic engineering**, and promoting **mutations**), we will look at **sterilizing**. We will conclude by looking at a cousin of trait modification: **extinction**.

Evolution relies on variation. This holds true for intentional as well as accidental evolution. To illustrate the extent of variation in domestic populations, let us begin with a thought experiment. Please imagine a map of the world. Now paint the four places where cotton was domesticated, with each site getting a different color of paint. Splash some red in Peru for *Gossypium barbadense*. Add blue to Central America for *G. hirsutum*. Scientists have found it harder to locate the origins of the two domestic Old World species, but for our purposes, it is sufficient to use hypothesized locations. Paint yellow in southern Africa for *G. arboreum* and black in south Asia for *G. herbaceum*.[1]

Now imagine that our map has an animation feature. Our paint highlights domestication sites of about five thousand years ago. With a click, we ask the map to disperse the paint to show how each of the four species spread in subsequent years. We will see colors emerge, spread, and shade into each other. This is because *Gossypium* is a randy genus, and species cross-fertilize each other. Purple emerges where *G. barbadense* and *G. hirsutum* overlap. We also see colors jump to new continents. Yellow (*G. arboreum*) and black (*G. herbaceum*) emerge in the Old World and, after A.D. 1500, pop up in the Americas when Europeans introduced them. Red and blue (the colors of the New World species) begin to speckle and spread in the Old World for the same reason.

Our map has emphasized variation in species composition, but species also vary within themselves. When populations of a species differ in traits, we often refer to them as **varieties, strains, cultivars, lines,** or **breeds.** We can illustrate varieties on our map using shades of color. With another click, our animated map subdivides each cotton-growing area into thousands of smaller areas of varying shapes and sizes, each with a different shade representing a different variety. Red now speckles the earth in tints ranging from the lightest hint of rose to the deepest, darkest red. The other three original colors do the same. Where colors overlap, the secondary colors (such as purple) explode into a greater range of shades as well.

Now our map looks as though Jackson Pollock has been in charge, for its outstanding feature is its riot of color. In 1907, for example, one survey found six hundred varieties of cotton growing in the United States.[2] An estimate of the world total for that year would begin with six hundred and add the varieties missed by the survey in the United States and elsewhere in the world. The number would surely reach the thousands, and easily more. Since varieties come and go, we would have to repeat the exercise for each of five thousand years to know the total number of varieties ever grown. I asked you to mix several thousand shades of color, but that was a lowball number designed not to scare you away. I suspect we would need orders of magnitude more tints for five thousand years of varietal maps.

Let us use the time-animation feature of our map again. We see shades of primary colors ebb and flow, jump around, appear in new variations, and fade away. The U.S. agricultural census of 1880 found fifty-eight varieties in use. Only six of those were still common fifteen years later, a number that dropped to zero by 1936. Most had gone extinct. An 1895 survey found 118 varieties in fields; two of those were in use by 1925. Of more than six hundred varieties growing in 1907, nine were growing extensively by 1925, and only twenty-five had avoided extinction.[3]

The point of this thought experiment is to emphasize the enormous variation that exists within domestic species. This variation is both the raw material for and the product of intentional evolution. It is the raw material because selection needs variation to act, and it is the product because people have used a variety of techniques to enhance it.

Although this chapter emphasizes human intentionality, it is important to keep in mind that the most of the time, human beings have depended on other species to generate variation. We may have decided to select for a trait, but another species had to originate the trait. We have developed a few techniques that create variation, such as mutagenesis, but the impact of these techniques has been infinitesimal compared to nature's handiwork.

Now we turn to ways that people have conceived of their efforts to change the traits of populations. Cotton continues to provide a good example. I asserted that people domesticated four species of cotton, which is the consensus view today (taxonomists in the past divided varieties into many more species). But historically, few growers, merchants, consumers, or even breeders knew or cared much about the species of cotton in their hands. They cared about the qualities of the plant and its product, and variety names told them more than a species name. We could not assign many historical varieties to species even if we wished, for they have disappeared without leaving behind the evidence taxonomists need for their work. Plus, species hybridized to produce fertile offspring, so understanding cotton evolution means organizing our ideas around varieties. Now let us look at techniques that have affected three key elements of Darwinian evolution: selection, variation, and inheritance.

One selective technique used by cotton growers and breeders is **culling** (also known as **selecting**), or choosing the individuals with desirable traits to use as breeding stock. We saw examples of accidental culling in Chapter 3, but people have also culled intentionally. One of the early upland cotton varieties in the United States emerged in this way. A single plant in a field owned by a Mr. Boyd was the progenitor, and its descendents became known as Boyd Prolific. By 1847, Boyd Prolific had become common in Mississippi.[4]

Another dramatic example came with the arrival of a disease, cotton wilt fungus, in the American Southeast in the late 1800s. The Sea Island cotton industry survived thanks largely to an enterprising grower on St. James Island, South Carolina, named E. L. Rivers, who walked through his fields looking for the exceptional plant not laid low by the wilt. Rivers found one such plant, gathered its seeds, and planted them on badly infected land the next year. The progeny survived, but they produced an inferior fiber. So Rivers tried a second time with another individual that happened to survive the wilt. This time the progeny produced good fiber, and a new variety known as Rivers was born. The U.S. Department of Agriculture purchased seed from Rivers and distributed it to other Sea Island growers. Sea Island cotton thus evolved in a classic Darwinian fashion. An inherited trait enabled some individuals to survive and reproduce, whereas kin without the trait perished, and the next generation bore the traits of the survivor. The population evolved.[5]

The second technique is **methodical selection**, also known as **breeding** and **selective mating** (because breeders select specific males and females with desirable traits to couple). Breeders might mate individuals within an existing variety, cross individuals from different varieties, or even hybridize different species. John Griffin of Greenville, Mississippi, produced the common Griffin variety this way in the mid-nineteenth century. Selective mating became common among professional breeders in the twentieth century. While animal breeding pairs specific males and females, plants that cross-pollinate (such as cotton) can be bred by growing varieties near each other (in alternate rows, for example).[6] It is hard to overestimate the importance of selective mating today because most of us rely on it to keep our food supply growing along with world population.

In recent centuries, science and industry have played increasingly important roles in evolution. Deborah Fitzgerald has traced the rise of corn breeding in the United States. In the nineteenth century, farmers improved their corn by saving the best seed to plant the next year. The arrival of government and industrial scientists shifted the locus of control from farmers to scientists. Responding to their own agendas as well as those of farmers, these scientists shifted from traditional, open-pollinated breeding methods to new, hybrid methods. Because hybrids did not "breed true," farmers had to buy new commercial seed each year. The result was a massive change in the nature of corn. In 1933, hybrids grew on 0.4 percent of the corn acreage in the United States. By 1945, the share of land devoted to hybrids had soared to 90 percent.[7]

For rural sociologist Jack Kloppenburg, the most important force driving breeding has been capitalism. In *First the Seed*, he highlights three processes that facilitated capitalistic penetration of plant **biotechnology** between 1492 and 2000. In his terminology, they are political economy – commodification, institutions – division of labor, and world economy – germplasm transfer. Kloppenburg notes that humans shaped the evolution of plants through dispersing, breeding, and patenting lifeforms. Traditional plant breeding was "applied evolutionary science." With new biotechnology, such as genetic engineering, humans started outdoing evolution by moving genes across species. The result was that genes became a form of property, further facilitating commodification and accumulation of wealth.[8]

The significance of breeding has extended well beyond farm fields. *Geopolitics* usually brings to mind national leaders, armies, alliances, and strategic resources; few would include plant breeding on the list. John Perkins, an environmental historian with a background in genetics, has challenged this view. Wealthy and poor nations alike, Perkins argues, saw increased food production as critical to their self-interest in the cold war. Leaders of poor countries feared that insufficient food for growing populations could lead to loss of hard currency (to pay for imports) and create fertile ground for revolutions against the government in power. Leaders of wealthy nations feared political and economic instability, the spread of hostile ideologies, and weakening of alliances against the Soviet Union. Using wheat as his case study, Perkins shows how these fears motivated rich and poor countries to fund programs designed to boost wheat productivity rapidly through locating and transferring germplasm. A green revolution would counter red revolutions.[9]

Breeding has also shaped social history. In *The Animal Estate*, cultural and environmental historian Harriet Ritvo argues that Victorians used animal breeding to resolve class anxieties. As industrialization twisted and strained the English class structure, breeders created elaborate class systems, replete with blue books and pedigrees, patterned after those of the nobility, for horses and dogs. Published breed standards and show rings created islands of control and predictability in a turbulent world. At the same time, shows offered breeders from lower rungs on the social ladder a rare and treasured chance to compete against and defeat so-called social betters.[10]

Now let us turn to intentional efforts to increase variation. We already peeked at one, **hybridizing**, under the heading of selective mating. Hybridizing generates novel traits by crossing individuals from different varieties or species, so in this case, breeders affect selection and variation at the same time. The most famous example of hybridizing comes from corn. Breeders developed high-yielding varieties by crossing two highly inbred lines; that is, by mating two varieties, they produced a third that differed from both parents.[11]

Another way to increase local variation is transportation, or transferring varieties from one place to another. In the 1830s, H. W. Vick of Vicksburg, Mississippi, created a cotton variety called Jethro via culling from fields growing the Belle Creole variety. In 1846, he mailed seeds to J. V. Jones of Henderson, Georgia, where Jethro became parent to the Jones Long Staple and Six-Oaks varieties.[12] Transportation might also link continents. In the 1850s, a German man sent cottonseeds from Algeria to his brother in Georgia. The seeds grew into plants that became parent stock for a number of important varieties. Transportation routes need not be direct. The imports from Algeria resembled Mexican big-boll varieties and probably descended from them (so the route might have been Central America to Algeria to North America). The U.S. federal government, too, imported seeds from other countries. In the nineteenth century, the government focused on introducing new varieties of cotton. In the twentieth, its emphasis shifted to breeding from varieties already in the country.[13]

It can sound easy to import varieties from elsewhere, but the realities of evolution make it a lot of hard work. Local environments often differ from those in the country of origin, so new varieties meet one of two fates. One is extinction in the new locality. Plants often fail to grow, grow poorly, or develop traits so different from ancestral stock that importers give up on the variety. The other is **adaptation**. In a process known as **acclimatizing**, farmers or researchers grow a variety, select seeds from the individual plants that perform best, use those seeds the next year, and repeat the process until the variety outperforms the local competition. Then the variety spreads.[14]

We can see both these processes at work in the effort to grow Egyptian cotton in the American South. The first effort was a by-product of warfare. During the American Civil War, the Union cut the economic feet out from beneath the Confederacy by blocking exports of cotton from Southern ports. English spinners encouraged other countries, such as Egypt, to plug the gap in production. The Egyptians grew high-quality *G. barbadense*, the same New World species as Sea Island cotton, and mills developed a taste for what became known as Egyptian cotton. In 1867, the United States tried to recapture some of the market by importing seeds from Egypt and planting them across the traditional cotton belt. All efforts failed, though not for lack of trying. The Department of Agriculture staged fifty experiments over five years before allowing those varieties to go extinct in the United States. This failure led the Department of Agriculture to ignore Egyptian varieties for twenty years.[15]

Economics sparked renewed efforts, and this time, Egyptian varieties adapted successfully. Around 1890, the rising price of Egyptian cotton imports prompted American mills to push for more research and domestic production. The Department of Agriculture tried the three most popular Egyptian varieties across the cotton states, and again, the experiments failed. The turning point came in 1897, when a federal breeder decided to try a larger number of Egyptian varieties in the American Southwest. A hot climate and irrigation made conditions in this part of the country similar to those in the Nile Valley. The first generation produced low yields and poor fiber quality, but years of selecting for early ripening, yield, and fiber quality produced two varieties (Yuma and Somerton) that differed substantially from their Egyptian parent (Mit Afifi). In 1912, the Department of Agriculture distributed Yuma seeds to farmers in Arizona and California, and production increased rapidly.[16]

But evolution did not stop there. In 1910, a sharp-eyed observer noticed a single Yuma plant with longer, finer, and lighter-colored fibers than other plants of that variety. Researchers selected seeds from that plant, which gave rise to a new variety known as Pima. The cotton growers of the Salt River Valley of Arizona agreed that Pima seemed superior to Yuma, so they decided that all of them would switch to Pima in 1918. In 1920, production of Pima reached ninety-two thousand bales. Today, Pima, Egyptian, and Sea Island are the three best-known names for varieties of *G. barbadense* and their long, fine, strong fibers.[17]

Transportation does not increase the global genetic diversity of a species, but another technique – **mutation** – does. This technique comes in handy when a species does not possess a desired trait at all. In Uzbekistan, researchers wanted to extend the growing season for cotton by inducing plants to flower at a different time of year than normal. By exposing seeds to radiation and electromagnetism, they induced the mutations they desired.[18] Mutagenesis affects many genes, not just the ones researchers want to target, so it is only the first step in creating useful varieties. Researchers need to raise plants to adulthood, see which have the desired traits, and cull them. Then they can use the new varieties in a breeding program.

Breeders also rely on genetic **recombination** to spur variation in traits. Sexual reproduction scrambles and unites genes of parents to endow offspring with genetic combinations unseen in either parent. New combinations of genes can generate new traits. In 1998, a study found that the cultivars growing over 89 percent of the cotton acreage in the United States derived from closely related parents. The puzzle was to explain how close relatives carried enough variation for breeders to change traits of populations in substantial ways. The researchers concluded that "a minimal amount of recombination resulted in sufficient genetic variance to make breeding progress."[19]

Breeders sometimes have recombined genes by crossing individuals from different species or genera. An example is the beefalo, a mixture of three-eighths American bison (*Bison bison*) and five-eighths cattle (*Bos taurus*) that produces fertile offspring. Beefalo advocates have identified many traits that distinguish the breed from full-blooded cattle, including lower production costs, greater adaptability to varying climates, longer life span, greater growth rates, and the ability to consume a wide variety of food and forage.[20]

The most remarkable new technique for increasing variation is **genetic engineering,** or the transfer of genes among individuals using molecular techniques. The key difference between genetic engineering and traditional breeding is the ability to move genes across taxonomic groups that otherwise could not produce fertile offspring. Breeding limits breeders to the traits that interbreeding populations possessed. Genetic engineering, in contrast, makes traits generated by all species available to breeders. Genetic engineers can even move genes across kingdoms of organisms such as from animals to plants. Tobacco plants can now glow in the dark thanks to a gene for luminescence from a firefly. Genetic engineering's impact on evolution will only increase in the future. For such a young technique, it is astonishing how much of the world's surface it has already modified. By 2010, genetically engineered crops accounted for 93 percent of the soybeans, 78 percent of the cotton, and 70 percent of the corn grown in the United States.[21]

Let us delve more deeply into the genetic engineering of cotton to understand this new way of managing evolution, and especially the way it intersects with corporate goals. Genetic engineering enables cotton researchers to unite two contrasting (if complementary) strategies for pest control. Breeders have long adapted plants to their environments by changing their traits; pesticide researchers have adapted environments to plants by changing their ecology. The two strategies merged when researchers at Monsanto transferred a gene from a bacterium (*Bacillus thuringiensis*, or Bt for short) to cotton. The gene carried instructions for manufacturing a compound poisonous to insects. Now cotton plants made and dispersed their own insecticides, which held the promise of reducing pest losses and pesticide use. The researchers changed the traits of a population of cotton (the strategy of breeders) to change the ecology of cotton fields (the strategy of pesticide researchers).

These efforts sparked rapid evolution in cotton. In 1996, Monsanto began selling Bollgard, a cotton variety with a Bt gene inserted into its DNA. It resisted cotton bollworms, pink bollworms, and tobacco budworms. An EPA study found that farmers planting Bollgard sprayed insecticides less often than growers raising other varieties of cotton, adding up to a reduction of 1.6 million pounds of pesticides applied in 1999. Monsanto later introduced Bollgard II, which carried a second Bt gene that enabled it to fend off beet and fall armyworms and soybean loopers as well as those pests targeted by Bollgard. Dow introduced a cotton variety with similar properties called WideStrike. Massive and quick evolution in farm fields came when farmers switched to these transgenic cottons, growing them on 24.2 million acres worldwide by 2005.[22]

At the same time that companies were promoting the ability of insect-resistant cotton to reduce pesticide spraying, they were also using genetic engineering to *increase* pesticide use. Monsanto and Bayer Crop-Science sold herbicides (Roundup and Liberty, respectively) designed to clear vegetation altogether from fields. (*Pesticides* is an umbrella term for herbicides, insecticides, and fungicides.) When it came to fields with crops, Roundup and Liberty were too effective – they killed desirable plants as well as weeds, which blocked off huge markets. Genetic engineering solved the problem by making cotton immune to the herbicides. Monsanto introduced Roundup Ready Cotton and Roundup Ready Flex Cotton, while Bayer developed LibertyLink Cotton.[23]

Researchers developed herbicide-resistant cotton by looking far away taxonomically and close by geographically. Roundup (the trade name for glyphosate) works by derailing a plant enzyme called EPSP synthase. Knowing that Roundup annihilated virtually all members of the plant kingdom, researchers at Monsanto realized they might want to look in a different kingdom for a gene that conferred resistance to the herbicide. They turned to bacteria in the hope of finding a version of EPSP synthase that could survive glyphosate.

They found their prey by hunting close to home – the waste stream of a factory making glyphosate. It was brilliant reasoning because the waste stream selected for resistance. Researchers bagged a bacterium (*Agrobacterium* sp.) carrying a Roundup-resistant version of EPSP synthase (called C4 EPSP synthase), which they inserted into the cotton genome to create Roundup Ready Cotton. Bayer Crop Science also relied on a bacterial gene to create LibertyLink Cotton, though the gene came from a different species (*Streptomyces hygroscopicus*) and worked in a different way (by disabling the active ingredient in Liberty, glufosinate ammonium).[24]

As corporate strategy goes, creating these varieties of cotton was brilliant. Cotton uses more pesticides than any other crop, so cracking the cotton market was a coup for Roundup and Liberty makers. Plus, these varieties force growers to buy herbicide and cotton seeds from the same company. Roundup and Liberty work in different ways, and so do their protective genes. Roundup Ready cotton dies if sprayed with Liberty, and LibertyLink cotton dies if sprayed with Roundup. The lack of cross-resistance makes each company's products a package. If you want the benefits of one variety of cotton (say, Roundup Ready), you have to buy the same company's herbicide (Roundup, not Liberty). The principle works in the opposite direction, too. If you like one company's herbicide (say, Liberty), you have to buy the same company's cotton (LibertyLink, not Roundup Ready). Evolution management via genetic engineering, then, provides a subtle but powerful way to control grower behavior in the marketplace.

By now you can predict what happened when farmers drenched their fields with herbicides: weeds evolved resistance. Herbicide makers hated seeing this happen with their own product because their market dried up. But evolving resistance to a competitor's product is welcome news because it gives one's own product a competitive advantage. The evolutionary ball took a bounce in Bayer CropScience's favor when weeds evolved resistance to Monsanto's Roundup. Bayer CropScience pounced. On its Web site, it posted this text: "Liberty®/LibertyLink® provides the convenience, ease and cost effectiveness of glyphosate [Roundup]. But Liberty also takes out weeds resistant or tolerant to glyphosate with its unique, non-selective chemistry. . . . Get a true alternative to glyphosate, plus manage weeds and resistance – choose Liberty. . . . Unique mode of action – no known resistance."[25] The overt message was to substitute Liberty for Roundup. The subtle message, implied in the first, registered trademark–laden words, was that choosing Liberty also meant choosing LibertyLink plant varieties.

Transgenic plants have sparked heated debate. On one side are seed companies, scientists, and farmers who support their use. For corporations, transgenic seeds offer a competitive advantage in the marketplace. Company representatives also speak of higher goals, especially increasing the world's supply of food and reducing the burden of disease. While economic self-interest is clearly in play, there is no reason to doubt the sincere desire of these individuals to improve the world's lot. For farmers, the plants offer the chance to increase yields and income by reducing losses to pests. Growers also see the potential for insect-resistant crops to save money, guard the health of workers, and protect wildlife by reducing pesticide use.[26]

On the other side of the debate are activists, scientists, farmers, and consumers. They object to genetic engineering for many reasons, including concerns about ethics, economics, and health. Here we will focus on only one concern: the evolution of resistance. Well before Monsanto went looking for genes to kill insects, organic farmers had relied on Bt (*Bacillus thuringiensis*) as a biological alternative to chemical pesticides. They mixed up a soup of the bacteria and sprayed it on their crops, usually after they saw enough pests to worry about. Bt was also popular in government-run aerial spray programs against the gypsy moth in the United States because it killed butterflies and moths but not birds, fish, or mammals.[27]

The idea of inserting Bt genes into plants terrified advocates of Bt bacteria because it threatened to crumple a useful tool. Bt users knew the history of chemical pest control, in which pests had evolved resistance to every chemical introduced. Plus, diamondback moths in Hawaii had evolved resistance to Bt, showing it could happen.[28] They feared that widespread use of Bt genes in plants would accelerate the effect, making sprays of live bacteria useless. In response, government and corporations worked out a plan to manage the evolution of resistance. The plan featured the planting of susceptible cotton varieties near the resistant strains. The susceptible plants would not select for resistance in pests. When pests feeding on the two types of cotton mated, the pests feeding on susceptible plants would dilute the genes for resistance, slowing its evolution.[29]

By now you can predict what happened: as transgenic crops spread, they selected for resistance. Farmers in India began growing genetically modified cotton in 2002 and planted it on 83 percent of the country's cotton fields (8.3 million hectares) by 2009. In 2010, Monsanto announced that pink bollworm (*Pectinophora gossypiella*) populations in India had evolved resistance to Bollgard, its first commercial variety of Bt cotton.

India is the world's second largest producer of cotton (after China), giving this development global significance. The company described resistance as "natural and expected," and it had a solution at hand: Bollgard II, which carries two genes for resistance. The company expected 90 percent of cotton farmers in India's Gujarat state, where resistance to Bollgard emerged, to plant Bollgard II in 2010. It should not be long before insects evolve resistance to the latter variety as well.[30]

The program may have worked, as field surveys have not turned up resistant populations.[31] But I have to predict that these programs will not prevent resistance, especially knowing that cotton pests carry genes for resistance.[32]

Now we turn from efforts to broaden variation to efforts to narrow it. Once breeders create a variety they like, they usually try to narrow its genetic variation so that it breeds true (produces offspring very like the parents). Traditional breeding accomplishes this goal through **inbreeding,** or mating close relatives (parents with offspring or siblings with each other). We can think of inbreeding as a specific case of the **sampling effect** (Chapter 3). By using a small number of individuals to create an isolated breeding pool, breeders dramatically narrow genetic variation. So long as subsequent generations of the variety mate only with each other (something people try to control), the genetic variation remains narrow. Purebred dogs provide a familiar example.

Another method of narrowing genetic variability is **cloning,** or creating offspring genetically identical to parents. One of the most common methods of cloning is grafting, or inducing a twig from one plant to grow on another so that it will bear fruit identical to the parent's. Apple growers rely on this method because trees grown from seeds vary wildly (some trees easily cross-pollinate). Novel techniques from molecular biology have made it possible to clone species that previously resisted this method. Dolly the sheep is the most famous example, but researchers have also cloned pigs, goats, horses, and cats.[33]

It can be tricky to differentiate the human impact on **inheritance** from our impact on selection and variation. Breeding, to pick one example, affects selection as well as inheritance. The key is to recognize the role of inheritance in the evolutionary process. It supplies a mechanism for passing traits from one generation to the next. So here we want to focus on ways people have influenced that mechanism – that is, how organisms inherit traits, more than what they inherit. We begin with techniques we studied under the headings of variation and selection.

Cloning and genetic engineering affect inheritance by replacing sexual with asexual reproduction. Cloning enables individuals of sexual species to pass along all their genes to each descendent rather than just the half that sexual reproduction would permit. The next generation includes genetic replicas of the parent, which sexual reproduction would not create. This pattern holds true whether the cloning technique depends on grafting or molecular biology. Whereas cloning bypasses sexual reproduction to narrow variation, genetic engineering bypasses it to increase variation. This technique enables individuals to inherit traits from organisms that might not belong to the same kingdom. The next generation includes individuals (and populations) with genetic traits unseen in preceding generations of the same species.

Another method of generating variation, mutagenesis, also qualifies as a way of modifying inheritance. By disabling or altering some genes, mutations prevent offspring from inheriting some traits. The next generation has fewer individuals with some traits than normal reproduction would have created. Mutations also enable offspring to inherit traits their parents did not possess, producing subsequent generations with traits unseen in their ancestors.

Scientists have also modified inheritance by inducing sterility. The screwworm fly plagued cattle on the island of Curacao, in the Netherlands Antilles. Entomologists decided to control the pest by slashing its ability to reproduce. They irradiated fly eggs, which sterilized the males but otherwise seemed to leave the flies unharmed. Researchers let the eggs hatch, then released the adults into the wild. Sterile and fertile males mated at the same rate, but only fertile males fathered fertile eggs. Massive releases of sterile males led females to lay so many infertile eggs that the screwworm disappeared from the island. So in this case, researchers altered the traits of a population (and eventually eradicated it) by increasing the frequency of a mutation-generated trait, male sterility, that interfered with inheritance.[34]

Eradication via trait modification takes us to a cousin of intentional evolution: intentional extinction. The difference between eradication and extinction is one of scale. Eradication eliminates a species from a place (also known as local extinction). Extinction without an adjective refers to the elimination of a species from the earth. Groups of organisms by any other name – variety, genus, family, and so on – can also go extinct. Intentional evolution and intentional extinction are cousins because of their common ancestor: intentionality. They differ in that intentional evolution aims to modify traits of a species while keeping it alive, whereas intentional extinction aims to eliminate the traits of a species by exterminating the species altogether. Extinction brings the process of evolution to an end in the same way that death brings life to an end, so extinction belongs in the evolutionary history of a species in the same way that death belongs in the biography of a person.

The best example of intentional extinction is the campaign against smallpox. As with the screwworm, the effort relied on halting reproduction of the target species. But the mechanism differed. With smallpox, investigators altered traits of the hosts rather than of the disease. Infecting human beings with a related but mild disease, cowpox, mobilized the human immune system in a way that also conferred resistance to smallpox. Global vaccination efforts succeeded so well that in 1980, the World Health Organization declared the disease extinct. It would have been more accurate to declare it extinct in the wild, as medical and military laboratories kept the virus alive. Many urged the destruction of those stocks, too, but researchers resisted on practical and moral grounds (do we have the right to eliminate a species from the earth?). It looks like the disease survived in the wild, too, because it later reappeared, but certainly the campaign came close to exterminating the species.[35]

This chapter has argued that human beings have developed a variety of techniques to shape evolution intentionally. Accidental evolution usually occurs via impacts on selection, but intentional evolution affects variation and inheritance as well as selection. One should not misconstrue *intentional* to mean complete control. Except for a few recent exceptions, other species have initiated the changes on which human beings then capitalized in intentional ways. And human actions have certainly produced unintended consequences. But the principle remains: whether people thought in these terms, much of human history has been an effort to control evolution.

8

Coevolution

The idea of coevolution originated in evolutionary biology to describe the process by which pollinators and plants developed traits that seemed to suit each other astonishingly well. Why is the tongue of the hummingbird just long enough to reach the nectar in a flower, and the flower tube just long enough to force the bird's head to bump into pollen grains that the bird transfers to the next plant it visits? The idea emerged that the two species continually evolved in response to each other; biologists dubbed this process **coevolution**. If hummingbirds evolved a longer tongue that enabled the head to avoid contact with pollen, they created a selective advantage for plants with longer-tubed flowers that forced hummingbirds to brush against pollen stalks once again. Longer flower tubes created a selective advantage for birds with longer tongues, and so on, with flower tubes and bird tongues both lengthening over time.[1]

This chapter argues that populations of people and of other species have coevolved; that is, a human population has caused changes in the traits of a population of another species, and those changes have in turn reshaped traits in the human population, and so on. Because we have been emphasizing genetic evolution so far in this book, I will start out with examples involving the evolution of two genetic traits of human beings: light skin and lactose tolerance. Then I will turn to another way of thinking about evolution and coevolution that involves culture.

Many of my days begin with a run, so I don clothes best suited to the temperature. In the summer, this means wearing a singlet, shorts, socks, and shoes. This outfit leaves a lot of skin exposed, which helps keep me cool. The freedom to wear so little clothing is one of the motives for running first thing in the morning. I have fair skin that burns easily, and early-morning sunlight is too weak to cause damage. My behavior changes when I run mid-day. Then I don a hat and long-sleeved shirt or slather on sunscreen. The dangers of sun-damaged skin hit home all too clearly for my wife when, as a thirteen-year-old, she watched her father die of melanoma. I run the risk of the same fate. I have the light, freckled skin that is most susceptible to sun damage and burned frequently as a boy.

Not everyone has the same problem. We know a family with a range of skin hues in their house. The African American father has dark skin, the Caucasian mother has light skin, and their four children fall in between. On the basis of skin color alone, the risk of melanoma is lowest for the father, intermediate for the children, and highest for the mother. The father can enjoy hours in the same sunlight that would burn his wife in minutes. I envy the father and children. I love spending time outdoors. Protective clothes are hot and sticky, and sunscreens make a slimy mess.

Given its disadvantages, why does light skin exist at all? It is a question that would take many of us by surprise. I grew up surrounded by light-skinned people who, to my memory, never posed the question. Light skin seemed normal, and people rarely question the normal. Certain social forces have guided our attention away from the question. Adherents to the biblical account of creation believe God created people as they are. Every image I have seen of Adam and Eve shows them with light skin, which implies that all of us descended from light people. Racists are convinced light people are superior to people of other colors.[2]

But is light skin normal? One meaning of *normal* is "most common." Most of the world's people have so-called black or brown skin, so the idea that numerical dominance makes lightness normal is out. Another meaning of *normal* is "standard," with everything else being considered a variant from the standard. For skin, the closest we might come to a standard is the color of the first human beings. I am afraid the painters of Adam and Eve will have to do some retouching. All human beings descended from African ancestors, and those ancestors were almost certainly dark.[3] We also use *normal* to refer to something that works as expected. We have seen that dark skin performs better than light at protecting one from sunburn in Charlottesville, so lightness does not seem to work as well as the alternatives.

Dark skin is also normal, in the sense of common, across species exposed to bright sunlight. Fur and feathers protect the skin of most mammals and birds, but many species have patches of dark, uncovered skin on faces, hands, feet, and so on. Darkness comes from a pigment, melanin, produced by special cells in the epidermis. A variety of genes regulate melanin production, and their blending explains why children have skin color intermediate between their parents' skin tones. If a single gene regulated production, we would see two different states (either dark or light) rather than intermediates. Exposure to sunlight also increases melanin production (which we call *tanning*).[4]

Given that light skin looks abnormal by all these measures, it seems to need some explaining. Evolutionary biologists so recoiled from eugenics after World War II that they avoided questions of race. Recently, however, we have seen a surge of publications that have produced a credible explanation for skin color. This explanation has nothing to do with universal superiority or inferiority and instead regards skin color as an adaptation to specific climates. A color suited to one climate can pose problems in another, and vice versa.

Let us look first at the advantages of dark skin. Melanin screens out ultraviolet rays that damage DNA and cause melanoma. This disease may or may not have acted as a strong selective force. It usually strikes individuals after they have produced offspring, which would reduce its impact on reproduction and inheritance of the trait (requirements for genetic evolution). But it could have a selective impact because human beings rely on parents to survive until they reach sexual maturity. Grandparents, too, contribute to the survival of grandchildren, so their presence could have provided a selective advantage.[5]

Another advantage of melanin is preventing ultraviolet radiation from breaking down vitamin B (folate) in the skin. Cells need folate to make red blood cells and to make, repair, and follow instructions of DNA. Rapidly dividing cells, which abound in reproductive organs and in fetuses, vacuum up large amounts of folate. Shortages can cause birth defects (such as neural tube defects) and reduce sperm production. These problems dramatically reduce reproduction, making folate deficiency a strong selective force.[6] So dark skin would provide a strong selective advantage compared to light skin in bright sunlight.

Given these benefits of dark skin, why would light skin evolve at all? Light skin has one clear advantage: it produces more vitamin D than dark skin. Vitamin D is a child of the sun. Plants and animals produce it, but only in sunlight. Melanin screens out the ultraviolet B rays that stimulate vitamin D synthesis, and individuals with dark skin might need twenty

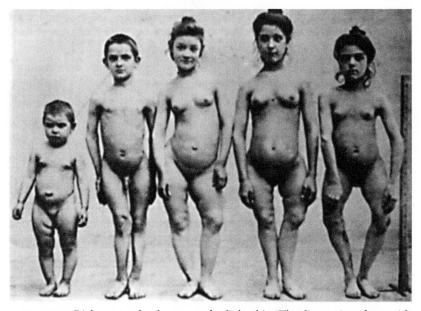

FIGURE 8.1. Rickets may be the reason for light skin. The disease interferes with the development of bones, including the pelvis, which creates problems in childbirth. Rickets results from a deficiency of vitamin D. Light skin makes vitamin D more quickly than dark skin when exposed to sunlight. In the scarce light of northern Europe, people with lighter skin may have suffered rickets less often than those with darker skin, giving them a selective advantage. Urbanization and industrialization in the nineteenth and twentieth centuries reduced sunlight so dramatically that even light-skinned people, such as these five siblings photographed in Paris in 1900, came down with rickets. (Image 139481 from the History of Medicine Collection, National Library of Medicine.)

times more sunlight than those with light skin to meet their needs. Vitamin D is important for skeletal development, regulation of metabolism, inhibition of cancer, and cell growth. A lack of vitamin D causes rickets (the disease characterized by small, weakened, and bowed bones) by interfering with absorption of calcium and phosphate (Figure 8.1). Women with rickets develop small pelvises, experience obstructed labor, and give birth to babies with rickets. Because a shortage of vitamin D harms reproduction, natural selection might well have favored light skin in areas where sunlight was in short supply.[7]

A reasonable hypothesis, then, is that skin color evolved as a balancing act. On one hand, natural selection would have favored dark skin to protect against folate shortages (and perhaps melanoma). On the other, it would have rewarded light skin that increased vitamin D production.

Human beings evolved in Africa, where the abundance of bright sunlight made protection from its damaging effects important. Sunshine was so plentiful that even with abundant melanin, enough ultraviolet rays entered the skin to power vitamin D production. Near the poles, the situation reversed itself. The shortage of sunlight reduced the risk of skin cancer and folate damage, and it increased the importance of capturing ultraviolet light to produce vitamin D. This environment favored light skin. For people in between, we would predict a gradual lightening of color as one moved from the equator to the poles.[8]

The data support this prediction. Skin color of peoples who have lived a long time in a given region correlates strongly with the amount of ultraviolet radiation the region receives. The stronger the solar radiation, the darker the inhabitants. The weaker the solar radiation, the lighter the inhabitants. In areas of intermediate radiation, inhabitants have skin of intermediate shades. Furthermore, women overall have lighter skin than men in all regions. This is consistent with women needing more vitamin D and calcium during pregnancy and lactation. It is also possible that sexual selection played a role. Males may have preferred to mate with lighter females or females with darker males.[9]

The idea that skin color evolved under natural selection as a balancing act is an appealing explanation, but you might have spied an iceberg in its path. People living farthest north and south should have the lightest skin. Yet Inuits, who live in the Arctic, have brown skin. How have they stayed healthy? The answer is diet. Although human beings need vitamin D, we do not have to produce it ourselves. Our bodies are happy to absorb vitamin D produced by plants and animals. Marine mammals, which make up a large part of the traditional Inuit diet, supply plenty of vitamin D. Recent events add support to this explanation. Inuits who have switched from their traditional diet to supermarket food now suffer some of the worst vitamin D deficiencies in the world.[10]

Observations like these led Luca Cavalli-Sforza to hypothesize in 1972 that the adoption of agriculture, and the nutritional shortages that arrived in its wake, selected for light skin in Europeans. Geneticists have calculated that the European alleles for lightness developed fifty-three hundred to twelve thousand years ago. This was roughly the time that Europeans adopted agriculture. It may be that Europeans performed the same experiment on themselves thousands of years ago that Inuits essayed in the last few decades. So long as they lived as hunters and gatherers, Europeans could have ingested enough vitamin D from wild plants and animals to stay healthy. The narrowing of diet that came with agriculture cut out many of these sources, creating a selective pressure for lighter skin that had not existed previously.[11]

If this hypothesis is correct, it is an example of coevolution. It is often easier to see the back-and-forth of this process if we arrange the steps in a sequential list:

- A human population evolved with a certain set of traits. Human beings evolved with dark skin in Africa and migrated into Eurasia. They met their vitamin D requirements by hunting wild animals and gathering wild plants.
- Actions by human beings altered the inherited traits of populations of other species. Domestication by human beings reduced vitamin D production in domestic species.
- Changes in partner populations encouraged evolution in human populations. Reduced vitamin D production by domestic species created a vitamin D shortage among farmers, leading to rickets. By chance, a few individuals carried mutations for lighter skin, which produced more vitamin D than darker skin, giving them a selective advantage in reproduction. Light skin became more common, and dark skin less common, among human populations in Eurasia. The strongest selection for the lightest skin came for farmers living at high latitudes such as northern Europeans. A countervailing selection for darker skin as protection against folate loss created a latitudinal gradient in skin color.

Now we can add another evolutionary step: the narrowing of genetic diversity among Europeans. In general, populations with less genetic diversity are more susceptible to health problems. In a real blow to racists, a recent study found that European Americans carried more harmful versions of genes than African Americans. The reason is unknown, but the most likely explanation is that European populations squeezed through population bottlenecks that reduced genetic variation. Small populations would have been more susceptible to genetic drift that increased the frequency of certain gene versions even in the absence of strong selection.[12]

The bottleneck may have occurred in several ways, and current evidence is inconclusive as to the reason. One possibility is that the benefits of light skin dramatically increased odds of survival. Beneficial mutations are rare, and probably only a small number of people carried the

European-specific gene for lightness. If the advantage of lightness was strong enough, this small number of people might have fathered and mothered most Europeans despite carrying other, less desirable genes. Bottlenecks could also have occurred because of famine, disease, or genocide. The few survivors would have passed along whatever genes they carried.[13]

In addition to perhaps encouraging light skin, agriculture appears to have altered human genetics by selecting for the ability to digest milk into adulthood. Our bodies cannot absorb lactose, an important sugar in milk, at any age. Infants, however, produce an enzyme, lactase, that splits lactose into two smaller sugars that the small intestine does absorb. (Please note the small but crucial difference of one letter between *lactose*, the name of a sugar, and *lactase*, the name of an enzyme.) After weaning, most human bodies stop producing lactase. So if they drink milk as adults, these people develop digestive problems (such as nausea, cramping, flatulence, and diarrhea). This condition, known as lactose intolerance, posed no problem during most of our evolutionary history because, like other mammals, people drank milk only when small. It poses no problem for most people in the world today, either, because adults in their cultures do not drink milk.[14]

In some places, however, adults today drink milk without problems because their bodies continue to produce lactase. Called lactose tolerance (or lactase persistence), this condition is common in northern Europe and some places in Asia and Africa. Eighty-five percent or more of Finns, Swedes, and some Arab and African populations tolerate lactose. The trait appears with intermediate frequency among southern Europeans (about 50 percent of people in Spain and France) and some Africans and Asians. It is also common among descendents of lactose-tolerant populations who migrated elsewhere such as European Americans in the United States. In other regions, it is rare. Only about 1 percent of Chinese adults tolerate lactose.[15]

Genetic differences among populations create this variation. A reasonable first hypothesis might be that populations carry different alleles of the lactase gene. One allele could carry accurate instructions for making lactase and another allele faulty instructions, but, so far as I know, they do not. Because infants rely on milk to survive, selection strongly favors lactase genes that carry accurate instructions, and because genes stay the same throughout a person's lifetime (except for rare mutations), virtually all adults carry perfectly good lactase genes.

A second hypothesis, which the evidence supports, is that people vary in the way their bodies control the lactase gene. Many of us are used to thinking of DNA as telling the body to produce some trait – brown eyes or lactase, for example. Many stretches of our DNA do just that. But other stretches of DNA have a different job – regulating the operation of genes. They are like the people (managers) who decide whether to put other people (employees) in a given factory to work.

It turns out that the key difference between lactose-tolerant and lactose-intolerant individuals usually lies in a control region on the same strand of DNA as the lactase gene. In most people, this stretch allows the gene to function during infancy, shuts it off in childhood, and keeps it off in adulthood. The result is lactose intolerance. Other people carry a different allele in this control region. Their allele never switches off the lactase gene, so the latter continues to crank out lactase throughout an individual's lifetime. The result is lactose tolerance.[16]

If you have not brushed up on genetics in a while, a refresher might help in understanding differences between these alleles. Just four molecules make up DNA. They are abbreviated G, C, A, and T. In the same way that rearranging twenty-six letters allows us to spell thousands of English words with different meanings, so rearranging G, C, A, and T enables DNA to tell cells to do thousands of different things. When geneticists sequence someone's DNA, they report the data in long strings of the four letters, parts of which look like this: ATCGGGTTAC. We can think of these strings of letters as sentences in DNA language. Genes are words (shorter stretches) of DNA within the sentence.[17]

Tiny differences in DNA distinguish the alleles responsible for lactose tolerance and intolerance. Recall that the substitution of a single letter converts the word for a sugar (*lactose*) into a word for an enzyme (*lactase*). Similarly, changing one or two letters in the spelling of a DNA sequence can alter the function of a gene. In the regulatory region of DNA near the lactase gene, lactose-intolerant people have a C in a certain slot (−13910). Lactose-tolerant Europeans and their descendents, on the other hand, have a T there. This is the case for 82 percent of Swedes and Finns, 77 percent of European Americans, 69 percent of Orkney Islanders, and 43 percent of the French. Although cell biologists are still working out the exact mechanism by which the C and T alleles (at −13910) affect the lactase gene, several lines of indirect evidence support the hypothesis that this difference can account for lactose tolerance or intolerance.[18]

The allele common among Europeans does not, however, explain lactose tolerance everywhere. Some populations in northern China, sub-Saharan Africa, and Saudi Arabia tolerate lactose, but few of their members carry T at position −13910. They do, however, differ from lactose-intolerant populations at nearby DNA locations (G vs. C at −14010, T vs. G at −13915, and C vs. G at −13907). Because different mechanisms can create the same trait in multiple populations, it appears that lactose tolerance evolved at least twice in different locations in the world; that is, populations developed at least two different ways to keep the lactase gene from turning off after weaning.[19]

Why did lactose tolerance evolve? It could have emerged by accident and spread by drift in small populations, but its independent origin in at least two places suggests that this trait might have conferred a selective advantage. The advantage is not hard to find. Lactose-tolerant populations share a **cultural trait**: a history of dairying. The ability to digest milk from cattle or camels would have added to the supply of protein, calories, and calcium available to these populations, especially after poor harvests.[20]

A coincidence in time lends further support to the selection hypothesis. A test of skeletons showed that early Neolithic Europeans lacked the T allele at −13910, so Europeans did not always have this trait. Instead, it appears to have originated around the same time as the introduction of domestic cattle breeds. The same coincidence in time holds in other regions, with other alleles, as well. Because the trait apparently originated and spread in just five to ten thousand years, its rate of spread would suggest some of the strongest selection for any human trait.[21] Given that the lightest-skinned Europeans are also lactose tolerant, I have to wonder whether combined selection for light skin and lactose tolerance helped create the population bottlenecks mentioned earlier.

In sum, it appears that populations of people and other mammals repeatedly shaped each other's genetic makeups in ways that created lactose-tolerant human groups and specialized breeds of cattle. Here is a plausible sequence:

- Mammals (including people) evolved to digest milk as infants. A control region of DNA allowed the lactase gene to operate in infancy and shut it off in childhood.
- Human actions shaped the inherited traits of populations of other species. People developed a domestic relationship with other mammals

such as cattle and camels. Domestication selected for docility (a partly genetic trait) in domestic mammals, which made it possible to milk them.

- Evolution in populations of partner species encouraged evolution in human populations. People consumed animal milk, perhaps initially as a food supplement for infants. Adults and children tried drinking milk, got sick, and avoided fresh milk thereafter. By chance, some individual person's DNA mutated in a way that allowed the lactase gene to continue functioning after weaning. That individual continued to drink milk in childhood and adulthood; did not get sick from the practice; and derived a selective advantage in the form of increased protein, calories, and/or calcium. The selective advantage for lactose-tolerant individuals led the trait to spread in human populations with domestic animals to milk. Mutations with similar effects might well have occurred in nondairying populations, but they would have provided no selective advantage and might have created a metabolic cost.
- Evolution in human populations encouraged further evolution in populations of partner species. People selected for cows that produced large amounts of milk, resulting in distinctive breeds, such as Jerseys and Guernseys.

Scholars from biology, anthropology, and other fields now study the impact of behavior on human genetics. They have identified genes that seem to have undergone strong, recent selection, and they have proposed ways in which human behavior may have caused some of those genes to become more or less common over time. Genes that contribute to digestion of carbohydrates, proteins, fats, and alcohol (as well as lactose) appear to have become more common in human populations recently, which could have resulted from domestication of plants and animals. Genes for stronger immune systems and resistance to crowd diseases have increased in frequency, perhaps as a consequence of settlement and urbanization. The evolution of relatively small, weak jaws may have become possible once cooking relaxed selection for large, strong jaws.[22]

Scholars have also realized that we can study behavior from an evolutionary perspective. Although many of us might not think in these terms, behaviors are traits of organisms, so they have the potential to evolve like other traits. It is easiest to see the application of this idea for behaviors controlled by genes such as cocoon building by caterpillars. Natural selection should favor caterpillars that spin strong, protective cocoons and weed out those that do not. Mechanisms other than natural selection, such as sexual selection, also affect the evolution of behavior. Males of some species of birds attract more mates if they sing or dance in certain ways than if they do not. Sampling effects and drift may also influence the frequency of behaviors in populations.[23]

The going gets steeper when we look at behaviors under less rigid genetic control. Complex interactions among genes affect behaviors in many species, and often genes do not determine behaviors so much as set boundaries. Genes do not force horses to move in one specific way; instead, they create a variety of options. Their genes enable horses to move in many ways within wide boundaries – horses cannot fly (a boundary), but they can walk, trot, canter, gallop, or swim. One look around the world makes it clear that human genes do not force us to behave in one certain way, either; our genes enable us to choose from an astonishing array of behaviors and to invent new ones. And it is clear that ideas about how to behave pass among individuals through mechanisms other than genes. My genes do not force me to write this book in English. I am doing so because I happened to be born into an English-speaking culture. If I had been born in France, I probably would be writing in French. I could do either one with no change in my genetic makeup.

Some scholars have developed ways to analyze the evolution of behaviors with no clear genetic basis (beyond making the behaviors possible). They point out that behaviors fit the definition of evolution as changes in inherited traits of populations over generations. Behaviors are traits of organisms. They can be inherited (e.g., through learning). The frequency of behaviors in a population can change over generations. Ergo the behavioral traits of populations evolve.

A stumbling block is defining the unit of inheritance. If I teach my daughter to kick a soccer ball, what exactly have I passed on? Clearly not a gene for kicking soccer balls. The best answer is perhaps that I conveyed an *idea about how to do something*. This description is similar to a definition that anthropologists have developed for **culture**. Anthropologists once thought of culture as a shared set of ideas that unite all individuals in a society. Over the past several decades, they have come to see culture as something more particularized, contested, and changing. They have defined culture as *ideas about how to do things*. Synonyms would include *recipes, routines, values, rules, laws,* and *instructions* (among other things). This definition distinguishes culture (an idea about how to behave) from behavior (an action). The idea that adults should drink milk is an example of culture; milk drinking by adults is an example of behavior.[24]

This concept of culture makes it possible to see parallels between genes and culture and between genetic inheritance and cultural inheritance. Genes and culture both consist of instructions for how an organism can or should do things. Both lead to visible traits (what biologists call *phenotype*) when organisms carry out the instructions. Both originate in individuals. Both can both be inherited, or passed from one individual to the next. Both can be copied, sometimes inaccurately. Both can change and appear in new forms. Both can become more or less common, or go extinct, in populations over time. Both come in multiple versions that carry different instructions for doing the same task in different ways. Both may become more common if they confer benefits on those that carry them and less common if they harm their carriers. Both may become more or less common in a population by drift, even if they provide no selective advantage or disadvantage. Both can disappear if their carriers die before passing them along to others.[25]

To emphasize these similarities, an evolutionary biologist, Richard Dawkins, proposed the term **meme** for units of cultural inheritance. He intended that the term evoke a sense of imitation and memory. "Just as genes propagate themselves in the gene pool by leaping from body to body via sperms or eggs," he wrote, "so memes propagate themselves in the meme pool by leaping from brain to brain via a process which, in the broad sense, can be called imitation. If a scientist hears, or reads about, a good idea, he passes it on to this colleagues and students. . . . If the idea catches on, it can be said to propagate itself, spreading from brain to brain."[26] I have no great objection to memes, but I find the concept no clearer than the concept of culture.

Culture and genes also differ from each other in important ways. Genes pass from parents to offspring, but culture passes among nonrelatives, between individuals of the same generation, and even from offspring to parents. Genes usually stay the same throughout an individual's lifetime, but culture changes within lifetimes. We can pinpoint genes as sequences of DNA within cells, but it is harder to define the physical basis of culture. Is it a pattern of neural activity in the brain? Words on the pages of a book? We can identify genes as discrete units of DNA, but it is difficult to define the size of a meme. Is it a musical note on a page? The entire score of a symphony? Perhaps we need not settle the question now. Darwin did not understand genetic inheritance, but that did not stop him from developing his theory of evolution by selection.

Whatever terms we use, it is clear that human beings possess two interacting means of inheritance: genes and culture. When we saw human behaviors affecting the frequency of lactase persistence, we were seeing the impact of cultural inheritance on genetic inheritance. As lactase persistence became more common, it probably encouraged dairying to become more common. So here genetic inheritance influenced cultural inheritance. These ideas enable us to see coevolution as not just an interaction between two gene pools (populations of separate species) but also between a gene pool (human populations) and a culture pool.

It is also possible for coevolution to occur between genetic traits in one population and cultural traits in a population of another species. Our cod example from earlier provides an example:

- Cod evolved under natural selection to have large bodies (genes).
- Human fishers selectively harvested larger individuals (culture).
- Cod populations evolved smaller bodies, which, when paired with heavy harvesting, reduced population size and catches (genes).
- Fishers responded by using nets with smaller mesh (culture).
- Cod populations collapsed.
- Government responded with a ban on fishing (culture).
- Preban evolution of smaller fish (genes) likely retarded the ability of cod populations to rebound once fishing pressure disappeared.
- The cod population's decline, fall, and failure to rebound led to social changes in fishing villages. Residents shifted their focus to harvesting other species of fish and invertebrates, and they stayed in school for more years than before the collapse, but nevertheless they experienced increases in unemployment, stress, and out-migration (culture).[27]

This sequence describes what did happen, not what had to happen. Each time cod populations changed, human beings had their choice of ways to respond. They chose to respond in a certain way, such as by reducing the size of the mesh in their nets, which had a certain effect on cod populations (smaller and fewer fish in the sea). People could have chosen to respond differently, such as by increasing the size of the mesh, which would have had a different effect (more and bigger fish would have survived). People's choices at one step then circled back to influence their choices at the next step. Hastening the collapse of cod populations left little choice but to halt fishing. Leaving more and bigger fish in the water might have made it possible to continue some fishing.

Let us return to the introduction to see another example of coevolution between populations of people (evolving culturally) and other species (evolving genetically). It may have appeared brazen for me to suggest that we could predict what happened in a hospital in Omaha. My confidence grows out of the knowledge that pathogens have evolved resistance to every antibiotic ever produced. The medical community has responded primarily by introducing new antibiotics. The result has been a coevolutionary arms race. I do not know what pathogen infected my grandfather, but it might have been a staphylococcus (a large group of bacterial species and strains that we will treat generically). Let us spell out the coevolution of cultural traits in human populations with genetic traits in staphylococcus populations:

- Staphylococcus populations evolved the ability to live in human populations (genes).
- Human populations treated staphylococcus populations with penicillin in 1943 (culture).
- Staphylococcus populations evolved resistance to penicillin in 1946 (genes).
- Human populations substituted methicillin for penicillin to kill staphylococcus (culture).
- Staphylococcus populations evolved resistance to methicillin in 1961 (genes).
- Human populations substituted vancomycin for methicillin (culture).
- Staphylococcus populations evolved resistance to vancomycin in 1986 (genes).
- Human populations substituted linezolid (Zyvox) for vancomycin (culture).
- Staphylococcus populations evolved resistance to linezolid in 2001 (genes).[28]

This example demonstrates the arbitrariness of grasping an impact in one direction and making it stand for the whole. For example, we could write an article about how penicillin enabled people to conquer staphylococcus. We could write another about how staphylococcus evolved resistance to penicillin. Both portrayals would be true but incomplete. Saying that people cured staphylococcus infections with penicillin implies a permanence of victory that did not exist. Saying that staphylococcus evolved resistance obscures the extraordinary but temporary efficacy of penicillin. Only by describing the reciprocal effects can we understand the relationship.[29]

A coevolutionary perspective also encourages us to notice the long-term, repetitive nature of reciprocal impacts. In addition to narrowing our understanding to half an interaction, focusing on one-way impacts makes it easy to narrow a study in time. Noting one or two reciprocal impacts improves our understanding but still leaves us shy of crucial insights. Let us say we wrote an article about how (1) penicillin cured staphylococcus infections, (2) staphylococcus populations evolved resistance to penicillin, and (3) doctors cured staphylococcus infections with methicillin. Although we now have three impacts, we would be telling essentially the same story as if we had stopped at the first impact: doctors cured staphylococcus with antibiotics. The overall story remains a tale of human triumph over nature (despite a temporary setback) thanks to technological ingenuity.

But if we expand our study to include all nine steps in the example, a very different story emerges. Now we would have to say that people and nature continually adapted to each other. Neither gained the upper hand permanently.

This conclusion is significant for scholarship in almost all fields. The most common way scholars try to explain the world is by describing the impact of one thing on another. Scientists and social scientists make this framework explicit in two-dimensional graphs that show the effect of one variable (plotted on the horizontal x axis) on another variable (plotted on the vertical y axis). Though humanists (including historians) use such graphs less frequently, we, too, focus on one-way impacts. Did profits from the slave trade spark the Industrial Revolution? How has the Internet influenced politics? How did World War I shape English poetry? Is class struggle the major driver of economic change? An evolutionary history approach encourages us to continue to analyze one-way impacts, but in addition to trace subsequent, reciprocal effects.

This conclusion has profound implications for medicine and public policy. If we end the story with penicillin conquering staphylococcus, or even with methicillin curing penicillin-resistant staphylococcus infections, one could conclude that antibiotics offered an effective technological solution to a problem. A reasonable public policy lesson would be that we should pour money into finding other antibiotics so that we can eliminate bacterial diseases.

But if we conclude that history shows a pattern of continual evolution rather than stasis, we might draw a different conclusion. We might decide to try to stay the course, keeping one step ahead of staphylococcus by introducing a stream of new compounds (which has been the main strategy). Or we might decide to increase research on other methods. My own inclination would be to accept evolution as inevitable – organisms have been evolving as long as life has existed on earth, they continue to do so now, and they will continue to do so until life ends. The question then becomes not how we halt evolution, as chemists looking for antibiotics hope to do, but how we adapt to it. This might lead us to look at the part of our bodies responsible for adapting to pathogens, the immune system, and see how we can mobilize it. We have a medical method that does just that – vaccination – and we might want to devote research to developing new vaccines for a range of diseases.

Once we see coevolution in one sphere, it encourages us to look for it in others. We noted in Chapter 4 that insects, like pathogens, are past masters at adaptation. Not surprisingly, the history of chemical pest control has also been one of a coevolutionary arms race. This has been true around the world, but let us use India as an example. As we saw, DDT sent hopes soaring for the eradication of insect-borne diseases after World War II. When DDT lost its efficacy against anopheles mosquito populations, public health officials substituted another insecticide. Mosquito populations evolved resistance to that insecticide, officials substituted another insecticide, and so on. Insecticides used in India included hexachlorocyclohexane, malathion, and deltamethrin. Today, *Anopheles culicifacies* populations in India resist all those insecticides.[30]

The introductions of new antibiotics and insecticides illustrate the rapid rate at which human culture can evolve, in contrast to the relatively slow rate at which human biology evolves. All the changes in these examples occurred within a human lifetime. Because culture can evolve rapidly, coevolution between people and other species involves human cultural change more often than human genetic change. The examples also illustrate the importance of technology. Human beings multiply their impact on other species through technology, so the more powerful and widespread a technology, the stronger the selective force it exerts. This means that one part of today's culture, the idea of constant innovation of more powerful technologies, almost guarantees an acceleration of the rate of coevolution between ourselves and other species.

These examples also reveal a problem with the historian's habit of attributing causation almost entirely to human initiative. This book's first argument (people shaped the evolution of populations of other species) reflects this bias because it emphasizes the impact of human beings on other species. My second argument does, too, though more subtly. Although it states that anthropogenic evolution in other species changed human history, it closes a human-initiated loop (people changed other species, and those changes circled back to shape human experience). But the staphylococcus and anopheles examples show that pathogens influenced human beings at least as often as human beings influenced populations of those species. For that reason, I let staphylococcus take the first step (by infecting people) in the preceding coevolutionary sequence.

We also need to recognize that populations of species have come in different versions in time and space, and those differences have influenced human experience. Many nonbiologists have a sense that species are, for practical purposes, uniform. Outside the breeding literature, historians usually treat horses as horses and wheat as wheat.

In many cases, this level of generality is appropriate, but not always. If a woman contracted a staphylococcus infection in 1960, penicillin would have cured her. If she contracted an infection a year later, penicillin could easily have failed, and she might have died. The two infections could have come from the same population of staphylococcus, but if that staphylococcus population evolved resistance in the intervening year (as some did), the difference between the 1960 version and the 1961 version would literally have been a matter of life and death for the patient.

Viewing culture through the lens of evolution has many advantages such as enabling us to see how populations have coevolved with each other. I would like to see more historians trace these sorts of reciprocal interactions over time. At the same time, this framework can lead into a trap. Although evolution is about variation and chance, too many people (mainly from outside evolutionary biology) think of it as a deterministic process. This has led to outlandish claims about genetic determinants of culture and behavior. These claims would be amusing if the consequences were not so serious. In the past, arguments about **genetic determinism** have been marshaled in favor of racism and eugenics policies.[31]

This chapter has emphasized the importance of coevolution between populations. We broadened our concept of traits to include those generated and transmitted by culture. The evolution of culture is a complex subject. I have not tried to address all its dimensions here, nor have I charted all the ways in which populations coevolve with each other. But we now have enough information under our belts to see how coevolutionary history might change our understanding of some of the most transformative events of the past. We take up that challenge in the next chapter.

9

Evolution of the Industrial Revolution

Previous chapters have focused primarily on ways that people have shaped the evolution of populations of other species. This chapter has a different purpose. It zeros in on one example to show how evolutionary history can revise our understanding of a well-studied episode in history. The Industrial Revolution provides an excellent case study. Historians agree it was important – second only to the agricultural revolution of about twelve thousand years ago in its impact on human history. A large, sophisticated literature has developed to explain its origins and consequences. Most of this literature attributes the revolution to human beings and their machines rather than to biology, nonhuman species, or evolution. Evolutionary history offers the chance to see the Industrial Revolution in a new light.

Most scholars agree that England underwent the world's first Industrial Revolution around 1760–1830. This episode transformed England's economy from one dominated by agriculture and trade to one fueled by factories and fossil fuels. A host of other changes – such as urbanization, expansion of markets, economic growth, and alterations in social relations – rode into the world along with industrialization. Many other countries have since followed Britain's lead, and modernizers around the world have seen industrialization as the key to economic and social progress.

Rather than taking on all aspects of the Industrial Revolution, we will focus on one of the most important sectors, cotton textiles, as a case study. Some historians have argued that the cotton industry caused the Industrial Revolution and others that it was one of several leading sectors rather than the sole cause. These are debates over degrees; for us it is sufficient to note that the industry was important. Historians have used the cotton industry as an exemplar to draw broader lessons about industrialization, and we will do the same. To simplify the prose, I will use "the Industrial Revolution" as shorthand for "the industrial revolution in cotton" in this chapter, except when I explicitly refer to broader processes.[1]

My overall hypothesis is that Amerindians, New World cottons, and anthropogenic evolution in the Americas made the Industrial Revolution possible, and the arrival of New World cotton in Lancashire sparked the invention of the transformative machines of the cotton industry. My hypothesis rests on four propositions. First, anthropogenic evolution facilitated the Industrial Revolution by enhancing the suitability of cotton fiber for spinning and weaving. Second, Amerindians working in the New World made the Industrial Revolution possible by developing fiber that was better suited to mechanization than Old World fiber. Third, New World and Old World cottons evolved with different traits partly because of differences in genomes. And fourth, the slave trade bolstered the Industrial Revolution by helping England tap the evolutionary inheritance of the New World.

Briefly, the story runs like this. People domesticated four species of cotton about five thousand years ago – two in the Old World and two in the New World. Anthropogenic selection by Amerindians, South Asians, and probably other peoples lengthened the fibers of all four species, but the two New World species evolved longer fibers than the Old World species did. A genetic difference may have been responsible. The two New World species have twice as many chromosomes and genes as do the Old World species. More genes meant more chances to develop mutations responsible for longer fibers, which in turn probably gave Amerindians more chances to select for longer fiber.

The arrival of New World cotton fiber in England appears to have catalyzed the Industrial Revolution. So long as England relied on imports from the Old World for fiber, its cotton industry depended on hand spinners and weavers to make thread and cloth. England's inventors developed machines to spin and weave cotton shortly after long-fibered New World cottons arrived. The difference in fiber length was probably responsible. Thread made from long fibers is stronger than thread made from short fibers. Long New World fiber made thread strong enough to withstand the rigors of machine processing, whereas short Old World fiber did not.

This hypothesis adds to the literature in several ways. First, it challenges the dominant view that Englishmen initiated the Industrial Revolution.

I am suggesting that English inventors *responded* to innovation by Amerindians working in the New World. Second, my hypothesis challenges the common view that mechanical innovation sparked the Industrial Revolution. I am suggesting that biological innovation by plants and Amerindians in the New World created the precondition for mechanical innovation in England. Third, my hypothesis adds a new twist to revisionist arguments that have stressed the importance of colonies for the Industrial Revolution. The revisionists have noted that England had to import cotton, which is true, and that the Industrial Revolution floated on a rising tide of imports from colonies, which is also true. But I argue that a focus on quantity has blinded historians to the critical role of quality. Economic historians have described cotton fiber as uniform and thus substitutable, but in fact, fiber varied widely. Fiber from New World species of cotton suited machine spinning far better than fiber from Old World species, and the arrival of New World cotton in Lancashire was critical for industrialization. Fourth, my hypothesis introduces a new perspective to the debate over the role of the slave trade for industrialization. This debate has focused mainly on capital formation (did profits from the slave trade finance industrialization?) and demand for industrial products. I am suggesting that the slave trade played a critical role by concentrating New World cotton fiber in Lancashire. Finally, my hypothesis offers an explanation for the timing of the Industrial Revolution by linking it with the introduction of New World cotton in Lancashire.

Let us begin with an overview of the literature. Joel Mokyr has grouped scholars of the Industrial Revolution into four schools. The *technological* school has stressed the importance of inventors and machines.[2] Cotton plays an important role in this school's studies, and scholars usually cite the same key inventions and argue that one led to the next in a stimulus-response fashion. In 1733, John Kay invented the fly shuttle, a device that enabled weavers to work hand looms faster than before. Faster weaving increased demand for thread, which spinners using traditional, hand-powered wheels could not satisfy. Lewis Paul took out a patent for machine spinning in 1738, but his device did not catch on. Two spinning machines burst on the scene in the 1760s and transformed the industry: James Hargreaves's spinning jenny (1764) and Richard Arkwright's water frame (1769). In 1779, Samuel Crompton invented another important spinning machine, the mule, which combined features of the jenny and the water frame (thus its name).[3]

Now the speed of weaving became the bottleneck. In 1787, Edmund Cartwright solved this problem by inventing a power loom. Accelerated spinning and weaving increased demand for raw cotton. Eli Whitney usually gets credit for fending off a shortage by inventing a machine to separate seeds from cotton fiber, which enabled the American South to become England's biggest cotton supplier. As Mokyr put it, the cotton gin "ensured the supply of cheap raw cotton to Britain's mills."[4] After that, no one could hold back the locomotive of industrialization.[5]

The *organizational* school has highlighted changes in the organization of work, especially the rise of the factory system. Paul Mantoux's classic book (and other works since) identified the cotton industry as a pioneer of the factory system.[6] The *macroeconomic* school has measured changes in aggregate statistics such as national income and economic growth.[7] Scholars in this school have identified the cotton industry as a leading sector when it came to growth. Walter Rostow believed that the cotton industry powered Britain's takeoff.[8] R. M. Hartwell identified the cotton industry as a sector showing spectacular growth, growing to 40 percent of all British exports by 1830.[9] Donald McCloskey called cotton textiles one of the most progressive sectors.[10] C. Knick Harley used cotton textile prices to understand the effect of the Industrial Revolution on prices.[11]

The *social* school has explored the impact of industrialization on class and other social structures. Social historians have been concerned with the impact of industrialization on class formation and class conflict. Karl Marx, E. P. Thompson, and Eric Hobsbawm are examples.[12] Classic works by authors such as Arnold Toynbee and Karl Polanyi highlighted the role of impersonal, competitive markets in industrial revolutions. More recent scholarship has stressed the role of the middle class and culture in creating an "industrious revolution."[13]

All four of Mokyr's schools have focused on the human sphere to explain the origin of the Industrial Revolution and its consequences. I would add a fifth school to the list, the *environmental*. This school emphasizes that the Industrial Revolution accelerated the use of natural resources, including fossil fuels. Some members have highlighted the role of agriculture. Rostow argued that an increase in food production was a precondition for takeoff. Among other things, this transition freed laborers for factory work.[14] Others, such as Alf Hornborg, have argued that England's ability to tap agricultural production elsewhere (especially of cotton) played an important role.[15] Several historians have identified the transition from wood to coal as a fuel source as an important, even defining, element of the Industrial Revolution. E. A. Wrigley has defined the Industrial Revolution as a shift from organic to mineral sources of energy. Kenneth Pomeranz brought together the emphases on coal and on imports of raw materials (including cotton) when he suggested that England's "coal and colonies" produced a "great divergence" in power between China and Europe in the nineteenth century.[16]

Members of this school disagree on the desirability of these changes. An optimistic wing, comprising largely economic historians, has regarded the Industrial Revolution as a glorious triumph over nature and an escape from Malthusian limits. Harold Perkin wrote that industrialization was a "revolution in men's access to the means of life, in control of their ecological environment, in their capacity to escape from the tyranny and niggardliness of nature.... It opened the road for men to complete mastery of their physical environment, without the inescapable need to exploit each other."[17] Mokyr identifies this passage as "the most eloquent" summary of the meaning of the Industrial Revolution.[18] A more pessimistic wing, comprising largely environmental historians, has tended to see the Industrial Revolution as an ecological disaster. They point out that industry placed unsustainable demands on natural resources, spewed out large amounts of pollution, and fueled climate change by burning fossil fuels. Notable names include John McNeill, Joachim Radkau, I. G. Simmons, Theodore Steinberg, Peter Thorsheim, and Stephen Mosley.[19] Some scholars have linked the Industrial Revolution with evolution. A landmark work was *Industrializing Organisms: Introducing Evolutionary History* (2004), edited by Susan Schrepfer and Philip Scranton.[20]

Alan Olmstead and Paul Rhode deserve special mention because this chapter builds on one of their arguments. In *Creating Abundance*, they note that historians usually credit the Industrial Revolution to English inventors and their machines. "However," they write, "this account neglects another set of innovators – the farmers and plant breeders who developed cotton varieties suited to the new spinning technologies and, as importantly, to the diverse North American environment. These innovations were essential for sustaining the Industrial Revolution."[21] Olmstead and Rhode use the term *biological innovation* to refer to changes people wrought in organisms and *mechanical innovation* to refer to changes in machinery. I will use these terms, too, but also subsume biological innovation under the broader rubric of anthropogenic evolution.

Olmstead and Rhode's emphasis on adapting cotton's traits to machinery contrasts with a common description of cotton as innately suited to machine spinning. This suitability, historians have suggested, explains why cotton industrialized before wool or linen. Makrand Mehta explains, "Cotton was uniform and, therefore, lent itself to machine treatment."[22] Patrick O'Brien writes that "cotton, a fibre of more uniform strength and elasticity than flax or wool, is easier to spin mechanically."[23] David Landes suggests that "cotton lent itself technologically to mechanization far more readily than wool. It is a plant fibre, tough and relatively homogeneous in its characteristics, where wool is organic, fickle, and subtly varied in its behavior."[24] Mokyr notes that "compared to its main competitors, wool and linen, cotton fibers lent themselves easily to mechanization."[25] This chapter suggests that cotton fiber was not uniform and that its suitability for machine spinning was not a given but rather the result of anthropogenic evolution.

My first proposition is the most basic: anthropogenic evolution facilitated the Industrial Revolution by enhancing the suitability of cotton fiber for spinning and weaving. Botanists believe that the wild ancestors of domestic cotton, like wild cotton today, bore short, coarse, convoluted fiber. It would have been challenging to spin this fiber into thread and weave it into cloth. Early domesticators may not even have tried. Fluffiness rather than spinnability might first have attracted human beings to cotton. We know this trait led Amerindians (peoples who inhabited the Americas before Europeans) to use cotton as stuffing (in beds and mummy bundles) and as arrow feathering. Five thousand years of domestication helped cotton evolve longer, more spinnable fiber. Cotton plants generated variations by chance, human beings selected for the variants they desired, and domesticated cotton populations evolved. Chance may have helped traits spread through populations, but on the whole, selection (unconscious or methodical) appears to have been more powerful because so many traits suit spinning so well.[26]

By the time of the Industrial Revolution, people were spinning cotton from four domestic species. Two originated in the Old World. Botanists are unsure exactly where *Gossypium herbaceum* (meaning "grass cotton") evolved. It may have developed as a perennial plant in southern Africa, traveled to Arabia, undergone major modifications, and spread across northern Africa. Traders are suspected of providing most of the transportation. When *G. herbaceum* moved north into Iraq, cold winters made being a perennial into a liability, and it evolved into an annual plant. As *G. herbaceum* wandered into northern India, short summers selected for the fastest-maturing varieties of this species.[27] So the ability of *G. herbaceum* to supply people with cotton depended on evolution in its agronomic traits (perennial vs. annual growth, longer vs. shorter time to maturity) as well as evolution in the traits of its fiber.

Another Old World species, *G. arboreum* (meaning "tree cotton"), also grew in India. It appears to have evolved somewhere along the

Asian-African coast of the Indian Ocean and undergone major change in the Indus Valley. The Chinese started growing a perennial version of this species as an ornamental in the seventh century, but development of large plantings and cloth production in China awaited the evolution of an annual form in the eleventh to thirteenth centuries. Both Old World species, then, underwent major anthropogenic evolution in centers of cotton production and manufacturing, especially in what is now India and Pakistan.[28]

The other two domestic species originated in the New World. *G. barbadense* (named after Barbados) probably evolved in present-day Peru and/or Ecuador before spreading more widely in South America and the Caribbean. *G. hirsutum* (meaning "hairy cotton") originated in present-day Mexico. It is the species that the American South grew most widely in the heady days of the nineteenth century, when King Cotton reigned.[29]

In addition to its impact on fiber quality and agronomic characteristics, anthropogenic evolution made the Industrial Revolution possible via its effect on quantity. Wild cottons produced only small amounts of fiber, both per species and per plant. They inhabited limited ranges, grew as perennial shrubs and trees, endowed the seeds with sparse hair (lint), produced small seeds (making them hard to separate from lint), and covered seeds with an impermeable coat (which limited germination). It would have taken a long time to gather a small amount of lint from these plants, and the harvest could not have come close to meeting the needs of industry.[30]

Under domestication, cotton populations evolved to produce much more fiber. They adapted to a wider range of environments than wild cottons tolerated, which increased the range and number of cotton plants. They evolved compact shapes, which made harvesting easier and faster. They evolved large bolls bearing abundant fiber, which increased yields per hectare and per hour invested. They evolved large seeds, which made it easier to separate them from lint. They evolved seeds that germinated well, which helped people spread cotton over wide areas. And they evolved long fibers, which made it possible to spin thread strong enough for cloth. All these developments laid the groundwork for spinning and weaving cotton by machine.[31]

One might challenge my proposition on the grounds of intentionality, sufficiency, or proximity, so let me address those concerns. I am not suggesting that preindustrial farmers intended to develop fiber for machines that had not yet been invented. To the extent they acted intentionally, they would have had hand spinning in mind. It happened that traits useful for hand spinning were also useful for machine spinning. I am not proposing that spinnable fiber was sufficient for industrialization. It was necessary but not sufficient. Nor am I averring that the key evolutionary steps in cotton were proximate, in space or time, with industrialization. Machine-spinnable fiber simply needed to evolve sometime before the Industrial Revolution.

My proposition contrasts with a long tradition of crediting the Industrial Revolution to inventors and their machines. In 1948, T. S. Ashton quoted approvingly a schoolboy who began an answer about the Industrial Revolution, "About 1760 a wave of gadgets swept over England."[32] More than a century earlier than Ashton, Edward Baines wrote that

a brilliant series of mechanical inventions, made during the last age, so economized labour, as to enable one man to do the work of a hundred. By this revolution in its processes the manufacture received an astonishing impulse, and in a single age eclipsed the greatest phenomena in the annals of commerce. These inventions were made in England; and they form at once the most splendid triumph of science applied to the useful arts, and an abundant source of wealth to the nation. It is not extravagant to say, that the experiments of the humble mechanist have in their results added more to the power of England than all the colonies ever acquired by her arms.[33]

Baines's story highlights the eighteenth century, mechanical inventions, England, and Englishmen. His argument may not have been wrong, but it was certainly incomplete. To his list we should add five thousand years of history, biological innovations, locations outside England (the Americas, Africa, Asia), and peoples other than the English (Amerindians, Africans, and Asians). A more balanced account might read like this (changes in italics):

A brilliant series of *biological and* mechanical innovations made *over five millennia* enabled one man to do the work of a hundred. By this revolution in *cotton traits and mechanical* processes the manufacture received an astonishing impulse.... These *biological innovations were made outside England, and the mechanical* inventions... in England; and they form at once the most splendid triumph *of biology and machinery joined in* the useful arts, and an abundant source of wealth to the nation. It is not extravagant to say, that the experiments of the humble *farmer and* mechanist have in their results added more to the power of England than all the colonies ever acquired by her arms.

This revision of the traditional story complements that of Olmstead and Rhode. I have proposed that anthropogenic evolution laid the groundwork for the Industrial Revolution. Olmstead and Rhode have argued that anthropogenic evolution was necessary for sustaining the

Industrial Revolution once it was under way. We agree that the Industrial Revolution depended on biological innovation just as much as on mechanical innovation.

These findings lead to a new answer to an old question: did England (or Europe) need help from other continents to industrialize? A long tradition has credited the Industrial Revolution to Western Europe in general and England in particular. The quotation from Baines reflects this view. Landes, Mokyr, and O'Brien provide more recent examples. But it is hard to argue that the cotton industry could have industrialized without reaching outside England because cotton does not grow in Britain. This fact has put some Eurocentric scholars in the uncomfortable position of suggesting that the cotton industry was not very important after all, which seems a stretch. In 1794 to 1796, cotton textiles made up 73 percent of British exports. I find it easy to agree with revisionist scholars, such as Kenneth Pomeranz and Alf Hornborg, who argue that colonies and the United States were essential for supplying raw materials.[34] To their work I would add this twist: England depended not just on cotton from other parts of the world but also on people (such as Amerindians and East Indians) and a process (anthropogenic evolution) that created spinnable cotton fiber and plants that grew in a variety of ecological conditions.

Now we turn from similarities among domestic cottons to their differences. As we saw earlier, many economic historians have seen cotton as uniform. Unfortunately, this view is mistaken (Figure 9.1). The four domestic species differed from each other, varieties within species differed from each other, populations within varieties differed from each other, and individuals within populations differed from each other. Variation was (and is) the rule in cotton, not the exception, and the differences mattered a great deal.

My second proposition is that anthropogenic evolution in the New World, in particular, made the Industrial Revolution possible. The New World developed cotton of the right quality and quantity for industrialization. The Old World might have done so, but it did not. One of the most important differences was the length of fiber, which led to big differences in the strength of thread. The success of machinery depended on spinning and winding long threads without breaking. New World cotton proved to be far better in this regard than Old World cotton.

Christopher Columbus helped introduce Europeans to New World cotton. On his first voyage to the New World, he met Caribbean islanders who showed him "vast quantities" of cotton thread, hammocks, nets, and clothing. Columbus was a mariner, but even he recognized that the

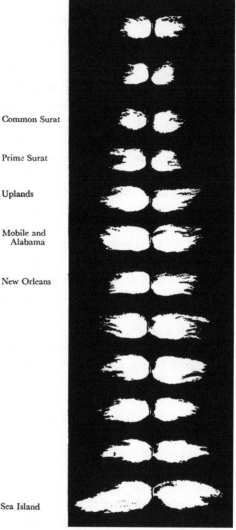

Common Surat

Prime Surat

Uplands

Mobile and
Alabama

New Orleans

Sea Island

FIGURE 9.1. Products of different evolutionary histories. In the seventeenth century, the English cotton trade relied on short-fibered Old World cotton like the first four examples from the top. Cotton from India (Surat) could be *G. herbaceum* or *G. arboreum*. In the eighteenth century, long-fibered *G. barbadense* surged into Lancashire from the New World. The sample on the bottom came from a variety of *G. barbadense*, Sea Island. Near the end of the eighteenth century, medium-fibered *G. hirsutum* from the New World arrived. The fifth through eleventh examples came from varieties of this species. (Image from Arthur W. Silver, *Manchester Men and Indian Cotton 1847–1872* [Manchester: Manchester University Press, 1966], 293.)

cotton had unusual traits, describing it as "very fine with an exceedingly long staple." The plants that produced this fiber seemed to Columbus to grow "spontaneously" in the mountains. As they pushed further into the Americas, Europeans came across more indigenous cotton growers and cloth makers in what is now the southwestern United States, Mexico, Central America, and South America.[35]

Since Amerindians had long grown cotton in the New World, it was no big step for Europeans to do the same. By 1700, Caribbean colonies surpassed southwest Asia as a source of cotton for English textile makers. In 1780, Britain imported ten times as much from the West Indies as from Asia. Place names today, such as Cotton Bay in St. Lucia, reflect the historic importance of this crop. Colonists in mainland British America also tried their hand at growing cotton in the sixteenth century, but they found it more profitable to focus on tobacco, rice, and indigo for market. Some mainland colonists did grow cotton for use in making homespun cloth.[36]

Plenty of accounts from the eighteenth and nineteenth centuries speak of the superiority of New World fiber over Old World fiber for machine spinning. I could not find quantitative data on strength from those centuries, so here I report the results of a twentieth-century study as a rough guide. The study compared the two New World species (*G. barbadense* and *G. hirsutum*) with one of the Old World species (*G. arboreum*). The other Old World species, *G. herbaceum*, does not appear in the study.[37]

New World cottons had longer fiber and made stronger thread than Old World cottons. Fibers from *G. barbadense* and *G. hirsutum* measured 3.25 centimeters and 2.92 centimeters in length, respectively, versus *G. arboreum*'s 1.88 centimeters. So the New World fibers were 70 percent and 55 percent longer than the Old World fibers. New World cotton was also stronger. Individual fibers of *G. barbadense* and *G. hirsutum* broke at 7.20 and 6.86 grams of weight, respectively, versus 6.23 grams for *G. arboreum*. The most striking contrast came when one bundled fibers together. Bundles of *G. barbadense* and *G. hirsutum* showed strengths of 48.1 and 39.8 grams per tex (tex is a unit of fiber density) versus 17.5 grams per tex for *G. arboreum*. So New World fiber bundles possessed 2.75 and 2.27 times the strength of Old World fiber bundles.[38]

These findings may resolve an anomaly in the literature about the Industrial Revolution. So far as we know, the English did not make all-cotton cloth before the eighteenth century because their cotton yarn broke too easily to use for warp. They did make all-cotton cloth in the last third of the eighteenth century. Some historians credit this transition to spinning machines. Mokyr writes, "Until Crompton, the cotton yarn spun in England was not strong enough to serve as warp and hence was used in combination with other yarns. The mule made all-cotton cloth possible."[39] Other accounts credit Arkwright's water frame.[40] Either way, historians have argued that new machines made it possible to spin cotton into thread strong enough for warp, which made it possible to weave all-cotton cloth, which opened up markets for English textiles. The problem is that the English began twisting cotton warp and making all-cotton cloth by 1726, and they made large amounts of all-cotton cloth in the 1750s. Arkwright's water frame (1769) and Crompton's mule (1779) appeared later.[41]

A better explanation emerges if we shift our focus from machines to biology. The traits of spinning devices did not change much in the 1720s, but the traits of cotton in England did. In the seventeenth century, England had relied on the Old World to supply its cotton. Raw cotton first arrived in England around 1601 from the Levant (eastern Mediterranean), where *G. herbaceum* grew. We lack aggregate data before 1697, but anecdotal accounts suggest that Levantine cotton continued to dominate imports through the seventeenth century. Much of this cotton went into stuffing, quilting, and candlewicks. Weavers wanted to make all-cotton cloth, but the weakness of cotton thread forced them to settle for fustian (cloth made of cotton weft and linen warp). *G. herbaceum* grew relatively short fibers, so it is not surprising that it made weak thread.[42]

In the eighteenth century, long-fibered cotton from the New World surged into England. Imports from the Levant sagged as those from the West Indies rose, both absolutely and as a percentage of total imports (Figure 9.2). In the 1720s, when cotton warp appeared, imports from the West Indies exceeded those from the Levant by 260 percent. The West Indies were home to *G. barbadense*, the long-fibered cotton whose bundles tested 2.7 times stronger than Old World fiber. Imports also increased from South America, where *G. barbadense* grew. The English would have spun stronger thread in the eighteenth century than in the seventeenth century simply by switching to *G. barbadense*, which provides a more realistic explanation for the appearance of cotton warp than machines that had not yet been invented.[43]

The geography of cotton warp and *G. barbadense* in England is consistent with this argument. New World cotton concentrated more heavily in Lancashire, where cotton warp arose, than in the rest of the country. Lancashire drew most of its cotton from the port of Liverpool, which imported fiber directly from the New World. Old World cotton arrived in

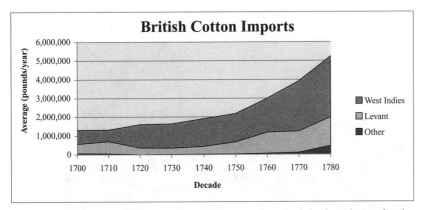

British Cotton Imports

FIGURE 9.2. New cottons, then new machines. Biology laid the foundation for the Industrial Revolution. In the seventeenth century, the Lancashire textile industry relied heavily on short-fibered Old World cotton from the Levant. In the eighteenth century, imports of long-fibered New World cotton from the West Indies surged into Lancashire. The West Indies grew some of the longest fiber in the world. Much of the Levant cotton in the graph went into candlewicks, stuffing, and other uses besides textiles. (Averages are calculated from data in Alfred P. Wadsworth and Julia de Lacy Mann, *The Cotton Trade and Industrial Lancashire, 1600–1780* [New York: Augustus M. Kelley, [1931] 1968], 520–521.)

England almost entirely at the port of London (where New World cotton also arrived). From London, cotton had to be transshipped or dragged over poor roads to reach Lancashire, which cost time and money, so only a portion of England's Old World cotton traveled to the northwest.[44]

Mechanical innovation, like cotton warp, followed the flood of New World cotton into Lancashire. In 1738, John Kay (born in Bury, Lancashire) invented the fly shuttle, which speeded up hand weaving, and Lewis Paul patented a spinning machine (though some believe John Wyatt deserved credit for the invention). Both devices were designed for wool but migrated into the cotton trade. Entrepreneurs set up mills for machine spinning in the 1740s, but the efforts failed, apparently because of mechanical problems. Then came the successful, transformative machines. James Hargreaves invented the spinning jenny around 1764 in Stanhill, Lancashire. Richard Arkwright developed his water frame around 1768 in Preston, Lancashire. Samuel Crompton invented his mule around 1779 near Bolton, Lancashire.[45]

It was no coincidence that spinning machines arose at the same time, and in the same place, that New World cotton concentrated. The

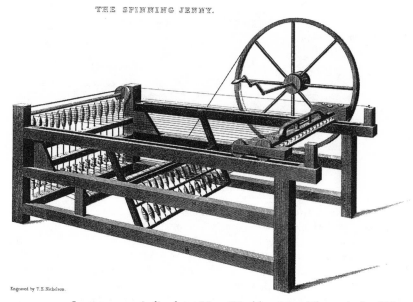

THE SPINNING JENNY.

Engraved by T. S. Nicholson.

FIGURE 9.3. Inventors capitalized on New World cotton. The arrival of New World cotton in Lancashire opened new doors for the cotton industry. A string of innovations requiring strong thread – cotton warp, all-cotton cloth, spinning machines, and weaving machines – followed the introduction of West Indies cotton in Lancashire. This image shows the spinning jenny. Hand spinsters could respond to variations in fiber as they worked, but a machine like this demanded fiber that could make consistently strong thread without the same deft touch. (Edward Baines, *History of the Cotton Manufacture in Great Britain*, 2nd ed. [New York: Augustus M. Kelley, [1835] 1966], 158.)

machines required long fiber. The point of machine spinning was to create a continuous thread of great length, so the big challenge was to avoid breakage. This was hard to do because machines lacked the touch and responsiveness of hand spinners (Figure 9.3). The added strength conferred by long fiber was crucial. Entrepreneurs in India (Ahmedabad) tried to spin cotton mechanically around 1848, long after the English had demonstrated proof of concept, but the effort failed because the thread kept breaking. The Indians were probably using one or both of the Old World species *G. arboreum* and *G. herbaceum*, which have short fibers. The first successful spinning mill in Gujarat, a center of Indian textiles, did not begin production until 1855.[46]

England's inventors and industrialists had the good fortune to inherit the longest fiber in the world (*G. barbadense*), which enabled them to develop and operate machines successfully despite the strain machines

CARDING, DRAWING, AND ROVING.

FIGURE 9.4. Industry relied on New World fiber. The shift from hand labor to machinery placed a premium on long fiber. This image shows English machines that carded (cleaned, disentangled, and aligned), drew (stretched and thinned), and roved (lightly twisted) cotton fiber in preparation for spinning and weaving. Longer fiber from the New World made stronger roving and thread that withstood the stresses of machine processing better than short fiber. (Edward Baines, *History of the Cotton Manufacture in Great Britain*, 2nd ed. [New York: Augustus M. Kelley, [1835] 1966], 182.)

placed on thread (Figure 9.4). Data from one of the largest spinning dynasties illustrate the reliance of industry on New World cotton. Between 1794 and 1803, the Strutt family mills consumed 24,833 bags of cotton. About 96 percent came from the West Indies and South America, home of *G. barbadense*. About 4 percent came from North America, which could have been *G. barbadense*, *G. hirsutum*, or both. Americans imported *G. barbadense* seeds from the Caribbean and planted them along the southeast coast, both in a strip near the ocean and on coastal islands. Known as Sea Island cotton, this fiber gained fame as some of the best in the world. We will discuss *G. hirsutum* later.[47]

Prices buttress the argument that industry needed New World cotton. If all cottons were uniform and fungible, we would expect manufacturers to buy whatever cotton was cheapest. This behavior would have kept prices in a narrow range for all varieties. But that is not what happened. New

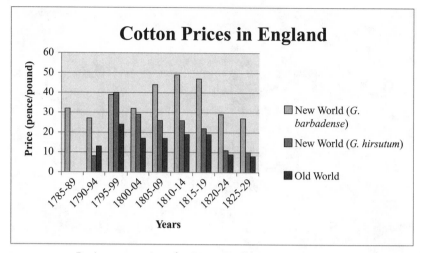

FIGURE 9.5. Paying a premium for New World traits. Prices for raw cotton in England reflected the importance of New World cotton for industrialization. Spinners paid most for long fiber from the New World species *G. barbadense*. They paid intermediate amounts for medium fiber from the New World species *G. hirsutum*. (Four years were exceptions, in which *G. hirsutum* fetched a higher price than *G. barbadense*.) Spinners paid least for short fiber from the two Old World species *G. arboreum* and *G. herbaceum*. The graph shows the average of the yearly high prices in England per pound of raw cotton. (Averages are calculated from data in Edward Baines, *History of the Cotton Manufacture in Great Britain*, 2nd ed. [New York: Augustus M. Kelley, [1835] 1966], 313–314. Prices in shillings were converted at 12 pence per shilling. For *G. barbadense*, Baines reports prices for the West Indies in 1782–1805 and Sea Island in 1806–1833. For *G. hirsutum*, he reports prices for Bowed Georgia in 1782–1805 and Upland in 1806–1833. Old World prices are for Bengal and Surat.)

World cotton cost much more than Old World cotton, but mill owners bought it because they had no choice (Figure 9.5). Prices for ginned cotton also speak to the importance of fiber length. Many of us learned that Eli Whitney invented the cotton gin, which replaced the slow, tedious picking of seeds from lint by hand, which sent cotton supplies soaring. In fact, other gins had been around a long time. The main model in use in the eighteenth century was called a roller gin, and it squeezed full-length fibers from seeds. Whitney's gin (which he may have copied from others) used a new principle: wires or saws that ripped fibers from seeds. The method was fast, but it also tore the fibers. The impact on price was dramatic. In 1796, an English merchant complained that Whitney's gin ripped 1.5 inch fibers into half-inch pieces. Roller-ginned cotton fetched twenty-seven pence per pound, whereas the same product processed on Whitney's gin brought only eighteen or nineteen pence.[48]

Mill owners hated paying high prices for New World cotton, which sent them in search of Old World substitutes, but the efforts failed for decades. The problem was not quantity or price but quality. India made superb cotton cloth, and England was growing stronger in South Asia, which led the search to concentrate on India. In 1788, Manchester spinners asked the East India Company to import more raw cotton. The company responded, sending 422,207 pounds to England in 1790. But the spinners found that the fiber would "by no means answer" their needs, and imports from India fell to nothing in 1792. High prices for New World cotton led the manufacturers to repeat the request at the end of the century, and imports from India in 1799 and 1800 averaged 6.4 million pounds per year. But no one bought the cotton. An embargo against American cotton in 1808 and 1809 sparked another effort, but so little Indian cotton sold that the East India Company described the supply as "a ruinous and unproductive burthen upon the Company and the private importers."[49] Unsuitable cotton was unsuitable cotton, even at a low price.

An excellent substitute did arrive from another part of the Old World, but it was New World cotton in disguise. By the mid-nineteenth century, English spinners considered the long fiber of Egyptian cotton to be second in quality only to American Sea Island cotton (*G. barbadense*). But this was no coincidence: Egyptian cotton descended from Sea Island cotton. Egypt's ruler decided to develop cotton suited for export in the 1820s, so it was logical to plant varieties that the English market valued most highly. Breeders crossed Sea Island with a variety called Jumel to create varieties that grew well in Egypt. Some authors have identified Jumel as an Old World species (*G. herbaceum*), but a 2009 study of cotton genetics labeled this suggestion "undoubtedly wrong" and classified Jumel as *G. barbadense*. It appears that crossing Jumel with Sea Island cotton united two varieties of the same species. So, although Egyptian cotton grew in the Old World, it extended industry's reliance on New World species.[50]

When another species did emerge to supply the cotton industry, it came from the New World. American farmers tried to spread *G. barbadense*'s range, but the plant grew poorly away from the ocean. So farmers turned to a Mexican species, *G. hirsutum*, that grew better inland (Figure 9.1). It spread across the South under a variety of names (Upland, Georgia Bowed, New Orleans, Green-Seed, and others). *G. hirsutum*'s fibers were shorter than *G. barbadense*'s but longer than those from Old World cottons, and they spun well. Imports of *G. hirsutum* arrived in England around 1800, and they soared in the nineteenth century. It was *G. hirsutum* that enabled King Cotton to rule the American South.[51]

The arrival of *G. hirsutum* enabled spinners to group cotton into three broad categories based on fiber length: long, medium, and short. (Spinners also subdivided these categories, but their broader grouping is sufficient for our purposes.) Long fiber from *G. barbadense* went almost entirely into warp. It made thread strong enough to withstand the tension of the loom and thin enough to pack into high-count cloth. (*Count* refers to the number of threads per inch of woven cloth. Count usually rises with quality and price.) Weavers could use long fiber for weft if they chose, but they usually did not because it produced harsh cloth. Medium fiber (*G. hirsutum*) went mainly into weft. Its soft, silky texture filled out and softened cloth. Weavers would have preferred to make all warp thread from long fiber and all weft thread from medium fiber, but the higher price of long fiber led them to use medium fiber for warp in lower-quality items.[52]

Short fiber came from the Old World. If the price of medium fiber and short fiber were the same, spinners chose medium fiber and avoided short fiber. But if medium fiber cost more, spinners used some short fiber. Aside from cheapness, short fiber had little to recommend it. The fiber was "blown away during the various processes of machine spinning." It created weak thread, which led to more breakage in spinning and weaving. Indian cotton needed twelve twists per inch to achieve the same strength that American cotton gained with eight twists. Items made of Indian cotton waned "poor and thin" because the short fibers "washed out" of cloth more easily than longer fibers. Short fiber went almost entirely into weft, though it was possible to spin it into the coarsest grade of warp if necessary. Usually spinners mixed it with medium-fibered American cotton, but short fiber "can only be blended with it with much caution, and in very moderate proportions."[53]

England's reliance on American cotton placed it in a precarious position. In 1857, the *Economist* noted that 90 percent of the cotton used in industry was medium fiber from the United States. Long fiber and short fiber together made up the other 10 percent. The magazine warned its readers that short-fibered Indian cotton (known as Surat) could not substitute for the others except in very limited ways. "Our desideratum is not simply more cotton," the *Economist* stressed, "but more cotton *of the same character and price* as that now imported from the States. If India were to send us two millions of bales of *Surat* cotton per annum, the desideratum would not be supplied, and our perilous problem would be still unsolved. We should be almost as dependent on America as ever."[54]

The magazine proved to be prescient. When the American Civil War slashed exports, England suffered what became known as the cotton famine. Many mills closed; others switched to short fiber from India, but with difficulty. Merchants at a prayer meeting begged God for more cotton, but one added a qualification: "But not Surat, Lord, not Surat."[55] India was able to supply some medium fiber cotton known as Dharwar American, which became known as the best cotton grown in India. Like Egyptian cotton, though, it was a New World cotton species growing in the Old World. As its name implied, it descended from American *G. hirsutum* introduced to Dharwar, India.[56]

The cotton industry's reliance on New World species has continued to the present. *G. hirsutum* produces about 90 percent of the world cotton crop, and *G. barbadense* supplies most of the remaining 10 percent. The two Old World varieties (*G. arboreum* and *G. herbaceum*) contribute tiny amounts.[57]

Why did New World cottons suit machine spinning better than Old World cottons? In some ways, their evolutionary histories look remarkably similar. In both worlds, people domesticated two species of cotton roughly five thousand years ago. In both places, skilled craftspeople spun fiber into thread and wove it into cloth. In both places, methodical or unconscious selection favored longer fiber. In both places, people changed the agronomic traits of cotton in similar ways (perennials became annuals, rangy plants became compact, sparse hairs became more numerous, impermeable seeds became permeable, and seeds became easier to separate from fiber). As for fiber length, differences in environments may have been responsible, though I know too little to speculate. People may have wanted different lengths of fiber in different places. And some people may have selected more skillfully than others, though I tend to assume that people are equally smart and creative everywhere.

It is also possible that nature presented people with different opportunities. Mutations are the raw material of evolution. They generate new traits that chance or selection can spread through populations. Mutations have no goal, and they appear at random, so people had no power to summon new traits in cotton. They could only work with the options cotton offered to them. The mutations responsible for the long fiber of *G. barbadense* and medium fiber of *G. hirsutum* may have appeared only in those species, making it impossible for people outside South America to select for fiber of such lengths.

My third proposition is that differences in genomes gave New World cottons better odds for evolving long fiber than Old World cottons enjoyed. The fifty or so cotton species in the genus *Gossypium* grow in tropical and subtropical areas around the globe. Owing to common ancestry, species that evolved in the same region have similar sets of genes and genomes. Geneticists refer to such groups of species as genome groups. They have identified eight such groups, located their geographic origins, and named them for letters of the alphabet (A, B, C, D, E, F, G, and K). Taxonomists continue to revise their understanding of the cotton genus, but a recent effort has allocated wild cotton species to genomes as follows. Three species have the B genome (Africa), two the C genome (Australia), thirteen the D genome (New World), seven the E genome (Africa-Arabia), one the F genome (Africa), three the G genome (Australia), and twelve the K genome (Australia).[58]

Nature dealt domesticated cottons in the Old World and New World different hands. All four of the domesticated species, from both the Old World and the New World, have the A genome. Research shows that the A genome originated the longer fiber that attracted the interest of human selectors (Figure 9.6). But the two New World domesticated species carry the D genome as well as the A genome, creating the AD genome. Fusing two (or more) genomes may sound odd, but it is a common phenomenon in plants. As a result, the two New World domesticated species have twice as many chromosomes as the Old World cottons. Most cotton species have thirteen pairs of chromosomes, whereas those with the AD genome have twenty-six pairs.[59]

The fusion of the A and D genomes poses a bit of a puzzle. Geneticists estimate that the A genome and the D genome fused perhaps one to two million years ago, well after the Americas and the Old World continents drifted apart. The A genome seems to have evolved in the Old World and nowhere else. Both the domestic Old World cotton species have the A genome. The D genome seems to have evolved in the New World and nowhere else. Wild cottons in the Americas have the D genome. One hypothesis is that seeds from an A genome plant drifted from the Old World to the New World, perhaps as part of a larger clot of vegetation. Some biologists have suggested a transatlantic voyage (the short route), whereas others have favored a transpacific route. Close relatives of the two New World domesticated species grow on Pacific islands, opening the possibility that the AD genome island hopped across that ocean after their fusion. Whatever the itinerary, cottonseeds seem capable of surviving the journey. In one experiment, seeds of a Hawaiian species germinated after soaking in salt water for three years.[60]

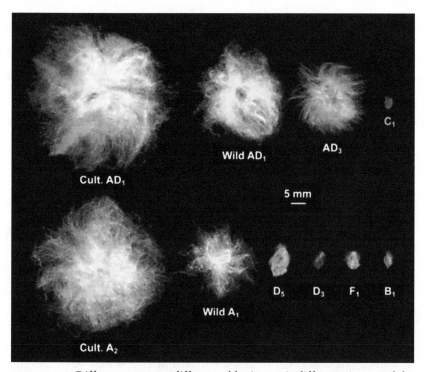

FIGURE 9.6. Different genomes, different odds. A genetic difference increased the odds that New World cottons would evolve new traits, such as extralong fiber, before Old World cottons. The two domesticated species of Old World cotton carry thirteen pairs of chromosomes; the two domesticated New World species carry twice as many. More chromosomes meant more genes, more mutations, and more chances to evolve new traits. The Old World domesticates carry thirteen chromosomes from what is known as the A genome group (bottom row). Perhaps one or two million years ago, an ancestor of the New World domesticates fused the A genome with another group (the D genome), creating the AD genome with twenty-six chromosomes (top row). Note the contrast in fiber from wild species belonging to the A and AD genome groups as well as the short fiber from wild species in other genome groups (B, C, D, and F). (Photograph courtesy of Jonathan Wendel. Reproduced by permission.)

The marriage of the A and D genomes increased the odds that New World cottons would generate new traits, and evolve faster, than Old World cottons. Doubling the number of genes doubled the chance of beneficial mutations. (It also doubled the chance of harmful mutations, but those had a smaller likelihood of surviving selection.) Doubling also increased the chance of generating a trait via different means. The genes of *G. barbadense* and *G. hirsutum* share commonalities, but they also differ in ways that make it possible they use different genes to grow relatively long fiber. And doubling reduced the risk created by mutations. One genome could continue to do everything the plant needed to survive and reproduce, while the other generated novel traits. So it is very likely that the AD genome gave human selectors in the New World a wider range of options from which to choose than the A genome gave to Old World selectors. And because variation is the raw material of evolution, genome doubling probably enabled New World cottons to evolve faster than Old World cottons.[61]

My hypothesis is probabilistic, not deterministic. I am not suggesting that inheriting the AD genome guaranteed that New World cottons would evolve longer fiber, nor that the AD genome conferred a unique ability to evolve longer fiber. I am proposing that inheriting the AD genome increased the chances that New World cotton would evolve longer fiber than Old World cotton did – and it did.

I have found one example that suggests Old World cottons also might have been able to supply fiber of the right quality for machines. In 1787, some of England's more talented mule spinners used a scarce, high-quality Indian variety called Amood to make yarn for muslin.[62] I have been unable to find out the species to which this variety belonged, but there is a good chance it was one of the Old World species. So although harder to work than West Indies cotton, Old World cotton may have had the genetic capacity to produce machine-spinnable fiber. But the Old World did not supply fiber of the right quality *and* quantity to support English industrialization.

It was not for lack of trying. Britain tried over and over again to get India to supply cotton suitable for its machines. One list shows seventy-five different initiatives to improve Indian cotton between 1788 and 1850, or about one per year. Improvement efforts included the introduction of new machinery, such as cotton gins, and instruction in farming methods. But the most common strategy was to disseminate seeds, both from one part of India to another and from other parts of the world to India. Seeds came from the best varieties in the world. Almost all these programs failed. The American Civil War sparked even more efforts, but they, too, failed. An exception was a program that introduced American upland cotton (*G. hirsutum*) to Dharwar in the 1840s. That effort petered out before being successfully revived in the 1860s, when it became known as the best cotton grown in India and the mainstay of exports to Britain during the cotton famine created by the American Civil War.[63]

Why did these programs fail? British observers in the nineteenth century usually blamed Indians and especially what they perceived as backward beliefs and economic systems. One commenter wrote, "Nothing seems more unaccountable than the opposition thrown in the way of improvement by the natives themselves." Another said, "A *ryot* [peasant] has the greatest disinclination to every kind of innovation; it is not only that he has a disinclination to change, but it is not to the interest of the Brahmin part of society to allow of any innovation." Yet another found "the Brahmins discouraging the cultivation, as it would cause the disappearance of the native plant, and that, therefore, 'the evil eye' would be upon all their efforts." Many critics thought it would be essential to counter the "baneful influence" of Indian middlemen, who focused on selling cotton to the Indian market, by replacing them with European agents in the growing districts.[64]

The world looked very different through the eyes of the *ryots*. Traditional cotton varieties brought several advantages. They had adapted to the soils and climates of specific regions, so they produced crops reliably. They required little labor. They grew in the same fields as other crops, such as rice (a practice today called *intercropping*), and matured at a different time than other crops, which spread out labor demands. The cotton could be cleaned cheaply on simple, hand-operated roller gins. The fiber found a ready market in the Indian textile industry, which had long since mastered the arts of spinning and weaving short-fibered cotton.[65]

Skill and time underpinned the success of the Indian cotton industry. The hands of skilled spinners imparted just the right amount of stretch and twist to each inch of the yarn to create thread strong enough for hand-operated looms. The men who laid the warp handled it gently; two men took ten to thirty days to lay warp for a single piece of cloth. Weavers worked slowly and carefully to avoid breaking the yarn; they also devoted ten to thirty days (depending on quality) to make one piece of cloth (Figure 9.7). After washing and bleaching, needleworkers repaired broken threads.[66]

Indian textile makers also knew how to capitalize on variation in cotton by using specific varieties to make specific types of cloth. Few of the names for the varieties or cloths made it into English, but a brief list gives us a sense of the specialization. *Narma* cotton went into *gurrahs*, *bafta*, and *khas*; *photi* into *malmal*, *allaballi*, *duriya*, *tanjeb*, and others; *latchi* into *tanjeb* and *malmal*; *bogra* into *bafta*, *gazzy*, and *duriya*; and *muhri* into *sanas*, *dimti*, *peniascos*, and gingham. This is just part of the list for one region: Bengal. Indian cloth spanned the range from the cheap and durable to the expensive and fine. Even the English admitted that their machine-made cloth was inferior to Indian handmade cloth.[67]

FIGURE 9.7. Old World cottons were superior in India. New World cottons
thrived in the Atlantic economy of the early nineteenth century, but that did
not make them superior in any universal way. Efforts to introduce American
varieties to India in the early nineteenth century failed repeatedly because Old
World cottons performed better in that environment. Compared to their American relatives, Indian varieties were cheaper to obtain as seeds, tolerated a wider
range of ecological conditions, required less labor and water, enabled farmers to
grow more crops in the same field, produced crops more reliably, and cost less
to gin. They found a ready market in the Indian textile industry, which made
finer cloth than English machines could produce. Superior skill, and willingness
to invest large amounts of time, enabled Indians to achieve this feat using simple technologies. (Edward Baines, *History of the Cotton Manufacture in Great
Britain*, 2nd ed. [New York: Augustus M. Kelley, [1835] 1966], 70.)

The English market offered *ryots* only one incentive – potentially higher prices – and many risks. Imported varieties often grew poorly or failed altogether in the Indian climate and soil. (Indian cottons grew long taproots, enabling them to survive frequent droughts, while the imported varieties had shallow roots. American plants survived in Dharwar because that region receives rain from dual monsoons, vs. the single monsoons experienced elsewhere.) American varieties grew in a different season and required a different method of planting (seeding in rows rather than broadcasting) from traditional varieties. American varieties required more labor. They cost more to gin because the seeds clung more tightly to the fibers. They would be sold to a distant market (Liverpool) with unpredictable swings in price (determined largely by the supply of cotton from the United States). And to top it all, if they did not fail, the imported varieties often fetched a lower price than the local varieties. Improvement, as defined by the English, meant impoverishment for the *ryots*.[68]

Situating organisms in environments helps us understand why traditional, long-fibered varieties of Indian cotton did not spread more widely in the eighteenth and nineteenth centuries. Demand outstripped supply, which should have encouraged its spread, but Indians grew long-fibered varieties only in tiny areas. This suggests that such varieties tolerated a narrow range of environmental conditions – the type of soil, amount of moisture, and range of temperatures all could have come into play.[69] The wider genetic tool kit of the New World cottons probably helped them adapt to a wider range of environments as well as to evolve longer fiber than the Old World cottons.

Some of the most important innovators for the Industrial Revolution were plants and long-dead Amerindians. New World cotton plants doubled their chromosome number from twenty-six to fifty-two, increasing the chance they would mutate in ways that lengthened fiber. Amerindians capitalized on plant-generated variation and selected for the long fibers that inventors and their machines needed. Mechanical inventors did not conjure the Industrial Revolution out of nothing but their own imaginations; they relied on genetic accidents and anonymous innovators on the other side of the Atlantic Ocean to create the preconditions for the success of their machines. Nor did the dependence of industry on biological innovation halt with the first generation of textile machinery; it continues to the present.

Traditional histories stop at the doorstep of biology, at most acknowledging differences between species but rarely seeking to explain them. In this case, the traditional approach would consider it sufficient to note that New World cottons had longer fibers than Old World species. But an evolutionary history approach walks right into the house of biology to reach a deeper understanding. One of the questions it encourages us to ask is why species have the traits they do. It reminds us that species are not givens; they have histories.

The evolutionary history of cotton enables us to take a fresh look at a long-standing debate: did slavery make the Industrial Revolution possible? In 1944, Eric Williams argued in *Capitalism and Slavery* that profits from the slave trade provided the capital England used to industrialize. Historians have argued over the Williams thesis ever since. Critics have charged that factory owners drew little capital from slave traders and that profits were too small to make much of a difference. Others have countered that profits flowed indirectly to industry such as through the banks that the slave trade helped found. Others yet have argued that Williams might have been mistaken about capital investment, but the slave trade supported industrialization in other ways such as by boosting demand for the products churned out by industry.[70] For the most part, these debates have turned on questions of quantity, whether of capital, raw materials, or demand. Shifting our focus to quality suggests a new line of thinking.

My fourth proposition is that the slave trade contributed to the Industrial Revolution by helping England to tap the evolutionary inheritance of the New World. The triangular slave trade brought New World cotton to England, which enabled England to industrialize. Slave traders were not unique, for other merchants also imported New World cotton to England, but they did play an critical role. The rise of Liverpool as a slave port concentrated New World cotton in Lancashire, which helps explain why all-cotton cloth, spinning machines, and cotton factories arose when and where they did. The slave trade also boosted demand for cloth made of New World cotton.

This proposition builds on the work of Alfred Wadsworth and Julia de Lacy Mann. In 1931, they noted that the triangular trade route helped the Lancashire cotton trade by increasing demand for cloth and supply of cotton fiber. Ships leaving on the first leg of the triangle carried cloth from England to Africa to trade for human beings. Textiles made up about two-thirds of the cargo of these ships.[71] On the second leg, these ships transported human beings from Africa to the New World to sell as slaves. On the third leg, the ships carried cotton from the New World back to England. Textile makers spun and wove the cotton into cloth, which they sold to merchants setting out for Africa to begin the next circuit around the triangle. By sitting at the intersection of the first and third legs of the triangle, Lancashire benefited from both.[72]

Lancashire owed much of its fortune to Liverpool. The London-based Royal African Company dominated the British slave trade in the late seventeenth century but lost its royal monopoly in 1698. As private merchants took over, the trade's geographic center migrated from London to western ports – first to Bristol and then to Liverpool. By the end of the eighteenth century, Liverpool was the busiest slave port in the world. About 80 percent of all English slave ships embarked from Liverpool in the last decades before England abolished its slave trade in 1807.[73] Cotton arriving in Liverpool from the New World flowed into surrounding Lancashire, and finished cloth traveled right back to Liverpool for export.[74]

Liverpool's rise as a slave port helps explain why New World fiber flooded Lancashire in the eighteenth century. *G. barbadense* grew in the West Indies and South America, the regions where the slave trade concentrated, and it thrived near the ocean, putting it close to water transportation and ports. So after selling off slaves, traders often found cotton close at hand to carry back to Liverpool. To some extent, this was no accident. Cotton planters bought slaves, which guided slavers to cotton-growing regions. In these cases, slavery and cotton helped pull ships around all three legs of the triangle. Slave ships took Africans to the New World to sell to cotton planters; slaves raised cotton that flowed back to Liverpool; and cloth made of slave-grown cotton left England for Africa to help enslave more Africans. But often, slavers found themselves near cotton regions by accident. The range of *G. barbadense* happened to overlap with that of an introduced plant, sugarcane (members of the genus *Saccharum*). Sugar growers created the biggest market for slaves, which drew traders to regions where *G. barbadense* grew as well.[75]

The timing of Liverpool's rise as a slave port helps explain the surge of innovations in Lancashire in the second half of the eighteenth century. The Liverpool slave trade took off after 1747, and Lancashire began making large quantities of all-cotton cloth in the 1750s – just when the amount of New World cotton increased.[76] Inventors launched their new spinning machines in the following decade, and the rising tide of *G. barbadense* enabled entrepreneurs to open factories that helped lead the Industrial Revolution. The slave trade, the cotton industry of Lancashire, and the port of Liverpool grew up together.

The slave trade would not have played the same role had it linked England, Africa, and India in the eighteenth century. That triangle would

TABLE 9.1. *Alternative Explanations for Industrialization of Cotton*

Element	Common Interpretations	Evolutionary History
Sphere of change	Human	Natural and human
Direction of impact	People conquered nature	Reciprocal
Types of innovation	Mechanical	Biological and mechanical
Location of innovation	England	India, Americas, England
Innovators	English	Cotton, Indians, Amerindians, English
Period	Late eighteenth century	Last five thousand years
Catalytic event	New machines	New World cottons, then new machines
Trade importance	Debatable	Essential
Cotton bottleneck	Quantity	Quality and quantity
Variation in cotton	Absent or trivial	Critical
Cotton evolution	Absent or trivial	Critical
Cotton genetics	Absent or trivial	Critical
Slavery	Debatable importance	Significant

Note: This table compares ideas that have appeared in many histories of the Industrial Revolution with ideas developed in this chapter. An evolutionary history approach widens our understanding of the causes and consequences of historical change, which in turn leads to new understanding of well-studied topics.

have limited England to the evolutionary inheritance of the Old World – two short-fibered species that could not support the Industrial Revolution. The slave trade enabled England to benefit from a radically different cotton genome, chance mutations that generated long fibers, and the work of Amerindians that selected for those long fibers. In linking New World evolution with Old World industry, the slave trade helped make the Industrial Revolution possible.

None of this provides justification for the slave trade, nor does it suggest that the slave trade was unique in its ability to supply Lancashire with raw cotton and to carry finished cloth to Africa. Some merchants traveled on two-legged journeys between England and the New World. My proposition simply notes what did happen, not what should or could have happened.

The story told in this chapter contrasts not only with other interpretations of the cotton industry (Table 9.1) but with interpretations of the Industrial Revolution as a whole. As we saw earlier, Harold Perkin believed that the Industrial Revolution enabled humanity to escape the "tyranny and niggardliness of nature." Was that true? New machines clacked and groaned only because cotton plants supplied fiber of sufficient length in sufficient quantity. Every other industry depended just as much on nature to supply its raw materials. Industrialization might have hidden our reliance on nature, but we remain as dependent on it now as we have ever been. A more balanced account would describe industrialization as a revolution in the ability to capitalize on the variation and abundance of nature.

IO

History of Technology

In Chapter 9, I hypothesized that a product of anthropogenic evolution (long cotton fiber) sparked the invention of machines that helped lead the Industrial Revolution. This chapter also explores ways in which evolution has affected technology, but it has a different goal. Here my purpose is to show how evolutionary history can help us identify understudied topics in existing fields, offer a new framework for analysis to existing fields, and benefit from applying insights developed by existing fields. We will use **biotechnology** and the history of technology as examples.

The next section describes how evolutionary history led me to recognize that it was important for historians of technology to study biotechnology, a topic that had received very little attention from that field. Then I will discuss ways in which evolutionary history helps us revise our understanding of the relationship between nature (here meaning organisms) and technology. Then I will reverse field to show ways in which insights developed in the study of other technologies can help us understand the history of biotechnology.

It took hard work to see how evolutionary history could intertwine with the history of technology, which is a comment on the feebleness of my imagination and on the strength of tradition in scholarly fields. After finishing my previous project (on the environmental history of war), I decided to make anthropogenic evolution the centerpiece of my next undertaking. I had been working in environmental history and the history of technology for a decade, and I wanted to continue to engage both in my next study. It was easy to see how to anchor evolutionary history in environmental history (the subject of the next chapter) because that field focuses on the interaction between people and other species. But finding a purchase in the history of technology proved difficult.

The main reason was the assumption that nature had to be inert to be technology. Living organisms have entered the history of technology literature mainly in two main ways. Nature often appears as something on which technology acted: trees (nature) cut down by chainsaws (technology) would be an example. Nature also plays the role of power source for machinery: oxen turning the wheels of flour mills would be an example. In both cases, organisms interacted with technology but were not themselves technology.

At the time, I was thinking about dogs as a case study of evolutionary history, so I applied these ideas to canine history to see how well they worked. It was not hard to recognize how technology acted on dogs (chains, collars, kennels) or, less commonly, how dogs had powered machinery (squat dogs had walked inside wheels to turn spits of meat in front of fireplaces). But these technologies, while important, lay outside my core interest: how the traits of dogs (and other species) changed over time. Without ten years of commitment to the history of technology, I probably would have abandoned the effort to position my new project in the field.

Loath to surrender, I asked some friends for help. Historians interested in the overlap between environmental and technological history have formed a group called Envirotech, which, among other things, hosts a Listserv.[1] In desperation, I posted a query to the list: "Can animals be technology?" I explained my quandary, then sat back to see what would happen. A vigorous debate followed, with historians coming down on both sides of the issue. Some participants objected that technology acted on nature but nature was not technology. Others argued that we demeaned animals (and ourselves) by thinking of them as machines, which opened them and us to exploitation. On the other side, several participants used horses bred for particular jobs as examples of animals used as technology. Another suggested that if something can be patented, as some life-forms now are, it is technology. Overall, supporters seemed to outnumber objectors.[2]

This discussion helped me find an argument that, in retrospect, seems obvious. When people modify organisms to provide human beings with goods and services, those organisms become tools. All tools are technologies, so domestic plants and animals are technologies. They are living technologies, or **biotechnologies** in the literal sense (*bio* means "life"). I had previously thought of biotechnology as genetic engineering, or the tools and techniques from molecular biology that are used to transfer genes among organisms without sexual reproduction. Now I saw the products (as well as techniques) of genetic engineering as biotechnologies. From there, it was not hard to see that organisms modified using classic breeding also qualified as biotechnologies. We readily see alarm systems as technologies for protecting homes from burglars. Why not see guard dogs as technologies designed for the same purpose? Because all technologies are fair game for historians of technology, living technologies qualified for study just as much as machinery.[3]

Then friends did another favor. Paul Israel, Susan Schrepfer, and Philip Scranton read the debate on the Envirotech Listserv and organized a 2002 conference at Rutgers on "Industrializing Organisms." They asked me to make introductory remarks, which helped me tease out more ways to position anthropogenic evolution and its products in the history of technology. The conference papers by other scholars opened up other new ways of thinking. Schrepfer and Scranton edited the collection of papers from the conference, titled *Industrializing Organisms: Introducing Evolutionary History*.[4] The appearance of that book marked the debut of self-described evolutionary history in the history of technology literature.[5]

Bringing biotechnologies more forcefully into the history of technology will enable us to contribute more effectively to current debates. (Throughout this essay, I use *biotechnologies* to refer to organisms that people have shaped to provide us with goods and services, no matter the era in which the shaping took place.) The Biotechnology Industry Organization's Web site implies that widely accepted goals drive development of biotechnology: feeding the world, improving health, cleaning up the environment, defending against biological warfare, and so on.[6] These goals are important, but are they the only ones? The virtue of evolutionary history is that it focuses on the why of human-induced evolution. Historians of technology are perfectly situated to address these questions because they have developed ways of understanding why humans have shaped machines and technological systems; now the task is to apply these insights to living technology.

The stakes are high. In 2002, with twelve million citizens on the brink of famine, Zimbabwe rejected emergency shipments of food from the United States because the shipments contained genetically engineered corn. Zimbabwean leaders feared that some of the corn might be planted, contaminate other corn plants with its pollen, and doom its export trade. In a major export market, Europe, fears of damage to health and environment had led to sharp limits on imports of bioengineered food. Between the jaws of advocacy of biotechnology, on one side, and criticism, on the other, twelve million hungry Zimbabweans found themselves squeezed in a dilemma not of their creation.[7] If genetic engineering does not convince us that organisms sometimes are technology, with as much potential for good or ill as any other technology, it surely will convince our successors.

In the classic story of industrialization, machines replaced human and animal muscles. Waterwheels replaced the oxen that had turned grindstones in mills. Steam engines replaced the mules that had pulled boats upstream. Gunpowder replaced the arms that had drawn bows or flung spears. Gasoline engines replaced the horses that had drawn plows, wagons, and carriages. Electricity replaced the hands that had beaten eggs and scrubbed clothes. Somewhere along the way, our understanding of technology followed suit. In the minds of many historians, technology has consisted of machines and, more recently, systems of machines and humans.

Hiding behind this view is an assumption about the relationship between technology and nature: technology replaced or modified nature, but nature was not technology. But because machines are always made from metal, wood, rubber, petroleum, and other products of nature, the assumption boils down to the idea that nature has to be inert to be technology. It might be inert because it had died (think wood in axe handles) or because it had never lived (think iron ore in axe heads), but either way, it did nothing under its own power.

One of the most enduring metaphors in the history of technology expresses this idea neatly. Leo Marx famously argued that the locomotive epitomized the intrusion of technology into the American countryside in the nineteenth and twentieth centuries. "The machine in the garden," he called such intrusions. Even cattle, sheep, and horses recognized that technology radically changed nature, Marx suggested.[8] While disagreeing on the desirability of such change, most historians before and since Marx have seen the relationship between technology and nature (wild as well as pastoral) in much the same way: as technology intruding into nature.

But the smoke of industrialization (along with romanticism and the Cartesian dichotomy between nature and humans) has obscured our view. Yes, machines brought radical changes to nature. But no, cattle, sheep, and horses did not simply witness the intrusion of technology into nature. Their ancestors had walked among the vanguards of technology. They were not machines but biological artifacts shaped by humans to serve human ends. They were technology and, in the root meaning of the word, biotechnology. To capture this reality, we need to reverse Marx's metaphor and see the garden (nature) in the machine (technology).

Now let us turn to ways in which technological history can help us understand anthropogenic evolution. Historians of technology have shown that many social factors shape the nature, development, and use of technology. Such factors include politics, labor-management relations, economics, warfare, science, institutional strategy, national identity, style, culture, gender, race, and class.[9] With that in mind, I have several suggestions for using ideas from the history of technology to analyze biotechnologies and thus anthropogenic evolution.

Suggestion 1: Conceptualize Biotechnologies as Factories

In analyzing the relationship between farming and industrialization, historians of technology have focused most closely on machinery and other tools produced by factories for farming. Such tools include tractors, plows, discs, harrows, combines, fertilizers, and pesticides. But farms are not just consumers of industrial products. As a 1916 textbook noted, farmers were manufacturers; they, too, transformed raw materials into useful products. Seeds, fertilizer, pesticides, calves, and feed were the inputs, and food and fiber were the products. A hog farmer referred to his operation as a "hog farrowing assembly line." As the twentieth century progressed, *factory farming* became a familiar term. It usually referred to farms relying on sheds to raise animals under controlled (and often crowded) conditions to maximize production and profit, but the concept was capacious enough to encompass whole farms.[10]

We can see a farm as one factory or as a complex of factories functioning on a variety of scales. Some of the factories are under roofs, but others are not. Smaller factories play essential roles in transforming raw materials into products. Plants convert carbon dioxide, water, nitrogen, and other elements into maize, and animals convert maize into beef, pork, and chicken. Agricultural scientists have long embraced this terminology. One agricultural scientist said that hogs needed to be modified because one should not use "poor machinery to put the raw product [feed] through."[11] Sugarcane stalks serve as factories to manufacture sucrose. Moreover, organismal factories carry out complex and difficult tasks. Fritz Haber and Karl Bosch received Nobel prizes for figuring out how to fix atmospheric nitrogen. We readily regard as factories the machinery that uses the Haber-Bosch process to make fertilizer. Why not legumes as well? Legumes are not machinery, but they do transform atmospheric nitrogen from one form to another, more useful form for humans.

Moreover, biological factories are essential in industrialized agriculture. No one has yet figured out how to transform sunlight, carbon dioxide, and a few nutrients into grain – except by subcontracting the job to plants. The same goes for meat production and animals. In a study of chicken breeding, including development of the "Chicken of Tomorrow," Roger Horowitz captures the need for keeping chickens at the center of production and fitting these animals to more technological settings.[12]

Suggestion 2: Think of Biotechnologies as Workers

One of the fascinating aspects of biotechnologies is their ability to perform a variety of roles. They resemble factories, but they also resemble workers in factories. Like human laborers, they cannot work all the time; need to eat and drink during the workday; require direction from managers; work well only if temperature, humidity, and light fall within certain ranges; have a limited life span; wear out with age; require special shelter; demand more resources to work harder; reproduce sexually (occasionally asexually); and even stop working all at once.

Historians of technology have learned much about workers in factories and workshops: who they were, where they came from, how they interacted with each other and with management, what conditions they encountered, and what impact they had on products and companies, to name just some of the dimensions. It would be fruitful to take these insights and apply them to organisms used as technologies. How have they interacted with each other and management? How have they convinced managers to alter the conditions of work? How have they been compensated for their work? What techniques have managers used to get them to do more work? How have human and organismal labor proved fungible?

For example, Stephen Pemberton has used the history of dogs to illustrate ways in which human and animal laborers resembled and substituted for each other. When medical researcher Kenneth Brinkhous began studying hemophilia, he relied on an itinerant human labor supply. If a hemophiliac happened to turn up in the hospital where Brinkhous worked, he would draw the blood he needed to carry out his studies. To overcome the unreliability of such labor, Brinkhous hired hemophiliac Jimmy Laughlin as a regular employee who washed equipment and supplied blood on demand. But even Laughlin was not ideal, for using him as a test subject threatened to kill him.[13]

Hemophilic dogs proved better workers than Laughlin. They lived in the laboratory around the clock, supplied hemophilic blood on demand

and in ever-growing quantities, drew no salary, and could die in tests without raising moral qualms. At the same time, the biological similarities of human and canine laborers placed some of the same demands on their employer. The life-threatening conditions for both types of laborers demanded surveillance, surgery, and ready blood transfusions. Industrialization made this type of canine labor possible by producing effective treatments to keep hemophilic dogs alive. The combination of machinery and biology increased the supply of a valuable product, hemophilic blood, in a way neither could have accomplished alone.

Pigs, too, became more productive workers when encased in a technological environment. Mark Finlay has shown that the introduction of feeds fortified with antibiotics and vitamins reduced the length of time sows needed to nurse their piglets. Meatpacker Jay Hormel noted that the sow could "immediately be put back to work producing another litter instead of performing no other service than milking her litter." Like human workers on assembly lines, sows found themselves in a speedup designed to boost productivity.[14]

Suggestion 3: See Biotechnologies as Products

Factory, worker, and product – biotechnologies have been all these things. Historians of technology have studied ways in which industrialization encouraged product standardization, mass production, brand marketing, and shared cultures of consumption spread over large areas. Some products have found their way onto the market as branded products, such as Fords and Apple computers, whereas others have been sold as commodities, such as screws and nails. Highly processed products have lent themselves most easily to such analyses, perhaps because they are most recognizably the products of industry. Biotechnologies, too, have become commodities and branded goods.

One of the aims or results (or both) of industrialization has been product standardization. This feature has been especially important for branded goods, for which quality control is crucial to maintaining the brand's reputation. Organisms also have undergone standardization while posing particular challenges. One of the most obvious is sexual reproduction, which rejiggers genetic endowments of offspring every time. A standard technique for producing certain characteristics more reliably is inbreeding, which reduces genetic variation. Switzerland set out in the nineteenth century to create a national cow. Out of countless varieties, Swiss authorities decided on the measurements and appearance of the Swiss cow. Herd books helped this process by recording pedigrees. A national brand, if you will, resulted.[15]

Roger Horowitz has demonstrated the speed with which the poultry segment of industrialized agriculture could change animals and markets. Concerted efforts by breeders and producers led to the postwar creation of a Chicken of Tomorrow, a meaty breed well suited to mass production. As this breed replaced older varieties on farms, marketers changed the bird's public identity as well. Rhode Island Red and other names of varieties disappeared from grocery store labels as broilers, fryers, breasts, and thighs arrived to take their place. One kind of product differentiation (based on chicken parts) superseded an earlier kind of product differentiation (based on breeds).[16]

As Gerard Fitzgerald reminded the participants in the Rutgers conference, some biotechnology products are valuable precisely because they are alive. He used the development of biological weapons as an example. One candidate, tularemia, would be of no use in an inert form. Tularemia pathogens needed to infect, reproduce themselves in, and overcome enemy soldiers. Industrializing this biotechnology demanded that researchers develop methods that would strictly govern when and where tularemia would be allowed to go about its business of reproduction, thereby advancing military and national interests.

Suggestion 4: Analyze Plant and Animal Breeding as Technological Innovation

When discussing technology, most historians take one of two approaches. The first treats technology as an externality, a deus ex machina that descends from the heavens to shape life on earth. A variation on this theme makes technology the inevitable by-product of science. "Science invents, technology applies, and man conforms" captures this view. The second approach treats technology as a simple response to a stimulus. In this "necessity is the mother of invention" view, people identify a problem and invent a technology to solve it. A variation on this theme recognizes that a solution can produce unexpected, even perverse effects. One common narrative in environmental history, for example, suggests that people developed the technology they wanted, which changed nature, which backfired to harm people and nature.[17]

Both these approaches tumble into technological determinism, a belief that historians of technology have spent the last couple decades debunking. The first, deus ex machina, treats technology as a juggernaut to which people must adapt. Historians have shown, however, that users adapt technologies to their own ends, often in ways the inventor never imagined. Plus, social goals drive the development of technology in the first place. It would be just as accurate to say that technology adapts to society as the reverse. The second, "necessity is the mother of invention," treats invention and design as a simple, technical process. Here the determinism is a bit subtler. It enters when we assume that technical choices are inevitable – technical criteria govern technical decisions, each step in design follows logically from the one before, and designers arrive at optimal solutions. But social factors influence technological innovation at every stage, from problem definition to design to production to marketing. So social choices shape design just as much as technical factors. When those technologies emerge into the world, their effects derive from the social assumptions built into the design as much as from technical considerations.[18]

As for innovation, so for evolution. In the same way that historians have debunked technological determinism, so we need to debunk biological determinism. In the same way that historians have demonstrated the complex interplay of social and technical considerations in mechanical design, so we need to demonstrate the complex interplay of social and biological considerations in organismal design. Breeders have not set out to create the perfect plant or animal in the sense of some Platonic ideal, and each step in breeding did not follow inevitably from the one before. If breeding had headed inevitably toward a universal ideal, the traits of domestic organisms would have long since stabilized.

Instead, a variety of social and environmental forces have led breeders to define goals in certain ways and to emphasize certain traits over others. As times and environments have changed, so have goals of breeders. In the twentieth century, one of the goals of seed companies has been to force farmers to buy new seeds every year (rather than replant seeds from their own crops year after year). Breeders obliged by producing strains that produced well one year and poorly the next. Biology and evolution did not determine this trait in crop plants. The trait embodied a social (economic) goal of producers: increased profit at the expense of farmers.

Some historians have already embarked on this path, albeit usually under the rubric of studying breeding rather than evolution. William Boyd, Deborah Fitzgerald, Jack Kloppenburg, Harriet Ritvo, and John Perkins have traced the rise of plant and animal breeding from less formal to more formal systems. They have identified many factors that have driven changes in breeding practices and effects, including craft knowledge, government sponsorship of research, the rise of the science of genetics, capital accumulation, commodification, national security, agricultural research stations and universities, institutional ambitions, international trade, rural economics and politics, class anxiety, and concern about hunger.[19]

Another reason to study breeding as innovation is that it corrects a striking misinterpretation of economic history. To explain the growth of farm productivity in the United States, economic historians have focused on innovation in machinery (tractors, plows) and chemicals (fertilizers, pesticides). Implicitly, they assumed that the biology of farming remained constant. The data seemed to support this view. Because yield per acre remained roughly constant while yield per worker increased, economic historians thought that they had good reason to credit this increase to new machinery. This view is consistent with the large body of literature showing that extending or replacing human labor with machinery increased productivity in a variety of occupations.[20]

Economists Alan Olmstead and Paul Rhode have shown, however, that the received view is only about half right. The flaw lies in the assumption that organisms in wheat fields stayed constant. They did not. Farmers knew that wheat varieties "wore out" after several years, forcing them to plant new varieties to maintain yields. Wearing out resulted not from change in the wheat but from change in the wheat's enemies. Insects, diseases, and weeds evolved to overcome a wheat variety's defenses, so breeders had to produce a stream of new varieties to keep pace.[21]

Without breeding, yields would have plummeted, and productivity gains attributed to machinery would have been far smaller. Evolutionary biologists call this phenomenon, in which an organism evolves just to stay in place, the Red Queen hypothesis. Olmstead and Rhode estimate that wheat breeding accounted for about 40 percent of the increase in wheat productivity between 1880 and 1940.[22]

The failure of economic historians to recognize the importance of biology suggests a striking asymmetry in attention to biological and mechanical aspects of farming. We would not dream of seeing increased productivity over decades if farmers were to buy a fixed number of tractors, never maintain them, never replace them, and never buy other implements for the next one hundred years. Without a second thought, we would predict a drop in productivity. We are not trained to predict the same pattern with organisms. *Continual innovation* is a term we usually associate with technology, but organisms are past masters at this process. Evolutionary history encourages us to look for the same in organisms.

Wheat is not unique. Industrialization has often relied on organic evolution. Along with Olmstead and Rhode's work, examples include the breeding of hogs and chickens suited to factories in the field, hemophiliac dogs suited to scientific laboratories, and trees adapted to industrial silviculture. Might future historians see mechanization as the first wave of industrialization, with biotechnology as the second wave that supplemented and replaced machines?[23]

Pushed another step, we might even reverse our assumption about the type of technology best suited to industrialization. Usually, we have seen machinery as compatible with (and driving) industrialization. But biotechnology might in fact be better suited than machinery. One way to increase efficiency in a factory is to reduce the number of steps required to make a product. Imagine we collapsed steps so much that the assembly line was also the product itself. So each time General Motors sold an automobile, it would sell the assembly line at the same time. General Motors would have to build a new assembly line for each car, an impossible proposition. But biotechnology has made this feat possible repeatedly. Organisms convert raw materials into products – feed into meat, for example – and then leave the factory as the product itself. Moreover, they leave behind new, self-organizing assembly lines that also will become products, ad infinitum. Perhaps, then, the future of industrialization lies in becoming ever more biological rather than less.

Suggestion 5: Deemphasize the Plant-Animal Dichotomy as a Primary Way of Organizing Ideas

Fifty years ago, most universities had a department of zoology and a separate department of botany. In the 1960s and 1970s, many merged into a single department of biology. Now they are fissioning again into departments of cellular and molecular biology, on one hand, and departments of organismal, ecological, and evolutionary biology, on the other. As a result, people who study plant cells feel a greater kinship with people who study animal cells than with people who study plant taxonomy or ecology. In the era of traditional breeding, the plant-animal dichotomy worked fine. As we move into the era of genetic engineering, though, it will work less well. Now that we can move genes across taxonomic groups, their origins in plants or animals matter far less. Tobacco plants that glow in the dark thanks to a firefly gene exemplify the kingdom-spanning potential of genetic engineering.[24]

Suggestion 6: Expand History of Technology's Reach via Evolutionary History

A common call among historians of technology is to link scholarship more closely to other fields, thereby demonstrating the importance of technology in history. Evolutionary history has the potential to suggest a number of such links and encourage integration. To understand why people have shaped other species as technology, we might well turn to history of science, cultural history, economic history, political history, and social history. The list could continue; it quickly becomes apparent that every field of history intersects this new approach, has something important to contribute, and might well gain in the transaction. Once we think coevolutionarily, we encourage ourselves to examine not just how humans shape organisms but how organisms shape humans. This perspective does not imply a return to the older tradition of technological determinism; rather, because of its emphasis on change, coevolution provides us with an unusually flexible way of thinking about ways humans, nature, and technology have shaped each other.

As we incorporate biology more fully into our understanding of industrialization, we shed light on the present as well as the past. Industries today continue to depend on plants, animals, and microorganisms. Industrialized agriculture would disappear without plants to capture and transform the sun's energy into sugars and proteins. Bakeries and breweries would have to close their doors without yeast to transform sugars into carbon dioxide and alcohol. The construction industry would have to undergo massive transformation without trees to change carbon dioxide and water into cellulose in lengths and densities useful for homes and offices. Pharmaceutical companies rely on plants to invent molecules with pharmacological properties that the companies can then copy. Genetic engineering, one of the most high-tech industries in the world, would shut down without organisms to supply and receive genes that do certain kinds of work. By the end of the twenty-first century, under the continued influence of the biotechnology industry, historians will likely take organisms for granted as forms of technology.

The significance of such an understanding will grow as climate change and biotechnology expand the scale of anthropogenic evolution. As we saw earlier, human beings have long changed regional environments and thus the evolution of species in those environments. Climate change means these experiments have become global. Biotechnology, in its root sense of living technology, is nothing new. But genetic engineering has introduced a novel ability to move genes across very different taxonomic groups and accelerated the rate of evolutionary change. If we are to understand how genetic engineering shapes human experience today and in the future, it behooves us to examine ways in which anthropogenic evolution has shaped us in the past.

This chapter has argued that evolutionary history can enhance fields that have defined evolution as outside their purview. Traditionally, historians of technology have studied machinery and other tools made of inert nature. Organisms might power technology, or they might be acted on by technology, but they were not technology. Evolutionary history challenges that paradigm. By encouraging us to look for the role of anthropogenic evolution in every part of our past, it helps us see that people have remodeled living organisms to do human work, making wild animals into technologies. Recognizing this link between traditional methods of modifying other species to do human work (breeding) and recent methods (genetic engineering) enables historians of technology to engage in public policy debates over the motives and possible impacts of biotechnology.

This chapter also used the history of technology to illustrate ways in which other fields can enhance evolutionary history. Historians of technology have developed sophisticated concepts for understanding factories, workers, products, and technological innovation. We can apply those concepts to biotechnologies as well. Doing so creates the chance to overthrow long-standing interpretations of the past such as the idea in economic history that mechanical and chemical innovation drove the rise of agricultural productivity in the United States. In fact, biological innovation played a critical role, shouldering responsibility for roughly half the rise in production of wheat. Now biological innovation can stand alongside mechanical innovation as a central concern of historians of technology, challenging the dominant narrative of the Industrial Revolution as the replacement of muscles with machine power.

In a genetically engineered world, distant branches on the evolutionary tree find themselves grafted together into hybrids that challenge our traditional notions about taxonomic divisions. Are rice plants that express human genes plants or human? The answer is that we need new ways of organizing our understanding of the world as anthropogenic evolution ushers other species and us into a new era.

Environmental History

In Chapter 10, I used the history of technology to illustrate the potential for evolutionary history to broaden fields that might seem to have little to do with evolution. The task of this chapter is easier. Environmental history is the field that studies the interaction between people and their environments over time. Environmental historians have always been interested in the impact of people on other species, and vice versa, so the relevance of evolutionary history seems clear.

One could consider evolutionary history a subfield or research program of environmental history, and I am comfortable with such terms. But evolutionary history can also be a subfield or research program in the history of technology (and, as I will argue in the next chapter, other fields). This realization led me to some awkward locutions. After suffering through a seminar in which I referred to evolutionary history as a cross-cutting subfield or research program in environmental history and other fields, a colleague recommended that I slice through the Gordian knot of terminology and call evolutionary history a *field*. I have followed his advice ever since.

This chapter begins by noting the curiously low profile that evolution has played in environmental history. It suggests some reasons that might be responsible for this pattern. We will contrast evolutionary history with efforts in disciplines outside history to apply evolutionary ideas.

Evolution has played a surprisingly small role in environmental history. In 2010, a search of over forty thousand works in the "Environmental History Bibliography" flagged just seventeen entries in which authors used evolution as an analytical tool. Authors from fields other than environmental history wrote most of them. The "Research Register of the

Documenting Environmental Change" database at Cambridge University lists only two individuals working on what may be termed biological evolution.[1] Searches always miss some sources, but even a perfect search engine would probably not produce radically different results. With a denominator of forty thousand, we would need orders of magnitude more articles and books about evolutionary history to change the proportion significantly.

Most of the works on anthropogenic evolution by self-described environmental historians have focused on plant and animal breeding. They include works by John Perkins, Deborah Fitzgerald, Harriet Ritvo, and Eric Stoykovich. Works on a few other topics have also appeared. Perkins and I have written about the evolution of resistance to insecticides. Joseph Taylor has described the impact of hatcheries on the genetic makeup of salmon populations.[2] Earlier chapters summarized arguments from most of these works. We could add a few more, but the list would not be long.

The low number appears even more puzzling given the interest shown by some of the most widely read figures in the field. Donald Worster has called on historians to understand culture as an adaptation, "a mental response to opportunities or pressures posed by the natural environment." John McNeill has argued that human beings created "selection for symbiosis with humanity" among populations of other species by remaking the world's ecology. Historians from other fields have also called for more use of evolutionary ideas. Philip Pomper and David Gary Shaw edited a book titled *The Return of Science: Evolution, History, and Theory*. Daniel Lord Smail used the term *evolutionary history* as part of a call to historians to recognize that evolution shaped human history via its impact on our brains. Like most efforts to link evolution with history, the Pomper and Shaw collection and Smail's book focus on human evolution with little discussion of nonhuman species.[3]

Scholars from fields such as geography and agricultural history have probably written more works than environmental historians about the impact of human beings on the evolution of populations of other species. Jared Diamond's *Guns, Germs, and Steel* makes the case that adopting agriculture was the most revolutionary act in human history. He stresses that unconscious selection was essential to that process. In *Like Engend'ring Like*, Nicholas Russell challenges the idea that pre-nineteenth-century breeders practiced methodical breeding. He found that "accidental, domestic-environmental selection," more than breeding for specific traits, drove increases in productivity of meat, wool, and other animal products. Domestication and controlled breeding selected for rapid growth and sexual maturation, Russell argues, simply because growers bred domestic animals as soon as they were ready.[4] As we saw in the previous two chapters, economic historians Alan Olmstead and Paul Rhode have written brilliantly about the way in which farmers and scientists shaped the evolution of agricultural species in the United States.

Many factors may have contributed to the lack of interest in evolution by environmental historians, but three seem likely. First, historians may have lacked familiarity with evolution in general and anthropogenic evolution in particular. Few graduate or undergraduate programs in history require courses in science, much less in evolutionary biology. Even scholars who have taken courses in evolutionary biology may have learned little about anthropogenic evolution. Some of the most popular textbooks have omitted discussion of the topic. Eric Pianka, author of the textbook *Evolutionary Ecology*, wrote that he had "always tried to present evolutionary ecology as a 'pure' science."[5] Small wonder, then, if historians have seen evolution as something that has happened outside historical time and separate from human activity.

Recent publications in evolutionary biology may help correct this problem. Pianka, who devoted previous editions of his textbook to "pure" science, wrote in the introduction of the sixth (2000) edition of *Evolutionary Ecology* that "humans now dominate ecosystems to such an extent that pure ecology has all but vanished from the face of the earth! Hence, in this edition, multitudinous anthropogenic effects are interwoven into every chapter." Pianka used loss of genetic variability, extinction, and evolution of microbes as examples of these effects.[6]

Second, historians may have seen evolution as less useful or important than other sciences in their work. The workhorse sciences of modern environmentalism, ecology and public health, have held pride of place in environmental history as well.[7] A search for "ecology" and its variants in the "Environmental History Bibliography" turned up 3,543 entries. "Health" appeared 1,442 times. Their preeminence is not surprising. Environmental concerns have drawn many scholars into environmental history, influenced their choice of research projects, and probably shaped their selection of intellectual tools.[8]

More precisely, historians may have seen some fields of ecology as more valuable than others. Two – evolutionary ecology and ecological genetics – have offered environmental historians bridges from ecology to evolution all along.[9] But environmental historians have tended to focus on community, ecosystem, and population ecology. Perhaps these fields (and public health) have appeared more useful in understanding problems of concern to environmentalists and environmental historians alike such as wilderness, national parks and forests, wildlife, human disturbance, plant and animal invasions, and pollution.[10] This book suggests that adding evolutionary ecology and genetics to the list enhances rather than replaces the fields already of greatest interest.

Third, historians may have opposed the use of evolutionary ideas for intellectual or political reasons. The field of science and technology studies has encouraged skepticism about truth claims by science. Sociobiologists and evolutionary psychologists have sought to attribute much of human behavior to genes and natural selection, a direct challenge to territory humanists and social scientists have thought their own. Any use of evolutionary ideas might seem to open the door to disciplinary takeover. Social Darwinists and eugenicists in the past have drawn on, and perhaps have been inspired by, evolutionary biology. It is all to easy to read human ideas into nature, read them back out again, and justify the original ideas on the grounds that they are natural. If historians use evolutionary ideas, might they find themselves justifying biological determinism?[11]

These concerns deserve consideration but pose no insurmountable barriers. Evolutionary biology has not subsumed any discipline with which it overlaps, even among the sciences. There is no reason to believe history is any more vulnerable than, say, ecology. Although sociobiologists and evolutionary psychologists have grabbed their share of headlines, we should not mistake them for evolutionary biologists as a whole. On the contrary, evolutionary biologists have marched among the shock troops against biological and genetic determinism. Their persuasiveness grows not out of rejecting evolution but the opposite: mastering evolutionary theory and evidence. Paul Ehrlich, Stephen Jay Gould, Luca Cavalli-Sforza, and Richard Lewontin have pointed out that humans carry nowhere near enough genes to encode every human trait, that applications of evolutionary biology in the past have been based on bad science, that race is a cultural rather than a biological construct, and that the environment deeply influences the expression of genetic as well as cultural traits. Imagine how much more powerful their arguments might be when joined with those from historians able to speak knowledgeably about the dimensions of human experience in which genes have or have not played important roles.[12]

Similarly, we should not let skepticism necessarily lead to rejection. Scholars in science and technology studies have demonstrated the social dimensions of what had been seen as objective endeavors. The outcome of this process should be to make us skeptical about all the analytical tools we use – whether from humanities, social sciences, or natural sciences – and at the same time welcoming of useful ideas, whatever their source. Finally, we must combat political misuses of any ideas, including those from evolution. My own conviction is that deeper knowledge makes citizens more, rather than less, politically effective.

Historians who have not read much science might be shocked to learn how much evolutionary biologists emphasize the roles of genetic variation, chance, environment, and historical contingency in creating the world we inhabit. In the standard textbook on evolutionary biology, Douglas Futuyma argues, "Thus there is an important element of *historical contingency* in evolution: the condition of a living system, or of its environment, at a certain time may determine which of several paths of change the system will follow. Historical explanation of the properties of living systems is one of the most important contributions of evolutionary science to biology."[13] Contingency, multiple potential paths, the impact of the past on the present – these sound an awful lot like the ideas that appear in history journals as arguments against one sort of determinism or another. Evolutionary biologists see organisms not as entities with fixed traits or destinies, as caricature would have it, but as wondrously varied and changing.

Although various disciplines outside biology have created evolutionary fields, none is identical to evolutionary history. Nearly all the existing fields focus on human evolution, whether genetic or cultural, to the exclusion of nonhuman species. One exception is evolutionary (or Darwinian) medicine. Proponents of evolutionary medicine have argued that most physicians see the human body as a machine designed by a careless engineer. The task of the doctor is to fix broken machinery. Evolutionary physicians, on the other hand, see the body as an organism that has evolved methods to meet challenges. Faced with an infection, ordinary physicians might seek to control fever because it appears to be a problem caused by a pathogen. Evolutionary physicians agree that fever might be a problem caused by a pathogen – but on the other hand, fever might be the body's means of killing off the pathogen by heating it to death. (Evolutionary physicians would keep the idea of coevolution front and center. They expect that humans have evolved defenses against a certain pathogen, and the pathogen may have evolved a way to circumvent the defenses, which might have led to further evolution in humans.) Keeping the fever down, then, might slow recovery. For our purposes, the important point is that human experience, in this case of disease, is the outcome of a long history of reciprocal evolution. The body has evolved defenses, and organisms have evolved ways to circumvent those defenses. (The rapid evolution of the HIV virus is an excellent example.) An ahistorical understanding of the biology of humans and other species leads to misperceptions about causes and effects of ailments, which in turn leads to suboptimal treatments. Effective medicine demands that we understand the history and biology of human beings and the organisms with which they coexist.[14]

There have been efforts across the social sciences to develop evolutionary models of culture, behavior, and institutions. Unlike sociobiology and evolutionary psychology, these efforts do not ground their analyses in genes; rather they treat genetic evolution as the source of useful analogies. Evolutionary economists have studied firms as analogues of organisms, markets as analogues of natural selection, and routines (repeated ways of doing things, e.g., marketing) as analogues of genes. As we saw in Chapter 8, anthropologists (and biologists) have treated genes and culture as parallel and interacting systems of information subject to selection. The two systems resemble each other in being heritable, shaping human behavior, and transmitting information imperfectly. They differ from each other in that genes pass information only from parents to children, whereas culture passes among nonrelatives, skips generations, and enables individuals to inherit acquired characteristics from others.[15]

Although different from each other in several ways, and although evolutionary historians need not adopt their ideas, these fields illustrate the value of defining a research program as a field. Attaching "evolutionary" to the names of disciplines has helped scholars define their approaches, find others with similar interests (including people in other fields), and develop coherent literatures. Several of these fields have grown large enough to merit their own subject headings in the Library of Congress catalog.[16]

Developing evolutionary history as a field of history should bring us similar advantages: self-definition, ideas for research, identification of common ground with other scholars, and development of a coherent literature. Ultimately, the field's value will lie in new or revised interpretations of history and biology. In the concluding chapter, we will take a quick look at ways in which evolutionary history can enhance fields outside technological and environmental history, including those as disparate and perhaps as surprising as the history of politics and the history of art.

12

Conclusion

I hope this book has convinced you of five ideas. First, evolution is ubiquitous. Second, people have shaped evolution of populations of human and non-human species. Third, anthropogenic evolution has shaped human as well as natural history. Fourth, human and non-human populations have coevolved, or repeatedly changed in response to each other. And fifth, uniting the insights of history and biology in evolutionary history enables us to understand the past more fully than either discipline does alone.

I like to think that these ideas can help resolve puzzles that we all encounter in our daily lives. Why do our relatives die of infections despite treatment with antibiotics? Why do we catch so many small fish? Why do mounted heads of game animals killed two hundred years ago sport bigger horns than we see today? Why do some of us have light skin and others dark skin? Why do insects in my garden survive insecticides? Why do adults in some countries avoid drinking milk? Why do I wear cotton clothes? Evolution supplies part of the answer to all these questions, and human history supplies another part. We all live in a world shaped by evolutionary history.

I also hope that these ideas will encourage scholars in a variety of fields to incorporate evolution into their work, and that is the subject on which I wish to focus in this conclusion. We saw in Chapter 9 that evolutionary history offers a dramatic revision of the history of the Industrial Revolution, an episode of interest to almost all fields of history that study the eighteenth through twenty-first centuries. In most accounts, something uniquely English sparked the Industrial Revolution. It might have been inventive brilliance, a preference for practicality over theory, government support for private property, fashion trends, a rising commitment to hard work, enclosures that forced rural laborers off the land, merchant banks, trading firms, or something else the English created. Revisionists have stressed the quantitative impact of colonies and the slave trade on supplies of raw materials, demand for finished goods, and capital. But even the revisionists tend to credit the English with initiating and controlling events.

Chapter 9 upended the received wisdom. It shifted the focus from England to the New World, from Englishmen to Amerindians, from inventors to farmers, from uniformity of cotton species to variation among them, and from English culture that encouraged invention to cotton genomes that encouraged and sustained innovation. English inventors and factory owners *reacted* to an opportunity created by Amerindians and New World cottons. The slave trade played a critical role by linking England with the evolutionary inheritance of the New World. The forces identified by other scholars might have been important and even necessary, but they were not sufficient. Industrialization of the cotton industry depended on long fiber from New World cotton species, and credit for the fiber goes to cotton genomes, Amerindians, and anthropogenic evolution in the New World.

Chapter 10 showed how evolutionary history can widen a field that, at first glance, seemed to have little to do with evolution. Historians of technology have long recognized that organisms are *affected by* technology, but rarely have we thought of organisms *as* technology. This blind spot will surely come as a surprise to historians a hundred years from now. Surrounded by products of genetic engineering, they will take it for granted that some organisms are technologies. Populations of species modified to provide goods and services to people are living technology, or *biotechnology*. Biotechnology did not originate with molecular biology; genetic engineering is but the latest in a long line of methods used to fashion populations of other species into tools put to human use. Historians of technology have developed a powerful tool kit of ideas for understanding the development, use, and impact of machines. A wealth of opportunities awaits historians who apply these ideas to the history of biotechnology.

Chapter 11 explored the intersection of evolutionary history with a field where the overlap is clear: environmental history. The interaction between people and other species has been a central concern of environmental historians, so we might expect members of this field to have made evolution an important part of their work. Yet, with a few exceptions, they have not. Environmental historians have frequently drawn on insights from ecology and public health but rarely on ideas from evolutionary biology. The downside of this pattern is that we know embarrassingly little about the role of evolution in history. The upside is that environmental historians who decide to study evolutionary history will find trees heavy with low-hanging fruit.

Chapters 9–11 discussed only a few fields that overlap with evolutionary history; historians in almost every other field can incorporate evolution into their work, too. One way is by thinking about evolution as one of the downstream consequences of human activity. In Table 12.1, the first column lists forces that historians study, such as politics, economics, art, and science. The second column lists examples from this book in which we saw how each social force has affected the evolution of some population. The rest of the columns identify fields that could use each example to show that the forces they study are important because they affect the evolution of nonhuman species. The spirit of Table 12.1 is that historians can develop a habit of mind in which they look for ways in which social forces have changed the very nature, the DNA, of populations of organisms as well as the aspects of human experience that historians have traditionally emphasized.

Ivory poaching, which appears in the first nine rows of Table 12.1, provides an example of how evolutionary history can help historians see the evolutionary consequences of social forces. State building is one of the central concerns of political historians. Tuskless elephants and shrinking mountain goats illustrate that state strength (or lack of it) affects the evolution of populations of nonhuman species. So when making the case for the significance of state capacity, political historians could highlight its evolutionary impact as well as its social and political importance. Social and art historians have studied the development of artistic taste and the role of art as a status symbol. In uncovering reasons why certain social groups have desired ivory carvings, historians in these fields are also discovering reasons why African elephants have evolved tusklessness. Perhaps we will someday read studies of aesthetics as an evolutionary force. Economic historians have long been concerned with income and trade. Since poverty and trade have encouraged elephant poaching for tusks, economists have been studying forces that have shaped the traits of populations of nonhuman species in Africa. Subsequent rows of Table 12.1 can be read in a similar spirit.

TABLE 12.1. *Social Forces Have Shaped Evolution*[a]

Social Force	Example[b]	Political History	Economic History	Diplomatic History	Social History	History of Technology	History of Science, Medicine	Environmental History	Evolutionary Biology
Weakness of state	Weak state allowed poaching, which led to tuskless elephants (3)	X	X		X			X	X
Strength of state	Strong state enforced game laws, reducing size of bighorn sheep and their horns (3)	X					X	X	X
Art	Demand for ivory for sculpture led to tuskless elephants (3)		X		X	X		X	X
Recreation	Demand for ivory for billiard balls led to tuskless elephants (3)		X		X	X		X	X

Music	Demand for ivory for piano keys led to tuskless elephants (3)		X	X	X	X	X
Fashion	Demand for ivory for cutlery handles led to tuskless elephants (3)		X	X	X	X	X
Poverty	Poverty encouraged poaching of tusked elephants, encouraging tuskless varieties (3)	X	X		X		X
Trade	Demand for ivory led to tuskless elephants (3)		X		X		X

(continued)

TABLE 12.1 (*continued*)

Social Force	Example[b]	Political History	Economic History	Diplomatic History	Social History	History of Technology	History of Science, Medicine	Environmental History	Evolutionary Biology
Scale of trade	Global demand created more poaching than local demand, encouraging tuskless elephants (3)		X	X				X	X
Hunting	Creation of plains bison from giant long-horned bison (3)				X	X		X	X
Fishing	Smaller salmon, salmon that avoid ocean (3)	X	X	X		X	X	X	X
Medicine	Resistance to antibiotics, pesticides (1, 4, 8)		X			X	X	X	X
Agriculture	Resistance to pesticides (1, 4, 8)		X			X	X	X	X

Drug policy	Coca resistance to glyphosate (4)	X		X		X	X
Political insurgency	Rebels grew coca to finance insurgency, which led to glyphosate resistance (4)	X		X		X	X
War	Development of DDT for military led to resistance; war against political insurgents led to coca resistance to glyphosate (4)	X			X	X	X
Profit motive	Sales of antibiotics and pesticides, which led to resistance in target species (4)	X	X		X	X	X

(continued)

Social Force	Example[b]	Political History	Economic History	Diplomatic History	Social History	History of Technology	History of Science, Medicine	Environmental History	Evolutionary Biology
Advertising	Promotion of antibacterial soap probably led to triclosan resistance (5)		X		X	X	X	X	X
Constitutional distribution of power	Two senators per state promoted federal support for corn, which encouraged obesity, which probably led to gut flora evolution (5)	X					X	X	X
Energy type	Coal burning led to darker peppered moths (5)		X			X		X	X
Price advantages	Coal cheaper than other energy sources, leading to dark peppered moths (5)		X			X		X	X

Government regulation	Clean air acts prompted switch from coal to cleaner fuels, and peppered moths became light again (5)	X	X		X	X		X
Transportation	Fossil fuels burned by cars and trucks raised earth's temperature, affecting evolution of mammals, insects, plants (5)	X	X		X	X		X
Garbage disposal	Motive to tolerate wolves around camps may have led to dogs (6)	X	X		X	X		X
Warning of danger	Motive to tolerate wolves around camps may have led to dogs (6)	X	X		X	X		X

(continued)

TABLE 12.1 (continued)

Social Force	Example[b]	Political History	Economic History	Diplomatic History	Social History	History of Technology	History of Science, Medicine	Environmental History	Evolutionary Biology
Convenience	Motive to collect seeds and keep animals most suitable for domestication (6)				X	X	X	X	X
Science	Researchers domesticated foxes (6), plant and animal breeding (7)					X	X	X	X
Genetic engineering	Changed traits of cotton, corn, soy (7)		X			X	X	X	X
Imperialism	Transported cotton to new climates, to which it adapted (7)	X	X	X		X		X	X
Desire for social status	Breeding of purebred cattle, dogs (7)		X		X	X	X	X	X

[a] Most historians do not think of social processes as evolutionary forces, but they are. This table illustrates ways in which historians in a variety of fields could increase the reach and significance of their work by exploring the evolutionary consequences of the topics they study. Political historians, for example, could show that high state capacity (the ability of a government to meet its goals) has shaped the evolution of mountain goats as well as the lives of citizens, and that low state capacity has shaped the evolution of elephants as well as the lives of Africans.

[b] See the chapter numbers in parentheses for examples in this book.

Table 12.2 shifts the focus from evolution as a downstream consequence of human activity to evolution as an upstream force shaping human history. As Jared Diamond showed, almost everything that historians study is a by-product of the anthropogenic evolution of domesticated plants and animals.[1] Here my emphasis is on finer-grained, more recent examples. The first column of Table 12.2 highlights evolutionary processes, and the second column provides examples from the book of that process. The rest of the columns identify fields that are well positioned to bring that evolutionary process into their understanding of forces shaping history. Social and economic historians studying the impact of fishery collapse on a region (such as New England) could add size selection to their list of causes. Fishers undercut their livelihood not just by catching a lot of fish, which reduced the number in the ocean, but also by harvesting the biggest fish, which selected for smaller fish. Historians of technology could study ways in which developing more efficient methods of fishing hastened the evolution of small size. Political historians could look at ways that size selection for small fish exacerbated tensions between the United States and Canada over salmon stocks.

Human beings have always swum in a sea of evolving populations. We tend to think of evolution as a process that happened out there in time and space, far from the human realm, but the opposite is true. Populations of organisms have always evolved, evolve today, and will continue to evolve in the future. Our own populations are no exception. We have shaped the evolution of populations of other species, they have shaped our evolution, and we will evolve together until we disappear from this earth.

In an age of climate change and genetic engineering, we cannot understand evolution without taking human complexity into account. We live in societies that depend on some products of anthropogenic evolution for survival (domestic plants and animals) and are threatened by others (pathogens and pests that resist our poisons, fish that evolve smaller sizes in response to fishing). History helps us understand human complexity, evolutionary biology helps us understand ways that populations coevolve, and the synthesis of history and biology enables us to understand the world around us far better than either field does alone.

TABLE 12.2. *Evolution Has Shaped Human History*[a]

Social Force	Example[b]	Political History	Economic History	Diplomatic History	Social History	History of Technology	History of Science, Medicine	Environmental History	Evolutionary Biology
Adaptation	Resistance to antibiotics led to sickness, death, new antibiotics; resistance to pesticides increased agricultural losses, raised costs (4)		X		X	X	X	X	X
Size selection	Collapse of fisheries, livelihood, and food supply (3)	X	X	X	X	X	X	X	X
Domestication	Made settled societies, hierarchical social structures, writing, European dominance of Americas, etc., possible (6)	X	X	X	X	X	X	X	X

Culling	New cotton varieties survived disease, allowing cotton raising and slavery to continue (7); development of long-fibered cottons in New World underpinned Industrial Revolution (9)	X	X	X	X	X		X	X
Breeding	Plant and animal breeding in agriculture made life possible for about five billion people (7); green revolution part of cold war strategy (10); industrialization of agriculture depended on breeding (7)	X	X	X	X	X		X	X

(continued)

163

TABLE 12.2 (continued)

Social Force	Example[b]	Political History	Economic History	Diplomatic History	Social History	History of Technology	History of Science, Medicine	Environmental History	Evolutionary Biology
Hybridization	Generated new cotton and corn varieties that supported corporations, farmers, agricultural economy (7)		X	X	X	X	X	X	X
Acclimitization	Transporting seeds enabled cotton culture and slavery to spread to new areas (7)	X	X	X	X	X	X	X	X
Mutagenesis	Produced screw worm flies with rate of male sterility, lowering costs of cattle production (7)		X	X		X	X	X	X

Genetic engineering	Moved genes (thus traits) across species and kingdoms, increasing plant yields, food supply, and corporate profits (7)	X			X	X	X	X
Inbreeding	Created purebred lines of plants and animals that increased production, profit (7)	X				X	X	X
Cloning	Created genetically identical individuals (7)	X		X		X	X	X
Extinction	Almost eliminated smallpox as cause of death (7)	X	X	X		X	X	X

---

[a] Historians rarely consider evolution as a historical force, but it is. This table shows examples of ways in which historians in a variety of fields can develop a fuller understanding of historical causation by widening the ambit of their study to include evolution. Chapter 9 provides an in-depth example by arguing that evolution played a central but unappreciated role in the Industrial Revolution.

[b] See the chapter numbers in parentheses for examples in this book.

Note on Sources

Evolutionary history, as described in this book, is an effort to synthesize the insights of history and biology. The spirits of the two disciplines are similar because both disciplines are interested in continuity and change over time. And the practices of the disciplines resemble each other because both disciplines value primary and secondary research. But the paths diverge once research begins. Historians usually burrow into archives and libraries to find data, whereas biologists huddle over lab benches, handle museum specimens, or hike to field sites. Scholars continue on separate paths as they analyze and summarize their findings. Historians like to organize their insights around narratives, whereas biologists prefer to test hypotheses using statistics or other quantitative methods. The paths veer closer to each other when publications from both disciplines find their way into the same libraries, but they do not quite meet. Science journals and books journey to one section of the library and history journals and books to another (or to a separate library altogether). A host of other forces, ranging from departmental reward systems to database design, help keep scholars from the disciplines apart.

This essay is an effort to nudge the two paths a bit closer together. I will not try to describe how to do primary research in either field. Graduate programs in each discipline are the best places to learn such skills. Nor will I tackle the way disciplines and departments reward scholarship, which is beyond my ability to change.

I will focus instead on two more realistic goals. The first and easier one is to help scholars find sources outside their field. The second and more difficult goal of this essay is to suggest ways for historians to learn to read scientific publications. The barriers to understanding are lower for scientists who want to read history, so I will not address that topic. This essay is intended for novices. Those who have been working in one field or the other will find much or all of what I have to say familiar.

The best advice I can give for finding sources outside one's own field is the simplest: talk to colleagues from other departments and to research librarians. Experts know the most important scholars and publications in their field, and librarians know the databases and how to search them.

There is an important cultural difference between history and biology that affects the way one approaches the literatures. Historians usually think of their research as multiyear book projects. They may publish articles along the way, but information in articles usually appears in books as well. And rather than revealing their best ideas too soon, historians often save their biggest and most important arguments for project-culminating books. Databases typically do not index sources cited in books, so citation searches are less useful than in the sciences (see later) for tracing ideas as they travel among scholars. Someone entering the historical literature for the first time would be well advised to ask colleagues for the titles of the most important books and begin research there.

Biologists, in contrast, are article oriented. A leading biologist may never publish a book. Rather than saving up their best ideas, biologists try to publish them quickly in journals. The review and publication process typically happens faster at a scientific journal than at a history journal. When biologists want to summarize findings from multiple articles (beyond the brief literature review that appears in most articles), they will usually publish a review article rather than a book.

Someone entering the biology literature for the first time would be well advised to ask a colleague for the names of the most important scholars and articles related to your topic. With these in hand, you can ask a research librarian for help running three types of searches. The first is an author search to find everything a key author has published. There is a good chance the author has not tried to summarize all her work in one place, so you will want to see all her publications on a given topic. The second is a forward citation search to see who has cited an article. This will bring you up to date on more recent work on a topic. The third is a backward citation search: databases will show you the articles and books cited in a given article, often along with their abstracts. With a series of clicks, you can quickly navigate your way from one relevant article to the next.

Now we turn to the second goal of this essay: helping historians read science. Many historians find science daunting. I understand that feeling, for I felt the same way. I graduated from college with a degree in English and the minimum number of science courses required for graduation (three). I am embarrassed to admit it, but science courses scared me. Later, I realized that I had cheated myself. The cure was drastic – I went back to school to get a PhD in biology.

Few historians will want to earn degrees in science, so let me recommend some other strategies. The first is to try reading scientific publications. It can take years of study before one understands everything in some scientific articles, but other articles are accessible to someone with no specialized training at all. And some scientists, including leading evolutionary biologists, have written books intended for wide audiences.

The second strategy is to learn enough science to understand the main arguments of scientific publications even if you cannot follow all the details. One year of college-level biology will equip you with the most important concepts and terms. Adding an introductory course in applied statistics will work wonders. Many fields of science, including ecology and evolutionary biology, rely heavily on statistics. Statistical conventions appear indecipherable to the uninitiated, but a single statistics course is all you need to understand the statistics in most scientific publications. Community colleges offer science and statistics courses at bargain prices and convenient hours.[1]

If these recommendations ring a bell, they should. They are almost identical in spirit to the foreign language requirements of PhD programs. Language requirements almost never demand fluency. They require students to master enough of a language to understand the main arguments of a professional publication. I am suggesting the same level mastery of the language of science, and for the same purpose: to open up important literatures that otherwise would remain mysterious. Ideally, graduate students should know both a world language and some science. If there is room for only one in a PhD program, a strong argument can be made that learning the language of science would be most useful for an evolutionary or environmental historian.

Glossary

Acclimatizing is the process of encouraging members of a species to grow in a new location and climate. The process may include genetic adaptations.

Adaptation is the evolutionary process in which traits of a population change over time to suit its environment.

Anthropogenic means "human caused" or "human shaped." The word appears in this book most often as an adjective modifying *evolution*. Anthropogenic evolution may work by itself or in concert with other processes (such as natural selection), may involve large or small changes in populations, and may be intentional or accidental.

Artificial selection is a process in which human actions increase or decrease the survival or reproduction of individuals because of their traits. For reasons explained in the text, I avoid *artificial selection* in favor of *anthropogenic evolution* and other terms.

Biological refers in this book to physical, physiological, or genetic traits of organisms. Its counterpart in the realm of ideas is *culture*.

Biology refers to the scientific discipline that studies living organisms and to the ways that organisms live and function.

Biotechnology is a noun that refers to organisms modified to supply goods or services to human beings. Biotechnologies may be produced by traditional techniques (such as methodical selection) or new techniques (such as genetic engineering).

Breed as a noun usually refers to a variety of animal, especially one developed through methodical selection.

Breeding is a form of selection in which human beings intentionally shape the traits of future generations by mating specific males with specific females. Breeders often use culling in addition to selective mating.

Chance is a critical element in evolution of all types and especially in sampling effects.

Change in inherited traits of a population over generations is the definition of evolution.

Cloning is the process of creating offspring that are genetically identical to their parents, typically bypassing sexual reproduction. Cloning techniques include those with a long history (such as grafting) as well as others that have arisen recently (such as those that rely on techniques from molecular biology).

Coevolution is the process in which traits of populations of different species repeatedly change in response to each other. The idea originated in the study of plants and their pollinators and focused on physical traits, but the meaning has expanded to include cultural as well as biological traits.

Culling is the process of keeping some individuals of a population because they perform well and weeding out those that do not. Darwin called this process *unconscious selection* and noted its similarity to *natural selection*. Both processes led the traits of populations to change over generations, even though the actors (human beings and what Darwin called Nature) had no conscious intent to do so.

Cultivar is a noun that usually refers to a variety of plant developed under partial or full domestication.

Cultural evolution refers to changes in the frequency of ideas in a population.

Cultural traits are traits (usually behaviors) grounded in culture rather than biology.

Culture refers in this book to ideas about how to do things. In other contexts, the word has other meanings.

Darwin, Charles, was a nineteenth-century English naturalist who developed the idea that species (and populations of species) evolved as a result of natural, sexual, methodical, and unconscious selection.

Darwinian evolution is a term used in various ways but most often today refers to evolution by natural selection and to rejection of the idea that organisms can inherit acquired traits. Both these ideas revise Darwin's thinking because he attributed evolution to four types of selection (natural, sexual, methodical, and unconscious) and believed in the inheritance of acquired traits.

Domestication refers to the process through which human beings altered the traits of populations of other species to supply people with goods and services. Domesticated animals usually live in captivity, and people often control the planting of domesticated plants.

Environment refers to the surroundings of any species, human or otherwise. Environments play a critical role in evolution because they select for and against traits.

Epigenetic refers to heritable changes in gene expression that do not affect the sequence of nucleotides (DNA) in a gene.

Evolution refers to changes in inherited traits of populations of organisms over generations.

Evolutionary history refers in this book to the field (or research program) that studies the way populations of people and other species have shaped each other's traits over time and the significance of those changes for people and other species.

Extinction is the disappearance of all members of a population, variety, species, genus, or other taxonomic group.

Founder effect is an evolutionary mechanism in which an unrepresentative subset of individuals of one population produces a new population, usually in a different place. The new population's traits differ from those of the ancestral population because it inherits only the genes its parents carry rather than the full range of genes in the ancestral population.

Genes are units of biological inheritance made up of stretches of DNA (deoxyribonucleic acids) that encode instructions for cellular functioning.

Genetic determinism refers to a belief that genes control all traits of organisms, especially human beings. Based on a poor understanding of genetics and evolution, this idea has underpinned malign social policies directed at less powerful human groups.

Genetic drift is an evolutionary mechanism in which the frequency of genes in a population fluctuates over generations as a result of chance rather than selection.

Genetic engineering is the use of molecular biology techniques to transfer genes from one individual to another (often across divergent taxonomic groups).

Genetic traits are those shaped by genes (in contrast to cultural traits).

Heritable is an adjective meaning that something can be passed from parents to offspring. Heritability of traits is essential for evolution.

Hybridizing refers to the mating of individuals belonging to different taxonomic groups such as varieties or species.

Inbreeding is the mating of closely related individuals (such as siblings). Breeders have used this technique, which reduces genetic variation, to increase their ability to produce individuals with desirable traits.

Inheritance refers to the passing of traits from some individuals to others (usually parents to offspring) and is essential for evolution.

Lamarckian evolution refers to evolution via inheritance of acquired traits (named for Jean Baptiste Lamarck, the French evolutionary biologist).

Line as a noun may refer to a variety of plant or animal developed through methodical selection and often inbreeding.

Master breeder narrative (or hypothesis) refers to the belief that people domesticated other species by imagining traits they wanted to develop in wild species of plants and animals and controlling the mating of plants and animals to reach their goal.

Meme is a term coined by Richard Dawkins to refer to a unit of cultural inheritance. He meant it as the cultural analogue of *gene*.

Methodical selection is Darwin's term for *breeding*.

Mutation refers to a change in the sequence of nucleotides that make up an individual's DNA. Mutations may be beneficial, harmful, or neutral in their effect. Mutation is the raw material for evolution because it generates new traits.

Natural selection is the evolutionary process in which variation in traits leads some individuals to survive and reproduce more than others. Darwin believed natural selection was the primary driver of speciation.

Population refers to an interbreeding group of individuals, usually living near each other. Evolution is a characteristic of populations, not individuals.

Recombination refers (roughly) to the process through which chromosomes swap genes during cell division, creating gene combinations and traits in offspring that did not exist in their parents.

Reproduction is the process through which organisms produce offspring. Biological evolution involves changes in traits of populations from one generation to the next (rather than within one generation), so reproduction is essential for evolution.

Resistance refers to the capacity of populations to survive poisons (such as antibiotics or pesticides) that killed earlier generations of their population. Resistance evolves by selection.

Sampling effects are processes that affect the evolution of populations by chance. Examples include genetic drift (random fluctuation in gene frequency) and the founder effect (in which an unrepresentative subset of individuals creates the next generation).

Selecting refers in general to the process of selection. When used by breeders, the term may refer to culling or to selective mating.

Selection is the differential survival and reproduction of individuals in a population resulting from differences in traits. Darwin identified four types of selection: natural, sexual, methodical, and unconscious.

Selective mating means breeding.

Sexual selection refers to differences in reproduction by individuals because their traits increase or decrease their ability to mate.

Speciation is the process of creating new species from old species.

Species is a group of similar organisms that can interbreed.

Sterilizing means eliminating an individual's ability to reproduce without killing it, usually by removing or altering reproductive organs.

Strain as a noun often refers to a variety of microorganism.

Susceptible is an adjective that refers to organisms capable of being killed by a poison (such as insecticides, pesticides, and antibiotics). *Susceptible* is the opposite of *resistant*.

Traits are characteristics of organisms. They might be physical, behavioral, or chemical.

Unconscious selection is Darwin's term for the process through which human beings affect the evolution of populations without intending to do so.

Variation refers to differences in traits among individuals in a population.

Varieties are populations of organisms believed to be different enough to merit separate names but similar enough that they belong to the same species. Synonyms include *strains*, *races*, *cultivars*, *lines*, and *breeds*. Varieties may be domesticated or wild.

Notes

Preface

1. Words in bold are defined in the glossary.
2. Charles Darwin, *On the Origin of Species by Means of Natural Selection; or The Preservation of Favoured Races in the Struggle for Life* (London: Odhams Press, [1859] 1872), 140.
3. Leigh van Valen, "A New Evolutionary Law," *Evolutionary Theory* 1 (1973): 1–30.

1. Matters of Life and Death

1. I am indebted to Tom Finger for capturing the common view of evolution in this phrase.

2. Evolution's Visible Hands

1. Jonathan Weiner, *The Beak of the Finch: A Story of Evolution in Our Time* (New York: Knopf, 1994), 70–82; Peter R. Grant, *Ecology and Evolution of Darwin's Finches* (Princeton, NJ: Princeton University Press, 1999).
2. Brian and Deborah Charlesworth define evolution as "changes over time in the characteristics of populations of living organisms." Brian Charlesworth and Deborah Charlesworth, *Evolution: A Very Short Introduction* (Oxford: Oxford University Press, 2003), 5.
3. Charles Darwin, *On the Origin of Species by Means of Natural Selection; or The Preservation of Favoured Races in the Struggle for Life* (London: Odhams Press, [1859] 1872), 96.
4. Ibid., 102.
5. Ibid., 52.
6. Ibid., 55.
7. Charles Darwin, *Variation of Animals and Plants under Domestication*, 2 vols. (Baltimore: Johns Hopkins University Press, [1868] 1998), 369–399.

8. Theodosius Dobzhansky, *Genetics and the Origin of Species* (New York: Columbia University Press, 1937); Ernst Mayr and William B. Provine, eds., *The Evolutionary Synthesis: Perspectives on the Unification of Biology* (Cambridge, MA: Harvard University Press, 1980), 487.

9. I thank Michael Grant for this definition. Douglas Futuyma's textbook offers a similar definition: "a change over time of the proportions of individual organisms differing genetically in one or more traits." Douglas J. Futuyma, *Evolutionary Biology*, 3rd ed. (Sunderland, MA: Sinauer Associates, 1998), glossary.

10. Alexander O. Vargas, "Did Paul Kammerer Discover Epigenetic Inheritance? A Modern Look at the Controversial Midwife Toad Experiments," *Journal of Experimental Zoology Part B: Molecular and Developmental Evolution* 312 (2009): 667–678; Eric J. Richards, "Inherited Epigenetic Variation – Revisiting Soft Inheritance," *Nature Reviews Genetics* 7 (2006): 395–401.

11. Futuyma, *Evolutionary Biology*, 765.

12. Helena Curtis, *Biology* (New York: Worth, 1983), 1088.

13. Stephanie M. Carlson, Eric Edeline, L. Asbjorn Vollestad, Thrond O. Haugen, Ian J. Winfield, Janice M. Fletcher, J. Ben James, and Nils C. Stenseth, "Four Decades of Opposing Natural and Human-Induced Artificial Selection Acting on Windermere Pike (*Esox Lucius*)," *Ecology Letters* 10 (2007): 512–521.

14. Jean-Marc Rolain, Patrice François, David Hernandez, Fadi Bittar, Hervé Richet, Ghislain Fournous, Yves Mattenberger, et al., "Genomic Analysis of an Emerging Multiresistant *Staphylococcus aureus* Strain Rapidly Spreading in Cystic Fibrosis Patients Revealed the Presence of an Antibiotic Inducible Bacteriophage," *Biology Direct* 4, no. 1 (2009), doi:10.1186/1745-6150-4-1, http://www.biology-direct.com/content/4/1/1.

15. Number of mentions based on a search of the first editions of these books at the Complete Work of Charles Darwin Online, http://darwin-online.org.uk/.

16. Darwin, *Variation of Animals and Plants*, 2: 176–236.

17. Ibid., 2: 408–409.

18. Ibid., 1: 6.

19. Ibid., 1: 6.

20. Darwin, *On the Origin of Species*, 74.

21. Ibid., 73.

22. Ibid., 31.

3. Hunting and Fishing

1. H. Jachmann, P. S. M. Berry, and H. Imae, "Tusklessness in African Elephants: A Future Trend," *African Journal of Ecology* 33 (1995): 230–235.

2. Eve Abe, "Tusklessness amongst the Queen Elizabeth National Park Elephants, Uganda," *Pachyderm* 22 (1996): 46–47.

3. Though the authors of the study cited here concluded that selective hunting was the most likely explanation, it is also possible that genetic drift played a role. We will examine this process with another elephant population later in the chapter.

4. Size also correlated with age, so seeing the average size of individuals in a population decline over time did not prove an evolutionary effect. But researchers controlled for this variable by comparing the weights of four-year-old rams across the period of their study. David W. Coltman, Paul O'Donoghue, Jon T. Jorgenson, John T. Hogg, Curtis Strobeck, and Marco Festa-Blanchet, "Undesirable Evolutionary Consequences of Trophy Hunting," *Nature* 426 (2003): 283–292.

5. Tim Flannery, *The Eternal Frontier: An Ecological History of North America and Its Peoples* (New York: Atlantic Monthly Press, 2001), 220–222.

6. But wait, you might say, what about longhorn cattle, the mascots of the University of Texas athletic teams? They, in fact, illustrate our point. Longhorns thrived in the nineteenth century, when ranchers let their cattle run free on the open range. Shorthorns replaced longhorns when ranchers forced cattle to spend more time in close quarters by erecting fences.

7. Flannery, *Eternal Frontier*, 224–225.

8. Ibid., 204, 222–223.

9. Ibid., 225–226. It is possible for other resources besides food to limit the size of populations, too, though in this case, food seems to be probable.

10. Ibid., 224–226; Douglas J. Futuyma, *Evolutionary Biology*, 3rd ed. (Sunderland, MA: Sinauer Associates, 1998), glossary.

11. Jared M. Diamond, *Guns, Germs, and Steel: The Fates of Human Societies* (New York: W. W. Norton, 1999), 42–47; Flannery, *Eternal Frontier*, 204; John Alroy, "A Multispecies Overkill Simulation of the End-Pleistocene Megafaunal Mass Extinction," *Science* 292 (2001): 1893–1896.

12. Diamond, *Guns, Germs, and Steel*, 42–47.

13. Dean Lueck, "The Extinction and Conservation of the American Bison," *Journal of Legal Studies* 31 (2002): S609–S652; Andrew C. Isenberg, *The Destruction of the Bison: An Environmental History, 1740–1920* (Cambridge: Cambridge University Press, 2000), 25–26; Dan Flores, "Bison Ecology and Bison Diplomacy: The Southern Plains from 1800 to 1850," *Journal of American History* 78, no. 2 (1991): 465–485.

14. Isenberg, *Destruction of the Bison*.

15. Anna M. Whitehouse, "Tusklessness in Elephant Population of the Addo Elephant National Park, South Africa," *Journal of the Zoological Society of London* 257 (2002): 249–254.

16. Ibid. Selection can affect populations at the same time as drift, though here the absence of hunting probably left drift as the more powerful process.

17. United Nations Food and Agriculture Organization, "The State of the World's Fisheries and Aquaculture – 1996," http://www.fao.org/docrep/003/w3265e/w3265e00.htm#Contents.

18. Joseph E. Taylor III, *Making Salmon: An Environmental History of the Northwest Fisheries Crisis* (Seattle: University of Washington Press, 1999), 203–206.

19. W. E. Ricker, "Changes in the Average Size and Average Age of Pacific Salmon," *Canadian Journal of Fisheries and Aquatic Sciences* 38 (1981): 1636–1656.

20. Mart R. Gross, "Salmon Breeding Behavior and Life History Evolution in Changing Environments," *Ecology* 72 (1991): 1180–1186.

21. P. Handford, G. Bell, and T. Reimchen, "A Gillnet Fishery Considered as an Experiment in Artificial Selection," *Journal of Fisheries Research Board of Canada* 34 (1977): 954–961, cited in Stephen R. Palumbi, *Evolution Explosion: How Humans Cause Rapid Evolutionary Change* (New York: W. W. Norton, 2001); Douglas P. Swain, Alan F. Sinclair, and J. Mark Hanson, "Evolutionary Response to Size-Selective Mortality in an Exploited Fish Population," *Proceedings of the Royal Society, Series B* 274 (2007): 1015–1022; Esben M. Olsen, Mikko Heino, George R. Lilly, Joanne Morgan, John Brattey, Bruno Ernande, and Ulf Dieckmann, "Maturation Trends Indicative of Rapid Evolution Preceded the Collapse of Northern Cod," *Nature* 428 (2004): 932–935.

22. Christian Jorgensen, Katja Enberg, Erin S. Dunlop, Robert Arlinghaus, David S. Boukal, Keith Brander, Bruno Ernande, et al., "Managing Evolving Fish Stocks," *Science* 318, no. 5854 (2007): 1247–1248; Olsen et al., "Maturation Trends," 932–935; Swain et al., "Evolutionary Response to Size-Selective Mortality," 1015–1022.

23. Matthew R. Walsh, Stephan B. Munch, Susumu Chiba, and David O. Conover, "Maladaptive Changes in Multiple Traits Caused by Fishing: Impediments to Population Recovery," *Ecology Letters* 9 (2006): 142–148.

24. Lawrence C. Hamilton, Richard L. Haedrich, and Cynthia M. Duncan, "Above and Below the Water: Social/Ecological Transformation in Northwest Newfoundland," *Population and Environment* 25, no. 3 (2004): 195–215.

25. Ibid.; Lan T. Gien, "Land and Sea Connection: The East Coast Fishery Closure, Unemployment, and Health," *Canadian Journal of Public Health* 91, no. 2 (2000): 121–124; Lawrence C. Hamilton and Melissa J. Butler, "Outport Adaptations: Social Indicators through Newfoundland's Cod Crisis," *Human Ecology Review* 8, no. 2 (2001): 1–11.

26. David O. Conover and Stephan B. Munch, "Sustaining Fisheries Yields over Evolutionary Time Scales," *Science* 297 (2002): 94–96; Richard Law, "Fishing, Selection, and Phenotypic Evolution," *ICES Journal of Marine Scientists* 57 (2000): 659–668; Jorgensen et al., "Managing Evolving Fish Stocks," 1247–1248; Stephanie M. Carlson, Eric Edeline, L. Asbjorn Vollestad, Thrond O. Haugen, Ian J. Winfield, Janice M. Fletcher, J. Ben James, and Nils Chr. Stenseth, "Four Decades of Opposing Natural and Human-Induced Artificial Selection Acting on Windermere Pike (*Esox lucius*)," *Ecology Letters* 10 (2007): 512–521.

27. Conover and Munch, "Sustaining Fisheries Yields," 94–96.

28. Phillip B. Fenberg and Kaustuv Roy, "Ecological and Evolutionary Consequences of Size-Selective Harvesting: How Much Do We Know?" *Molecular Ecology* 17 (2008): 209–220.

4. Eradication

1. Yoshihiko Sato, Tetsuo Mori, Toshie Koyama, and Hiroshi Nagase, "*Salmonella* Virchow Infection in an Infant Transmitted by Household

Dogs," *Journal of Veterinary Medical Science* 62, no. 7 (2007): 767–769; Erskine V. Morse, Margo A. Duncan, David A. Estep, Wendell A. Riggs, and Billie O. Blackburn, "Canine Salmonellosis: A Review and Report of Dog to Child Transmission of *Salmonella enteritidis*," *American Journal of Public Health* 66, no. 1 (1976): 82–84.

2. Colgate-Palmolive Company, "Healthy Handwashing with a Wide Variety of Hand Soaps," http://www.colgate.com/app/Softsoap/US/EN/Liquid HandSoap/Antibacterial.cvsp.

3. Allison E. Aiello, Elaine L. Larson, and Stuart B. Levy, "Consumer Antibacterial Soaps: Effective or Just Risky?" *Clinical Infectious Diseases* 45 (2007): 137–147.

4. Ibid.

5. A. M. Calafat, X. Ye, L. Y. Wong, J. A. Reidy, and L. L. Needham, "Urinary Concentrations of Triclosan in the U.S. Population: 2003–2004," *Environmental Health Perspectives* 116, no. 3 (2008): 303–307.

6. Aiello et al., "Consumer Antibacterial Soaps."

7. Maria Schriver to Edmund Russell, June 12, 2008.

8. Randolph E. Schmid, "Study: Women Lead Men in Bacteria, Hands Down," *Washington Post*, November 3, 2008.

9. Ibid.

10. R. Zhang, K. Eggleston, V. Rotimi, and R. J. Zeckhauser, "Antibiotic Resistance as a Global Threat: Evidence from China, Kuwait and the United States," *Globalization and Health* 2 (2006): 6.

11. M. Larsson, G. Kronvall, N. T. Chuc, I. Karlsson, F. Lager, H. D. Hanh, G. Tomson, and T. Falkenberg, "Antibiotic Medication and Bacterial Resistance to Antibiotics: A Survey of Children in a Vietnamese Community," *Tropical Medicine and International Health* 5, no. 10 (2000): 711–721.

12. R. Monina Klevens, Jonathan R. Edwards, Chesley L. Richards Jr., Teresa C. Horan, Robert P. Gaynes, Daniel A. Pollock, and Denise M. Cardo, "Estimating Health Care-Associated Infections and Deaths in U.S. Hospitals, 2002," *Public Health Reports* 122 (March–April 2007): 160–166.

13. David Brown, "'Wonder Drugs' Losing Healing Aura," *Washington Post*, June 26, 1995, A1. As the century closed, the World Health Organization launched a new effort called Roll Back Malaria, whose title suggested the more modest goals that seemed realistic in light of previous disappointments. R. S. Phillips, "Current Status of Malaria and Potential for Control," *Clinical Microbiology Reviews* 14, no. 1 (2001): 208–226; J. F. Trape, "The Public Health Impact of Chloroquine Resistance in Africa," *American Journal of Tropical Medicine and Hygiene* 64, no. 1–2 (2001): 12–17; J. A. Najera, "Malaria Control: Achievements, Problems, and Strategies," *Parassitologia* 43, no. 1–2 (2001): 1–89; Stephen R. Palumbi, *Evolution Explosion: How Humans Cause Rapid Evolutionary Change* (New York: W. W. Norton, 2001), 137–138.

14. David Brown, "TB Resistance Stands at 11% of Cases," *Washington Post*, March 24, 2000, A14; Stuart B. Levy, *The Antibiotic Paradox: How Miracle Drugs Are Destroying the Miracle* (New York: Plenum Press, 1992), 279; Palumbi, *Evolution Explosion*, 85.

15. "Columbia – Insurgency," http://www.globalsecurity.org/military/world/war/colombia.htm.

16. "U.N. Reports 27% Rise in Coca Cultivation in Columbia," *USA Today*, http://www.usatoday.com/news/world/2008-06-18-cocacolombia_N.htm.

17. Joshua Davis, "The Mystery of the Coca Plant That Wouldn't Die," *Wired* 12, no. 11 (2004), http://www.wired.com/wired/archive/12.11/columbia.html.

18. Ibid.

19. Emanuel L. Johnson, Dapeng Zhang, and Stephen D. Emche, "Inter- and Intra-specific Variation among Five *Erythroxylum* Taxa Assessed by AFLP," *Annals of Botany* 95 (2005): 601–608; Jorge F. S. Ferreira and Krishna N. Reddy, "Absorption and Translocation of Glyphosate in *Erythroxylum coca* and *E. novogranatense,*" *Weed Science* 48 (2000): 193–199.

20. Davis, "Mystery of the Coca Plant."

21. National Research Council, *Pesticide Resistance: Strategies and Tactics for Management* (Washington, DC: National Academy Press, 1986), 16–17. See also J. Mallet, "The Evolution of Insecticide Resistance: Have the Insects Won?" *Trends in Ecology and Evolution* 4, no. 11 (1989): 336–340.

22. Palumbi, *Evolution Explosion*; National Research Council, *Pesticide Resistance*, 16–17; David Pimentel, H. Acquay, M. Biltonen, P. Rice, M. Silva, J. Nelson, V. Lipner, S. Giordano, A. Horowitz, and M. D'Amore, "Environmental and Economic Costs of Pesticide Use," *BioScience* 42, no. 10 (1992): 750–760. See also Mallet, "Evolution of Insecticide Resistance."

23. Paul Colinvaux, *Why Big Fierce Animals Are Rare: An Ecologist's Perspective* (Princeton, NJ: Princeton University Press, 1978), 25–31.

24. Ecologists refer to these as *k* and *r* strategies. The letters refer to variables in a population growth model in which *k* stands for the carrying capacity of a place and *r* for the reproductive rate.

5. Altering Environments

1. Michael Shrubb, *Birds, Scythes, and Combines: A History of Birds and Agricultural Change* (New York: Cambridge University Press, 2003).

2. V. E. Heywood and R. T. Watson, eds., *Global Biodiversity Assessment* (Cambridge: Cambridge University Press, 1995); Edward O. Wilson, "The Encyclopedia of Life," *Trends in Ecology and Evolution* 18, no. 2 (2003): 77–80; R. Youatt, "Counting Species: Biopower and the Global Biodiversity Census," *Environmental Values* 17 (2008): 393–417.

3. William E. Bradshaw and Christina M. Holzapfel, "Genetic Shift in Photoperiodic Response Correlated with Global Warming," *Proceedings of the National Academy of Sciences of the United States of America* 98 (2001): 14,509–14,511; Sean C. Thomas and Joel G. Kingsolver, "Natural Selection: Responses to Current (Anthropogenic) Environmental Changes," in *Encyclopedia of Life Sciences* (London: Macmillan, 2002), 659–664.

4. Fredrik Backhed, Ruth E. Ley, Justin L. Sonnenburg, Daniel A. Peterson, and Jeffrey I. Gordon, "Host-Bacterial Mutualism in the Human Intestine," *Science* 307 (2005): 1915–1920.

5. Ruth E. Ley, Peter J. Turnbaugh, Samuel Klein, and Jeffery I. Gordon, "Human Gut Microbes Associated with Obesity," *Nature* 444 (2006): 1022–1023.

6. Peter J. Turnbaugh, Ruth E. Ley, Micah Hamady, Claire M. Fraser-Liggett, Rob Knight, and Jeffrey I. Gordon, "The Human Microbiome Project," *Nature* 449 (2007): 804–810; Jian Xu, Michael A. Mahowald, Ruth E. Ley, Catherine A. Lozupone, Micah Hamady, Eric C. Martens, Bernard Henrissat, et al., "Evolution of Symbiotic Bacteria in the Distal Human Intestine," *PloS Biology* 5, no. 7 (2007): 1574–1586.

7. Michael Pollan, *The Omnivore's Dilemma: A Natural History of Four Meals* (New York: Penguin, 2006).

8. Adam Rome, *The Bulldozer in the Countryside: Suburban Sprawl and the Rise of American Environmentalism* (New York: Cambridge University Press, 2001).

9. Russ Lopez, "Urban Sprawl and Risk for Being Overweight or Obese," *American Journal of Public Health* 94, no. 9 (2004): 1574–1579.

10. H. B. D. Kettlewell, "Selection Experiments on Industrial Melanism in the *Lepidoptera*," *Heredity* 9 (1955): 323; H. B. D. Kettlewell, "Further Selection Experiments on Industrial Melanism in the *Lepidoptera*," *Heredity* 10 (1956): 287–300; R. R. Askew, L. M. Cook, and J. A. Bishop, "Atmospheric Pollution and Melanic Moths in Manchester and Its Environs," *Journal of Applied Ecology* 8 (1971): 247–256. Recently, Kettlewell's methods have come in for criticism. See Judith Hooper, *Of Moths and Men: An Evolutionary Tale* (New York: W. W. Norton, 2002), 377.

11. Laurence M. Cook, "The Rise and Fall of the *Carbonaria* Form of the Peppered Moth," *Quarterly Review of Biology* 78, no. 4 (2003): 399–417.

12. Ibid.

13. Ibid.

14. Ibid.

15. Gregory Clark and David Jacks, "Coal and the Industrial Revolution, 1700–1869," *European Review of Economic History* 11 (2007): 39–72.

16. Cook, "Rise and Fall"; B. S. Grant and L. L. Wiseman, "Recent History of Melanism in American Peppered Moths," *Journal of Heredity* 93, no. 2 (2002): 86–90; Askew et al., "Atmospheric Pollution and Melanic Moths"; Congressional Budget Office, *The Clean Air Act, the Electric Utilities, and the Coal Market* (Washington, DC: U.S. Government Printing Office, 1982).

17. Scholars have come up with varying estimates of the degree to which people have altered the earth's ecosystems, so this note cites the sources of the numbers used in the text as well as studies with somewhat different estimates. The key point is not that the estimates vary but that all the studies conclude that the human impact is significant. Fridolin Krausmann, Karl-Heinz Erb, Simone Gingrich, Christian Lauk, and Helmut Haberl, "Global Patterns of Socioeconomic Biomass Flows in the Year 2000: A Comprehensive Assessment of Supply, Consumption, and Constraints," *Ecological Economics* 65 (2008): 471–487; Helmut Haberl, K. Heinz Erb, Fridolin Krausmann, Veronika Gaube, Alberte Bondeau, Christoph Plutzar, Simone

Gingrich, Wolfgang Lucht, and Marina Fischer-Kowalski, "Quantifying and Mapping the Human Appropriation of Net Primary Production in Earth's Terrestrial Ecosystems," *Proceedings of the National Academy of Sciences of the United States of America* 104, no. 31 (2007): 12,942–12,947; Stuart Rojstaczer, Shannon M. Sterling, and Nathan J. Moore, "Human Appropriation of Photosynthesis Products," *Science* 294 (2001): 2549–2552; Eric W. Sanderson, Malanding Jaiteh, Marc A. Levy, Kent H. Redford, Antoinette V. Wannebo, and Gillian Woolmer, "The Human Footprint and the Last of the Wild," *BioScience* 52, no. 10 (2002): 891–904; Benjamin S. Halpern, Shaun Walbridge, Kimberly A. Selkoe, Carrie V. Kappel, Fiorenza Micheli, Caterina D'Agrosa, John F. Bruno, et al., "A Global Map of Human Impact on Marine Ecosystems," *Science* 319 (2008): 948–952; Peter M. Vitousek, Paul R. Ehrlich, Anne H. Ehrlich, and Pamela A. Matson, "Human Appropriation of the Products of Photosynthesis," *BioScience* 36 (1986): 368–373; Peter M. Vitousek, Harold A. Mooney, Jane Lubchenco, and Jerry M. Melillo, "Human Domination of the Earth's Ecosystems," *Science* 277 (1997): 494–499; Will Steffen, Paul J. Crutzen, and John R. McNeill, "The Anthropocene: Are Humans Now Overwhelming the Great Forces of Nature?" *Ambio* 36, no. 8 (2007): 614–621; Core Writing Team, R. K. Pachauri and A. Reisinger, eds., *Climate Change 2007: Synthesis Report. Contribution of Working Groups I, II, and III to the Fourth Assessment Report of the Intergovernmental Panel on Climate Change* (Geneva, Switzerland: Intergovernmental Panel on Climate Change, 2007); Chris T. Darimont, Stephanie M. Carlson, Michael T. Kinnison, Paul C. Paquet, Thomas E. Reimchen, and Christopher C. Wilmers, "Human Predators Outpace Other Agents of Trait Change in the Wild," *Proceedings of the National Academy of Sciences of the United States of America* 106, no. 3 (2009): 952–954.

18. Steffen et al., "The Anthropocene."

19. Vitousek, "Human Appropriation of the Products of Photosynthesis"; Vitousek, "Human Domination of the Earth's Ecosystems."

20. William J. Ripple and Robert L. Beschta, "Wolf Reintroduction, Predation Risk, and Cottonwood Recovery in Yellowstone National Park," *Forest Ecology and Management* 184 (2003): 299–313; Robert L. Beschta, "Cottonwoods, Elk, and Wolves in the Lamar Valley of Yellowstone National Park," *Ecological Applications* 13, no. 5 (2003): 1295–1309.

21. Steven J. Franks, Sheina Sim, and Arthur E. Weis, "Rapid Evolution of Flowering Time by an Annual Plant in Response to a Climate Fluctuation," *Proceedings of the National Academy of Sciences of the United States of America* 104, no. 4 (2007): 1278–1282.

22. Francisco Rodriguez-Trelles and Miguel A. Rodriguez, "Rapid Microevolution and Loss of Chromosomal Diversity in *Drosophila* in Response to Climate Warming," *Evolutionary Ecology* 12 (1998): 829–838.

23. Bradshaw and Holzapfel, "Genetic Shift in Photoperiodic Response"; Thomas and Kingsolver, "Natural Selection."

24. Dominique Berteaux, Denis Reale, Andrew G. McAdam, and Stan Boutin, "Keeping Pace with Fast Climate Change: Can Arctic Life Count on Evolution?" *Integrative and Comparative Biology* 44, no. 2 (2004): 140–151.

25. Chris D. Thomas, Alison Cameron, Rhys E. Green, Michel Bakkenes, Linda J. Beaumont, Yvonne C. Collingham, Barend F. N. Erasmus, et al., "Extinction Risk from Climate Change," *Nature* 427 (2004): 145–148.

26. I am indebted to Tom Smith for this insight.

27. Everyone attributes extinction to human beings, but authors disagree about the proximate cause. The lack of scientific studies of the passenger pigeon in the wild makes it impossible to settle the debates with field studies. In addition to habitat destruction, hypothesized reasons include exotic diseases, inbreeding, and disruption of breeding by people. Schorger favors the last of these, but habitat destruction seems more likely because it is unlikely people could have disrupted breeding over the species' entire range. Disruption of breeding might have been the last straw, but only after cutting trees over large areas concentrated the remaining breeding pairs in small enough areas to enable human beings to disrupt all breeding sites. A. W. Schorger, *The Passenger Pigeon: Its Natural History and Extinction* (Norman: University of Oklahoma Press, 1973).

28. A. P. Dobson, J. P. Rodriguez, W. M. Roberts, and D. S. Wilcove, "Geographic Distribution of Endangered Species in the United States," *Science* 275, no. 5299 (1997): 550–553.

29. Stuart L. Pimm, Márcio Ayres, Andrew Balmford, George Branch, Katrina Brandon, Thomas Brooks, Rodrigo Bustamante et al., "Can We Defy Nature's End?" *Science* 293 (2001): 2207–2208.

6. Evolution Revolution

1. Jared M. Diamond, *Guns, Germs, and Steel: The Fates of Human Societies* (New York: W. W. Norton, 1999); David R. Harris, ed., *The Origins and Spread of Agriculture and Pastoralism in Eurasia* (London: UCL Press, 1996), ix; U.S. Bureau of the Census, *Statistical Abstract of the United States: 2003*, 123rd ed. (Washington, DC: U.S. Census Bureau, 2003), table 1319.

2. Alfred W. Crosby, *Ecological Imperialism: The Biological Expansion of Europe, 900–1900* (New York: Cambridge University Press, 1986), 8–40; Daniel Lord Smail, *On Deep History and the Brain* (Berkeley: University of California Press, 2008), 1–39; Diamond, *Guns, Germs, and Steel*.

3. International Labour Office, "Global Employment Trends Brief," http://www.cinterfor.org.uy/public/english/region/ampro/cinterfor/news/trends07.htm.

4. United Nations Food and Agriculture Organization, "Database on Macro-Economic Indicators," http://www.fao.org/statistics/os/macro_eco/default.asp.

5. Edward Hyams, *Animals in the Service of Man: 10,000 Years of Domestication* (London: Dent, 1972); H. Epstein, *The Origin of the Domestic Animals of Africa*, vols. 1–2 (New York: Africana, 1971); Frederick E. Zeuner, *A History of Domesticated Animals* (New York: Harper and Row, 1963), 560; Sándor Bökönyi, *History of Domestic Mammals in Central and Eastern Europe* (Budapest: Akadémiai Kiadó, 1974); Juliet Clutton-Brock, *A Natural History of Domesticated Animals*, 2nd ed. (Cambridge: Cambridge University Press, 1999).

6. Jack R. Harlan, *Crops and Man* (Madison, WI: American Society of Agronomy, 1975), 295; B. Brouk, *Plants Consumed by Man* (London: Academic Press, 1975), 479; Maarten J. Chrispeels and David E. Sadava, *Plants, Food, and People* (San Francisco: W. H. Freeman, 1977), 278.

7. Thomas Bell, *History of British Quadrupeds* (London: John van Voorst, 1837).

8. Hans-Peter Uerpmann, "Animal Domestication – Accident or Intention," in Harris, *Origins and Spread of Agriculture*, 227–237; Peter Savolainen, Yaping Zhang, Jing Luo, Joakim Lundeberg, and Thomas Leitner, "Genetic Evidence for an East Asian Origin of Domestic Dogs," *Science* 298 (2002): 1610–1613; Bridgett M. vonHoldt, John P. Pollinger, Kirk E. Lohmueller, Eunjung Han, Heidi G. Parker, Pascale Quignon, Jeremiah D. Degenhardt, et al., "Genome-Wide SNP and Haplotype Analyses Reveal a Rich History Underlying Dog Domestication," *Nature* 464 (2010): 898–903.

9. Uerpmann, "Animal Domestication," 227–237; *New York Times*, "Pedigree of the Dog: Prof. Huxley's Views of the Origin of the Animal," April 29, 1880, 2.

10. Raymond Coppinger and Lorna Coppinger, *Dogs: A Startling New Understanding of Canine Origins, Behavior, and Evolution* (New York: Scribner Press, 2001).

11. M. F. Ashley Montagu, "On the Origin of the Domestication of the Dog," *Science* 96 (1942): 111–112; Gilbert N. Wilson, "The Horse and Dog in Hidatsa Culture," *Anthropological Papers of the American Museum of Natural History* 15, part 2 (1924): 125–311.

12. Nicholas Wade, "Nice Rats, Nasty Rats: Maybe It's All in the Genes," *New York Times*, July 25, 2006, F1.

13. D. K. Belyaev, "Destabilizing Selection as a Factor in Domestication," *Journal of Heredity* 70 (1979): 301–308.

14. Ibid.; L. N. Trut, I. Z. Plyusnina, and I. N. Oskina, "An Experiment on Fox Domestication and Debatable Issue of Evolution of the Dog," *Russian Journal of Genetics* 40, no. 6 (2004): 644–655; L. N. Trut, "Experimental Studies of Early Canid Domestication," in *The Genetics of the Dog*, ed. A. Ruvinsky and J. Sampson (New York: CABI, 2001), 15–41.

15. Trut et al., "Experiment on Fox Domestication"; Trut, "Experimental Studies of Early Canid Domestication."

16. Brian Hare, Irene Plyusnina, Natalie Ignacio, Olesya Schepina, Anna Stepika, Richard Wrangham, and Lyudmila Trut, "Social Cognitive Evolution in Captive Foxes Is a Correlated By-product of Experimental Domestication," *Current Biology* 15 (2005): 226–230.

17. Trut et al., "Experiment on Fox Domestication"; Trut, "Experimental Studies of Early Canid Domestication."

18. Trut et al., "Experiment on Fox Domestication."

19. Ibid.

20. Ibid.

21. Diamond, *Guns, Germs, and Steel*; Nicholas Russell, *Like Engend'ring Like: Heredity and Animal Breeding in Early Modern England* (New York: Cambridge University Press, 1986); J. Milnes Holden, W. J. Peacock, and John

H. Williams, *Genes, Crops, and the Environment* (Cambridge: Cambridge University Press, 1993).

22. O. T. Westengen, Z. Huaman, and M. Heun, "Genetic Diversity and Geographic Pattern in Early South American Cotton Domestication," *Theoretical and Applied Genetics* 110, no. 2 (2005): 392–402.

23. Ibid.

24. Yi-Fu Tuan, *Dominance and Affection: The Making of Pets* (New Haven, CT: Yale University Press, 1984); John H. Perkins, *Geopolitics and the Green Revolution: Wheat, Genes, and the Cold War* (New York: Oxford University Press, 1997).

25. Raymond P. Coppinger and Charles Kay Smith, "The Domestication of Evolution," *Environmental Conservation* 10 (1983): 283–292.

26. Stephen Budiansky, *The Covenant of the Wild: Why Animals Chose Domestication* (New York: William Morrow, 1992); Stephen Budiansky, *The Truth about Dogs: An Inquiry into the Ancestry, Social Conventions, Mental Habits, and Moral Fiber of Canis Familiaris* (New York: Viking Press, 2000).

27. Michael Pollan, *The Botany of Desire: A Plant's Eye View of the World*, 1st ed. (New York: Random House, 2001).

7. Intentional Evolution

1. C. L. Brubaker, F. M. Bourland, and J. F. Wendel, "Origin and Domestication of Cotton," in *Cotton: Origin, History, Technology, and Production*, ed. C. Wayne Smith and J. Tom Cothren (New York: John Wiley, 1999), 3–31.

2. J. O. Ware, "Plant Breeding and the Cotton Industry," in *Yearbook of Agriculture 1936* (Washington, DC: U.S. Government Printing Office, 1936), 712.

3. Ibid.

4. Ibid., 666.

5. Ibid., 683–684.

6. Ibid.

7. Deborah Fitzgerald, *The Business of Breeding: Hybrid Corn in Illinois, 1890–1940* (Ithaca, NY: Cornell University Press, 1990).

8. Jack Ralph Kloppenburg Jr., *First the Seed: The Political Economy of Plant Biotechnology, 1492–2000* (New York: Cambridge University Press, 1988).

9. John H. Perkins, *Geopolitics and the Green Revolution: Wheat, Genes, and the Cold War* (New York: Oxford University Press, 1997).

10. Harriet Ritvo, *The Animal Estate: The English and Other Creatures in the Victorian Age* (Cambridge, MA: Harvard University Press, 1987).

11. Fitzgerald, *Business of Breeding*.

12. Ware, "Plant Breeding and the Cotton Industry," 666.

13. Ibid., 659, 675–676.

14. Ibid., 676.

15. Ibid.

16. Ibid., 676, 694.

17. Ibid., 694–695.

18. Ibrokhim Y. Abdurakhmonov, Fakhriddin N. Kushanov, Fayzulla Djaniqulov, Zabardast T. Buriev, Alan E. Pepper, Nilufar Fayzieva, Gafurjon T. Mavlonov, Sukama Saha, Jonnie H. Jenkins, and Abdusattor Abdukarimov, "The Role of Induced Mutation in Conversion of Photoperiod Dependence in Cotton," *Journal of Heredity* 98, no. 3 (2007): 258–266.

19. George Van Esbroeck and Daryl T. Bowman, "Cotton Improvement: Cotton Germplasm Diversity and Its Importance to Cultivar Development," *Journal of Crop Science* 2 (1998): 125.

20. American Beefalo Association, "All about Beefalo," http://americanbeefalo .org/all-about-beefalo/; Daniel D. Jones, "Genetic Engineering in Domestic Food Animals: Legal and Regulatory Considerations," *Food Drug Cosmetic Law Journal* 38 (1983): 273–287.

21. USDA Economic Research Service, "Adoption of Genetically Engineered Crops in the U. S.," http://www.ers.usda.gov/Data/BiotechCrops/; Stephen R. Palumbi, *Evolution Explosion: How Humans Cause Rapid Evolutionary Change* (New York: W. W. Norton, 2001), 143–161; Marc Kaufman, "'Frankenfish' or Tomorrow's Dinner? Biotech Salmon Face a Current of Environmental Worry," *Washington Post,* October 17, 2000, A1; Rick Weiss, "Biotech Research Branches Out: Gene-Altered Trees Raise Thickets of Promise, Concern," *Washington Post,* August 3, 2000, A1; Rick Weiss, "Plant's Genetic Code Deciphered: Data Called a Biological 'Rosetta Stone,' an Engineering Toolbox," *Washington Post,* December 14, 2000, A3; Michael Specter, "The Pharmageddon Riddle," *New Yorker,* April 10, 2000, 58–71; William Claiborne, "Biotech Corn Traces Dilute Bumper Crop," *Washington Post,* October 25, 2000, A3; David W. Ow, Keith V. Wood, Marlene DeLuca, Jeffrey R. de Wet, Donald R. Helinski, and Stephen H. Howell, "Transient and Stable Expression of the Firefly Luciferase Gene in Plant Cells and Transgenic Plants," *Science* 234 (1986): 856–859.

22. Biotechnology Industry Organization, *Guide to Biotechnology* (Washington, DC: Biotechnology Industry Organization, [n.d.]), 79, 83.

23. Ibid., 83.

24. Larry Moran, "Roundup Ready® Transgenic Plants," http://sandwalk .blogspot.com/2007/03/roundup-ready-transgenic-plants.html; Australian Government, Department of Health and Ageing, Office of the Gene Technology Regulator, "Application of Licence for Commercial Release of GMO into the Environment, Application no. DIR 062/2005," http://www.health. gov.au/internet/ogtr/publishing.nsf/Content/ir-1/.

25. Bayer CropScience, "Liberty Labels," http://www.bayercropscienceus.com/ products_and_seeds/herbicides/liberty.html.

26. Rachel Schurman and William Munro, "Targeting Capital: A Cultural Economy Approach to Understanding the Efficacy of Two Anti-genetic Engineering Movements," *American Journal of Sociology* 115, no. 1 (2009): 155–202; Keiko Yonekura-Sakakibara and Kazuki Saito, "Review: Genetically Modified Plants for the Promotion of Human Health," *Biotechnology Letters* 28 (2006): 1983–1991.

27. Palumbi, *Evolution Explosion,* 144–146.

28. Ibid., 149.

29. Bruce E. Tabashnik, Aaron J. Gassmann, David W. Crowder, and Yves Carriere, "Insect Resistance to Bt. Crops: Evidence versus Theory," *Nature Biotechnology* 26, no. 2 (2008): 199–202.

30. Pallava Bagla, "Hardy Cotton-Munching Pests Are Latest Blow to GM Crops," *Science* 327 (2010): 1439. Monsanto did not state the Linnaean name for pink bollworm in the announcement about resistance on its Web site (http://www.monsanto.com/monsanto_today/for_the_record/india_pink_bollworm.asp). It stated that it conducted the research with the Central Institute for Cotton Research, whose Web site (http://www.cicr.org.in/research_notes/insec_mite_pest.pdf) identified pink bollworm as *Platyedra gossypiella* (Saund.). The U.S. Department of Agriculture identified pink bollworm in India as *Pectinophora gossypiella* (Saunders). Steven E. Naranjo, George D. Butler Jr., and Thomas J. Henneberry, *A Bibliography of the Pink Bollworm Pectinophora gossypiella* (Saunders) (Washington, DC: U. S. Department of Agriculture, 2001).

31. Sakuntala Sivasupramaniam, Graham P. Head, Leigh English, Yue Jin Li, and Ty T. Vaughn, "A Global Approach to Resistance Monitoring," *Journal of Invertebrate Pathology* 95 (2007): 224–226.

32. R. J. Mahon, K. M. Olsen, K. A. Garsia, and S. R. Young, "Resistance to *Bacillus thuringiensis* Toxin Cry2Ab in a Strain of *Helicoverpa armigera* (Lepidoptera: Noctuidae) in Australia," *Journal of Economic Entomology* 100, no. 3 (2007): 894–902.

33. Barrie Edward Juniper and David J. Mabberley, *Story of the Apple* (Portland, OR: Timber Press, 2006), 92–94; Gabor Vajta and Mickey Gjerris, "Science and Technology of Farm Animal Cloning: State of the Art," *Animal Reproduction Science* 92 (2006): 211–230.

34. E. F. Knipling, "Control of Screw-Worm Fly by Atomic Radiation," *Scientific Monthly* 85, no. 4 (1957): 195–202.

35. Frank Fenner, "Smallpox: Emergence, Global Spread, and Eradication," *History and Philosophy of the Life Sciences [Great Britain]* 15, no. 3 (1993): 397–420; Derrick Baxby, "The End of Smallpox," *History Today [Great Britain]* 49, no. 3 (1999): 14–16.

8. Coevolution

1. Paul R. Ehrlich and Peter H. Raven, "Butterflies and Plants: A Study in Coevolution," *Evolution* 18 (1964): 586–608.

2. Daniel J. Kevles, *In the Name of Eugenics: Genetics and the Uses of Human Heredity* (New York: Knopf, 1985).

3. Luigi Luca Cavalli-Sforza, *Genes, Peoples, and Languages* (Berkeley: University of California Press, 2000), 57–59; Nina G. Jablonski, "The Evolution of Human Skin and Skin Color," *Annual Review of Anthropology* 33 (2004): 600; Nina G. Jablonski and George Chaplin, "The Evolution of Human Skin Coloration," *Journal of Human Evolution* 39 (2000): 57–106, esp. 58–59.

4. Jablonski, "Evolution of Human Skin and Skin Color," 588–591; Brian McEvoy, Sandra Beleza, and Mark D. Shriver, "The Genetic Architecture of Normal Variation in Human Pigmentation: An Evolutionary Perspective and

Model," *Human Molecular Genetics* 15 (2006): R176–R181; Jablonski and Chaplin, "Evolution of Human Skin Coloration," 58–59.

5. Jared Diamond, "Geography and Skin Color," *Nature* 435 (2005): 283–284.
6. Jablonski, "Evolution of Human Skin and Skin Color"; Diamond, "Geography and Skin Color."
7. Jablonski and Chaplin, "Evolution of Human Skin Coloration."
8. Ibid.; Jablonski, "Evolution of Human Skin and Skin Color."
9. Jablonski and Chaplin, "Evolution of Human Skin Coloration"; Jablonski, "Evolution of Human Skin and Skin Color"; Esteban Parra, "Human Pigmentation Variation: Evolution, Genetic Basis, and Implications for Public Health," *Yearbook of Physical Anthropology* 50 (2007): 85–105.
10. Diamond, "Geography and Skin Color."
11. Ann Gibbons, "American Association of Physical Anthropologists Meeting: European Skin Turned Pale Only Recently, Gene Suggests," *Science* 316 (2007): 364.
12. Kirk E. Lohmueller, Amit R. Indap, Steffen Schmidt, Adam R. Boyko, Ryan D. Hernandez, Melissa J. Hubisz, John J. Sninsky, et al., "Proportionally More Deleterious Genetic Variation in European Than in African Populations," *Nature* 451 (2008): 994–998.
13. David Brown, "Genetic Mutations Offer Insights on Human Diversity," *Washington Post*, February 22, 2008, A5; C. D. Bustamante, A. Fledel-Alon, S. Williamson, R. Nielsen, M. T. Hubisz, S. Glanowski, D. M. Tanenbaum, T. J. White, J. J. Sninsky, and R. D. Hernandez, "Natural Selection on Protein-Coding Genes in the Human Genome," *Nature* 437 (2005): 1153–1157.
14. J. Burger, M. Kirchner, B. Bramanti, W. Haak, and M. G. Thomas, "Absence of the Lactase-Persistence-Associated Allele in Early Neolithic Europeans," *Proceedings of the National Academy of Sciences of the United States of America* 104, no. 10 (2007): 3736–3741. Lactase splits lactose into glucose and galactose.
15. S. A. Tishkoff, F. A. Reed, A. Ranciaro, B. F. Voight, C. C. Babbitt, J. S. Silverman, K. Powell, et al., "Convergent Adaptation of Human Lactase Persistence in Africa and Europe," *Nature Genetics* 39, no. 1 (2007): 31–40.
16. F. Imtiaz, E. Savilahti, A. Sarnesto, D. Trabzuni, K. Al-Kahtani, I. Kagevi, M. S. Rashed, B. F. Meyer, and I. Jarvela, "The T/G 13915 Variant Upstream of the Lactase Gene (LCT) Is the Founder Allele of Lactase Persistence in an Urban Saudi Population," *Journal of Medical Genetics* 44, no. 10 (2007): e89.
17. The analogy is not exact. Unlike written English, no empty spaces separate words. Instead, like telegraph operators who spelled the word *stop* to indicate the end of a sentence, DNA uses certain arrangements of letters to mark the beginning and ending of words.
18. T. Bersaglieri, P. C. Sabeti, N. Patterson, T. Vanderploeg, S. F. Schaffner, J. A. Drake, M. Rhodes, D. E. Reich, and J. N. Hirschhorn, "Genetic Signatures of Strong Recent Positive Selection at the Lactase Gene," *American Journal of Human Genetics* 74, no. 6 (2004): 1111–1120. This study found

almost identical percentages for differences in position −22018, with lactose-intolerant populations having a G and the lactose intolerant an A. The study reported data on −22018 for all populations except Swedes and Finns.

19. H. M. Sun, Y. D. Qiao, F. Chen, L. D. Xu, J. Bai, and S. B. Fu, "The Lactase Gene-13910T Allele Can Not Predict the Lactase-Persistence Phenotype in North China," *Asia Pacific Journal of Clinical Nutrition* 16, no. 4 (2007): 598–601; N. S. Enattah, A. Trudeau, V. Pimenoff, L. Maiuri, S. Auricchio, L. Greco, M. Rossi, et al., "Evidence of Still-Ongoing Convergence Evolution of the Lactase Persistence T-13910 Alleles in Humans," *American Journal of Human Genetics* 81, no. 3 (2007): 615–625; N. S. Enattah, T. G. Jensen, M. Nielsen, R. Lewinski, M. Kuokkanen, H. Rasinpera, H. El-Shanti, et al., "Independent Introduction of Two Lactase-Persistence Alleles into Human Populations Reflects Different History of Adaptation to Milk Culture," *American Journal of Human Genetics* 82, no. 1 (2008): 57–72; Imtiaz et al., "The T/G 13915 Variant"; Tishkoff et al., "Convergent Adaptation of Human Lactase Persistence."

20. Enattah et al., "Independent Introduction of Two Lactase-Persistence Alleles"; Tishkoff et al., "Convergent Adaptation of Human Lactase Persistence"; S. Myles, N. Bouzekri, E. Haverfield, M. Cherkaoui, J. M. Dugoujon, and R. Ward, "Genetic Evidence in Support of a Shared Eurasian–North African Dairying Origin," *Human Genetics* 117, no. 1 (2005): 34–42; Enattah et al., "Evidence of Still-Ongoing Convergence Evolution."

21. Burger et al., "Absence of the Lactase-Persistence-Associated Allele"; Bersaglieri et al., "Genetic Signatures of Strong Recent Positive Selection"; Tishkoff et al., "Convergent Adaptation of Human Lactase Persistence."

22. Kevin N. Laland, John Odling-Smee, and Sean Myles, "How Culture Shaped the Human Genome: Bringing Genetics and the Human Sciences Together," *Nature Reviews Genetics* 11 (2010): 137–148.

23. Douglas J. Futuyma, *Evolutionary Biology*, 3rd ed. (Sunderland, MA: Sinauer Associates, 1998), 579–604.

24. William H. Durham, *Coevolution: Genes, Culture, and Human Diversity* (Palo Alto, CA: Stanford University Press, 1991), 3–10.

25. Ibid., 419–428.

26. Richard Dawkins, *The Selfish Gene* (New York: Oxford University Press, 1976).

27. Lawrence C. Hamilton and Melissa J. Butler, "Outport Adaptations: Social Indicators through Newfoundland's Cod Crisis," *Human Ecology Review* 8 (2001): 1–11.

28. Stephen R. Palumbi, "Humans as the World's Greatest Evolutionary Force," *Science* 293 (2001): 1788. Palumbi gives a date of 1999 for the evolution of resistance to linezolid, but I have used the date of the earliest report I could find of a clinical isolate resistant to *Staphylococcus aureus*. Sotirios Tsiodras, Howard S. Gold, George Sakoulas, George M. Eliopoulos, Christine Wennersten, Lata Venkataraman, Robert C. Moellering Jr., and Mary Jane Ferraro, "Linezolid Resistance in a Clinical Isolate of *Staphylococcus aureus*," *Lancet* 358 (2001): 207–208.

29. A balanced account is Robert Bud, *Penicillin: Triumph and Tragedy* (Oxford: Oxford University Press, 2007), 330.
30. Douglas J. Futuyma and Montgomery Slatkin, eds., *Coevolution* (Sunderland, MA: Sinauer Associates, 1983); V. P. Sharma, "Vector Genetics in Malaria Control," in *Malaria: Genetic and Evolutionary Aspects*, ed. Krishna R. Dronamraju and Paolo Arese (New York: Springer, 2006), 158–161; Laland et al., "How Culture Shaped the Human Genome."
31. Kevles, *In the Name of Eugenics.*

9. Evolution of the Industrial Revolution

1. Fernand Braudel, *A History of Civilizations* (New York: A. Lane, 1993); Joel Mokyr, "Editor's Introduction: The New Economic History and the Industrial Revolution," in *The British Industrial Revolution: An Economic Perspective*, ed. Joel Mokyr (San Francisco: Westview Press, 1993), 96–100; David S. Landes, *The Unbound Prometheus: Technological Change and Industrial Development in Western Europe from 1750 to the Present* (Cambridge: Cambridge University Press, 2003), 41–45; William H. McNeill, *A World History* (Oxford: Oxford University Press, 1999), 420; Walter W. Rostow, *The Stages of Economic Growth: A Non-Communist Manifesto* (Cambridge: Cambridge University Press, 1960), 54–55; Alfred P. Wadsworth and Julia de Lacy Mann, *The Cotton Trade and Industrial Lancashire, 1600–1780* (New York: Augustus M. Kelley, [1931] 1968); Paul Mantoux, *The Industrial Revolution in the Eighteenth Century: An Outline of the Beginnings of the Modern Factory System in England* (London: Jonathan Cape, 1928), 193–276; C. Knick Harley, "Cotton Textile Prices and the Industrial Revolution," *Economic History Review* 51, no. 1 (1998): 49–83; Phyllis Deane, *The First Industrial Revolution* (Cambridge: Cambridge University Press, 1979), 87–102; Phyllis Deane and W. A. Cole, *British Economic Growth 1688–1959: Trends and Structure* (Cambridge: Cambridge University Press, 1967), 182–214; James Thomson, "Invention in the Industrial Revolution: The Case of Cotton," in *Exceptionalism and Industrialization: Britain and Its European Rivals, 1688–1815*, ed. Leandro Prados de la Escosura (Cambridge: Cambridge University Press, 2004), 127–144.
2. David Landes has argued that "the heart of the industrial revolution was an interrelated succession of technological changes." Landes, *Unbound Prometheus*, 1. Joel Mokyr has suggested that one should see "the Industrial Revolution primarily in terms of accelerating and unprecedented technological change." Joel Mokyr, *The Lever of Riches: Technological Creativity and Economic Progress* (New York: Oxford University Press, 1990), 82. See also Braudel, *History of Civilizations*, 377; McNeill, *World History*, 420–423. Karl Marx captured this view in his aphorism, "The windmill gives you society with the feudal lord; the steam-mill, society with the industrial capitalist." Karl Marx, *The Poverty of Philosophy*, trans. H. Quelch (Chicago: Charles

H. Kerr, 1910), 119. Other translations use "handmill" instead of "windmill." William H. Shaw, "'The Handmill Gives You the Feudal Lord': Marx's Technological Determinism," *History and Theory* 18 (1979): 155–176. Here I am using *technology* to mean more than tools or machinery and to encompass the social systems surrounding them, making it roughly equivalent to Marx's *factors of production*. Friedrich Engels argued that "steam and the new tool-making machinery were transforming manufacture into modern industry, thus revolutionizing the whole foundation of bourgeois society." Friedrich Engels, "Socialism: Utopian and Scientific," in *The Marx-Engels Reader*, ed. Robert C. Tucker, 2nd ed. (New York: W. W. Norton, 1978), 690. Landes has suggested that "it was the Industrial Revolution that initiated a cumulative, self-sustaining advance in technology whose repercussions would be felt in all aspects of economic life." Landes, *Unbound Prometheus*, 3. Mokyr has argued that "technological creativity was at the very base of the rise of the West. It was the lever of its riches." Mokyr, *Lever of Riches*, vii.

3. Mokyr, *Lever of Riches*, 96–98; Landes, *Unbound Prometheus*, 84–85; Harley, "Cotton Textile Prices and the Industrial Revolution," 50.

4. Mokyr, *Lever of Riches*, 99.

5. James A. B. Scherer, *Cotton as a World Power: A Study in the Economic Interpretation of History* (New York: Frederick A. Stokes, 1916), 57–58; O. L. May and K. E. Lege, "Development of the World Cotton Industry," in *Cotton: Origin, History, Technology, and Production*, ed. C. Wayne Smith and J. Tom Cothren (New York: John Wiley, 1999), esp. 67–76.

6. Mantoux, *Industrial Revolution in the Eighteenth Century*, 25; Patrick O'Brien, Trevor Griffiths, and Philip Hunt, "Political Components of the Industrial Revolution: Parliament and the English Cotton Textile Industry, 1660–1774," *Economic History Review* 44, no. 3 (1991): 395–423; Patrick O'Brien, "Central Government and the Economy, 1688–1815," in *1700–1860*, vol. 1 of *The Economic History of Britain since 1700*, ed. Roderick Floud and Donald McCloskey (Cambridge: Cambridge University Press, 1994), 205–241; Douglas A. Farnie, "The Role of Merchants as Prime Movers in the Expansion of the Cotton Industry, 1760–1990," in *The Fibre That Changed the World: The Cotton Industry in International Perspective, 1600–1990s*, ed. Douglas A. Farnie and David J. Jeremy (Oxford: Oxford University Press, 2004), 15–55; John Singleton, "The Lancashire Cotton Industry, the Royal Navy, and the British Empire, c.1700–c.1960," in Farnie and Jeremy, *Fibre That Changed the World*, 57–83.

7. Rostow, *Stages of Economic Growth*, 8, 54, 57; Deane, *First Industrial Revolution*, 1–2; Deane and Cole, *British Economic Growth 1688–1959*; Peter Mathias and John A. Davis, eds., *The First Industrial Revolutions* (Oxford: Basil Blackwell, 1989); R. M. Hartwell, *The Industrial Revolution and Economic Growth* (London: Methuen, 1971); Leandro Prados de la Escosura, ed., *Exceptionalism and Industrialisation: Britain and Its European Rivals, 1688–1815* (Cambridge: Cambridge University Press, 2004); Floud and McCloskey, *Economic History of Britain since 1700*.

8. Rostow, *Stages of Economic Growth*, 8, 54, 57.
9. Hartwell, *Industrial Revolution and Economic Growth*, 122.
10. Donald McCloskey, "1780–1860: A Survey," in Floud and McCloskey, *Economic History of Britain since 1700*, 242–270.
11. Harley, "Cotton Textile Prices and the Industrial Revolution," 49–83.
12. Eric Hobsbawm, *Workers: Worlds of Labor* (New York: Pantheon, 1984).
13. Jan de Vries, *The Industrious Revolution: Consumer Behavior and the Household Economy, 1650 to the Present* (New York: Cambridge University Press, 2008).
14. Rostow, *Stages of Economic Growth*, 8.
15. Kenneth Pomeranz, *The Great Divergence: Europe, China, and the Making of the Modern World Economy* (Princeton, NJ: Princeton University Press, 2000); Alf Hornborg, "Footprints in the Cotton Fields: The Industrial Revolution as Time-Space Appropriation and Environmental Load Displacement," in *Rethinking Environmental History: World-System History and Global Environmental Change*, ed. Alf Hornborg, John R. McNeill, and Joan Martinez-Alier (New York: Altamira, 2007), 259–272.
16. Pomeranz, *Great Divergence*; E. A. Wrigley, *Continuity, Chance, and Change: The Character of the Industrial Revolution in England* (New York: Cambridge University Press, 1988), 17.
17. Harold Perkin, *The Origins of Modern English Society*, 2nd ed. (London: Routledge, 2002), 3, 5.
18. Mokyr, "Editor's Introduction," 5.
19. John R. McNeill, *Something New under the Sun: An Environmental History of the Twentieth-century World* (New York: W. W. Norton, 2000), 421; Joachim Radkau, *Nature and Power: A Global History of the Environment* (Cambridge: Cambridge University Press, 2008), 195–198, 239–249; I. G. Simmons, *An Environmental History of Great Britain: From 10,000 Years Ago to the Present* (Edinburgh: Edinburgh University Press, 2001), 148–191; Shepard Krech, John Robert McNeill, and Carolyn Merchant, *Encyclopedia of World Environmental History* (New York: Routledge, 2004), 687–691; Theodore Steinberg, *Nature Incorporated: Industrialization and the Waters of New England* (New York: Cambridge University Press, 1991); Peter Thorsheim, *Inventing Pollution: Coal, Smoke, and Culture in Britain since 1800* (Athens: Ohio University Press, 2006); Stephen R. Mosley, *The Chimney of the World: A History of Smoke Pollution in Victorian and Edwardian Manchester* (Cambridge, UK: White Horse Press, 2001), 288.
20. Philip Scranton and Susan R. Schrepfer, eds., *Industrializing Organisms: Introducing Evolutionary History* (New York: Routledge, 2004).
21. Alan Olmstead and Paul W. Rhode, *Creating Abundance: Biological Innovation and American Agricultural Development* (New York: Cambridge University Press, 2008), 100.
22. Makrand Mehta, *The Ahmedabad Cotton Textile Industry: Genesis and Growth* (Ahmedabad, India: New Order, 1982), 38.
23. Patrick O'Brien, Trevor Griffiths, and Phillip Hunt, "Political Components of the Industrial Revolution: Parliament and the English Cotton Textile Industry, 1660–1774," *Economic History Review* 44, no. 3 (1991): 415.

24. Landes, *Unbound Prometheus*, 83.

25. Mokyr, *Lever of Riches*, 100.

26. The desire to make cloth might not have motivated the first experiments in spinning. Archaeologists in Peru have uncovered fishing nets and line made of cotton string. C. L. Brubaker, F. M. Bourland, and J. F. Wendel, "Origin and Domestication of Cotton," in Smith and Cothren, *Cotton*, 3–31; Kara M. Butterworth, Dean C. Adams, Harry T. Horner, and Jonathan F. Wendel, "Initiation and Early Development of Fiber in Wild and Cultivated Cotton," *International Journal of Plant Sciences* 170 (2009): 561–574; Jonathan F. Wendel, Curt L. Brubaker, and Tosak Seelanan, "The Origin and Evolution of *Gossypium*," in *Physiology of Cotton*, ed. J. M. Stewart et al. (Netherlands: Springer, 2010), 1–18.

27. Brubaker et al., "Origin and Domestication of Cotton."

28. Ibid.

29. Wadsworth and Mann, *Cotton Trade and Industrial Lancashire*, 175–176; Brubaker et al., "Origin and Domestication of Cotton"; Jonathan F. Wendel and Richard C. Cronn, "Polyploidy and the Evolutionary History of Cotton," *Advances in Agronomy* 78 (2003): 139–186; Jonathan F. Wendel, Curt L. Brubaker, and Tosak Seelanan, "The Origin and Evolution of *Gossypium*," in *Physiology of Cotton*, ed. J. M. Stewart, D. Oosterhuis, J. J. Heitholt, and J. R. Mauney, J. R. (Dordrecht: Springer, 2010), 1–18.

30. Brubaker et al., "Origin and Domestication of Cotton."

31. Ibid.

32. T. S. Ashton, *The Industrial Revolution 1760–1830* (London: Oxford University Press, [1948] 1967), 58.

33. Edward Baines, *History of the Cotton Manufacture in Great Britain* (New York: Augustus M. Kelley, [1835] 1966), 53. Many scholars since Baines have echoed his belief that English inventors and inventions drove the Industrial Revolution.

34. Pomeranz, *Great Divergence*, 274–278; Hornborg, "Footprints in the Cotton Fields"; Kenneth Morgan, *Slavery, Atlantic Trade, and the British Economy, 1660–1800* (Cambridge: Cambridge University Press, 2000), 65.

35. Christopher Columbus, *The Journal of His First Voyage to America* (London: Jarrolds, [n.d.]), 64–65. Columbus mentions cotton at least twenty-three times in this journal. May and Lege, "Development of the World Cotton Industry."

36. Angela Lakwete, *Inventing the Cotton Gin: Machine and Myth in Antebellum America* (Baltimore: Johns Hopkins University Press, 2003), 21–37.

37. C. R. Benedict, R. J. Kohel, and H. L. Lewis, "Cotton Fiber Quality," in Smith and Cothren, *Cotton*, esp. 283.

38. Ibid.

39. Mokyr, *Lever of Riches*, 98.

40. May and Lege, "Development of the World Cotton Industry"; Thomas Ellison, *The Cotton Trade of Great Britain* (London: Frank Cass, 1968), 19; Baines, *History of the Cotton Manufacture in Great Britain*, 183.

41. Wadsworth, *Cotton Trade and Industrial Lancashire*, 175–176, 275.

42. Ibid., 15–17; Brubaker et al., "Origin and Domestication of Cotton"; Ellison, *Cotton Trade of Great Britain*, 16.
43. Wadsworth, *Cotton Trade and Industrial Lancashire*, 520–521.
44. This conclusion is based on deduction. Up to 1780, almost all cotton imports from the Old World went to the port of London. Cotton from the New World also flowed to London, but most of it arrived at the port of Liverpool. Since London received almost all the Old World cotton, Lancashire must have been receiving almost entirely New World cotton. Wadsworth, *Cotton Trade and Industrial Lancashire*, 155, 175. London transshipped Levant (and West Indies) cotton to Liverpool, but published accounts of Liverpool cotton merchants mention almost exclusively New World varieties and rarely Levant cotton (sometimes called Smyrna). In one of the few mentions of the latter, the merchant suggested that the cotton was destined for lining packages. Wadsworth, *Cotton Trade and Industrial Lancashire*, 188–189, 233, 268–272; James A. Mann, *The Cotton Trade of Great Britain: Its Rise, Progress, and Present Extent* (London: Simpkin, Marshall, 1860), 23; Ellison, *Cotton Trade of Great Britain*, 166–168.
45. Wadsworth, *Cotton Trade and Industrial Lancashire*, 411–503.
46. Partly this was due to restrictions on exports of English machines. Mehta, *Ahmedabad Cotton Textile Industry*, 12.
47. The Strutts consumed five bags classified as Bourbon cotton, which is *G. hirsutum*, a New World species. Twelve bags were classified "fine" without designating the origin, but the Old World species were not considered fine. The Strutts began using upland North American cotton (*G. hirsutum*) in 1800 and consumed 899 bags through 1803. The Arkwright family also created a spinning dynasty, but almost all records of the Arkwright mills have been lost. R. S. Fitton and A. P. Wadsworth, *The Strutts and the Arkwrights, 1758–1830* (Manchester, UK: Manchester University Press, 1958), 261–265. J. O. Ware, "Plant Breeding and the Cotton Industry," in *Yearbook of Agriculture 1936* (Washington, DC: U.S. Government Printing Office, 1936), 658; *Economist*, "Supply of Cotton: Various Descriptions of the Article" May 23, 1857, 559–560.
48. Lakwete, *Inventing the Cotton Gin*, 63.
49. Ellison, *Cotton Trade of Great Britain*, 83–86.
50. E. R. J. Owen, *Cotton and the Egyptian Economy 1820–1914: A Study in Trade and Development* (Oxford: Clarendon Press, 1969); Richard G. Percy, *Plant Genetics and Genomics: Crops and Models: Genetics and Genomics of Cotton* (New York: Springer, 2009), sec. 3.22.
51. Ware, "Plant Breeding and the Cotton Industry," 657–744.
52. *Economist*, "Supply of Cotton," 559–560.
53. Indian cotton did have a few desirable traits. It had a creamy color, dyed well, and filled out cloth by swelling when bleached. But these advantages did not outweigh the disadvantages. John Forbes Royle, "On the Culture and Commerce of Cotton in India. Part 1," *Knowsley Pamphlet Collection* (1850): 22–25; Frenise A. Logan, "India's Loss of the British Cotton Market after 1865," *Journal of Southern History* 31, no. 1 (1965): 44–45; Arthur W. Silver, *Manchester Men and Indian Cotton, 1847–1872* (Manchester, UK:

Manchester University Press, 1966), 295; *Economist*, "Supply of Cotton," esp. 560.

54. *Economist*, "Supply of Cotton," 560, emphasis in original.

55. L. S. Wood and A. Wilmore, *The Romance of the Cotton Industry in England* (Oxford: Oxford University Press, 1927), 249.

56. Royle, "On the Culture and Commerce of Cotton in India," 86–91, 99; Peter Harnetty, "The Cotton Improvement Program in India 1865–1875," *Agricultural History* 44, no. 4 (1970): 379–392; Silver, *Manchester Men and Indian Cotton*, 34–42.

57. Francis A. Wood and George A. F. Roberts, "Natural Fibers and Dyes," in *The Cultural History of Plants*, ed. Sir Ghillean Prance and Mark Nesbitt (New York: Routledge, 2005), 287–289; R. Hovav, B. Chaudhary, J. A. Udall, L. Flagel, and J. F. Wendel, "Parallel Domestication, Convergent Evolution and Duplicated Gene Recruitment in Allopolyploid Cotton," *Genetics* 179, no. 3 (2008): 1725–1733. The United States, China, India, Pakistan, Brazil, and Turkey are the world's largest cotton producers.

58. These figures come from Wendel et al., "Origin and Evolution of *Gossypium*." See also A. E. Percival, J. E. Wendel, and J. M. Stewart, "Taxonomy and Germplasm Resources," in Smith and Cothren, *Cotton*, 33–63; Wendel and Cronn, "Polyploidy and the Evolutionary History of Cotton."

59. Each genome (A–G and K) consists of thirteen pairs of chromosomes. Most cotton species have one genome, so they have thirteen chromosomes (one from each pair) in their sex cells and twenty-six chromosomes (two from each pair) in the rest of their cells. Species with the AD genome, on the other hand, carry thirteen pairs of chromosomes from the A genome and thirteen pairs from the D genome, for a total of twenty-six pairs of chromosomes. Their sex cells have twenty-six chromosomes, and the rest of their cells have fifty-two. Percival et al., "Taxonomy and Germplasm Resources"; Wendel and Cronn, "Polyploidy and the Evolutionary History of Cotton"; Wendel et al., "Origin and Evolution of *Gossypium*"; Brubaker et al., "Origin and Domestication of Cotton." The technical term for carrying four sets of chromosomes is *tetraploid*.

60. O. T. Westengen, Z. Huaman, and M. Heun, "Genetic Diversity and Geographic Pattern in Early South American Cotton Domestication," *Theoretical and Applied Genetics* 110, no. 2 (2005): 392–402; Wendel and Cronn, "Polyploidy and the Evolutionary History of Cotton."

61. Hovav et al., "Parallel Domestication"; Jeff J. Doyle, Lex E. Flagel, Andrew H. Paterson, Ryan A. Rapp, Douglas E. Soltis, Pamela S. Soltis, and Jonathan F. Wendel, "Evolutionary Genetics of Genome Merger and Doubling in Plants," *Annual Review of Genetics* 42 (2008): 443–461; Lex E. Flagel and Jonathan Wendel, "Gene Duplication and Evolutionary Novelty in Plants," *New Phytologist* 183 (2009): 557–564.

62. Michael M. Edwards, *The Growth of the British Cotton Trade, 1780–1815* (New York: A. M. Kell[e]y, 1967), 80–82; Hameeda Hossain, *The Company Weavers of Bengal: The East India Company and the Organization of Textile Production in Bengal 1750–1813* (Delhi: Oxford University Press, 1988), 24.

63. Royle, "On the Culture and Commerce of Cotton in India," 86–91, 99; Harnetty, "The Cotton Improvement Program in India"; Silver, *Manchester Men and Indian Cotton*, 34–42.

64. Royle, "On the Culture and Commerce of Cotton in India," 91–95.

65. Harnetty, "The Cotton Improvement Program in India"; Baines, *History of the Cotton Manufacture in Great Britain*, 63.

66. Harnetty, "The Cotton Improvement Program in India"; Baines, *History of the Cotton Manufacture in Great Britain*, 55–76; Hossain, *Company Weavers of Bengal*, 40–43.

67. Hossain, *Company Weavers of Bengal*, 22–35; Baines, *History of the Cotton Manufacture in Great Britain*, 74.

68. Harnetty, "The Cotton Improvement Program in India."

69. Hossain, *Company Weavers of Bengal*, 32.

70. Eric Williams, *Capitalism and Slavery* (Chapel Hill: University of North Carolina Press, 1944); Kenneth Morgan, *Slavery and the British Empire: From Africa to America* (Oxford: Oxford University Press, 2007); Morgan, *Slavery, Atlantic Trade, and the British Economy*.

71. Morgan, *Slavery and the British Empire*, 68.

72. Wadsworth, *Cotton Trade and Industrial Lancashire*, 148–161. Other scholars have also noted these links.

73. James A. Rawley and Stephen D. Behrendt, *The Transatlantic Slave Trade: A History*, Rev. ed. (Lincoln: University of Nebraska Press, 2005), 176–177.

74. Morgan, *Slavery, Atlantic Trade, and the British Economy*, 85–89.

75. Melinda Elder, *The Slave Trade and the Economic Development of Eighteenth-century Lancaster* (Halifax, NS, Canada: Ryburn, 1992), 28, 32, 95, 99, 170; Morgan, *Slavery, Atlantic Trade, and the British Economy*, 9–24.

76. The slave trade also increased Lancashire's desire to make all-cotton cloth. Africans strongly preferred all-cottons to fustians. English traders tried to fob off fustians as all-cottons, but Africans learned to detect the fraud by ripping samples of cloth (the linen warp in fustians made them hard to tear). Until they figured out a way to compete, Lancashire textile makers had to watch Liverpool ships load up with all-cotton cloth from the East Indies. Morgan, *Slavery and the British Empire*, 68; Wadsworth, *Cotton Trade and Industrial Lancashire*, 150–155, 175–176.

10. History of Technology

1. Jeffrey K. Stine and Joel A. Tarr, "At the Intersection of Histories: Technology and the Environment," *Technology and Culture* 39, no. 4 (1998): 610–640; Martin V. Melosi, *Garbage in the Cities: Refuse, Reform, and the Environment 1880–1980* (College Station: Texas A & M University Press, 1981); Jeffrey K. Stine, *Mixing the Waters: Environment, Politics, and the Building of the Tennessee-Tombigbee Waterway* (Akron, OH: University of Akron Press, 1993); Joel A. Tarr, *The Search for the Ultimate Sink: Urban Pollution in Historical Perspective* (Akron, OH: University of Akron Press, 1996); James C. Williams, *Energy and the Making of Modern California* (Akron, OH: University of Akron Press, 1997).

2. Envirotech, "Are Animals Technology?" http://www.udel.edu/History/gpetrick/envirotech; Envirotech, "More Animals as Technology," http://www.udel.edu/History/gpetrick/envirotech.

3. Clay McShane and Joel A. Tarr have since published a book suggesting that horses in cities were living machines: Clay McShane and Joel A. Tarr, *The Horse in the City: Living Machines in the Nineteenth Century* (Baltimore: Johns Hopkins University Press, 2007).

4. Philip Scranton and Susan R. Schrepfer, eds., *Industrializing Organisms: Introducing Evolutionary History* (New York: Routledge, 2004).

5. Stine and Tarr, "At the Intersection of Histories"; Brian Black, *Petrolia: The Landscape of America's First Oil Boom* (Baltimore: Johns Hopkins University Press, 2000); Adam Rome, *The Bulldozer in the Countryside: Suburban Sprawl and the Rise of American Environmentalism* (New York: Cambridge University Press, 2001); Edmund Russell, "'Speaking of Annihilation': Mobilizing for War against Human and Insect Enemies, 1914–1945," *Journal of American History* 82 (1996): 1505–1529; Edmund Russell, "'Lost among the Parts Per Billion': Ecological Protection at the United States Environmental Protection Agency, 1970–1993," *Environmental History* 2 (1997): 29–51; Edmund Russell, "The Strange Career of DDT: Experts, Federal Capacity, and 'Environmentalism' in World War II," *Technology and Culture* 40 (1999): 770–796; Edmund Russell, *War and Nature: Fighting Humans and Insects with Chemicals from World War I to Silent Spring* (New York: Cambridge University Press, 2001); Stine, *Mixing the Waters*; Tarr, *Search for the Ultimate Sink*; Richard White, *The Organic Machine* (New York: Hill and Wang, 1995); Williams, *Energy and the Making of Modern California*. Rutgers recently began a new PhD program in the history of technology, environment, and health. Paul Israel, "New Ph.D. Program Announcement," *Envirotech Newsletter*, September 2001, 1. The University of Virginia has created a Committee on the History of Environment and Technology, which is overseeing a new graduate field in the history of environment and technology. Jim Williams, "Envirotech an Official SIG," *Envirotech Newsletter*, September 2001, 1.

6. Biotechnology Industry Organization, "Bio," http://www.bio.org/.

7. Rick Weiss, "Starved for Food, Zimbabwe Rejects US Biotech Corn," *Washington Post*, July 31 2002, A12

8. Leo Marx, *The Machine in the Garden: Technology and the Pastoral Ideal in America* (Oxford: Oxford University Press, 1967), 195. Some prefer terms such as *second nature* to refer to gardens and other landscapes that human beings have shaped.

9. Examples of a huge literature include John K. Brown, "Design Plans, Working Drawings, National Styles: Engineering Practices in Great Britain and the United States, 1775–1945," *Technology and Culture* 41 (2000): 195–238; Ruth Schwartz Cowan, *More Work for Mother: The Ironies of Household Technology from the Open Hearth to the Microwave* (New York: Basic Books, 1983); Claude S. Fischer, *America Calling: A Social History of the Telephone to 1940* (Berkeley: University of California Press, 1992); Donna Jeanne Haraway, *Simians, Cyborgs, and Women: The Reinvention of Nature*

(New York: Routledge, 1991); Gabrielle Hecht, *The Radiance of France: Nuclear Power and National Identity after World War II* (Cambridge, MA: MIT Press, 1998); David A. Hounshell and John K. Smith, *Science and Corporate Strategy: Du Pont R & D, 1902–1980* (Cambridge: Cambridge University Press, 1988); Thomas Parke Hughes, *Networks of Power: Electrification in Western Society, 1880–1930* (Baltimore: Johns Hopkins University Press, 1983); Sheila Jasanoff et al., eds., *Handbook of Science and Technology Studies* (Thousand Oaks, CA: Sage, 1994); Nina E. Lerman, Arwen Palmer Mohun, and Ruth Oldenziel, "The Shoulders We Stand On and the View from Here: Historiography and Directions of Research," *Technology and Culture* 38 (1997): 9–30; Donald A. MacKenzie, *Inventing Accuracy: An Historical Sociology of Nuclear Missile Guidance* (Cambridge, MA: MIT Press, 1990); Philip Scranton, *Beauty and Business: Commerce, Gender, and Culture in Modern America* (New York: Routledge, 2001); Philip Scranton, *Endless Novelty: Specialty Production and American Industrialization, 1865–1925* (Princeton, NJ: Princeton University Press, 1997); Bruce Edsall Seely, *Building the American Highway System: Engineers as Policy Makers* (Philadelphia: Temple University Press, 1987).

10. Mark R. Finlay, "Hogs, Antibiotics, and the Industrial Environments of Postwar Agriculture," in Schrepfer and Scranton, *Industrializing Organisms*, 239, 248; Deborah Fitzgerald, *Every Farm a Factory: The Industrial Ideal in American Agriculture* (New Haven, CT: Yale University Press, 2003).

11. Finlay, "Hogs, Antibiotics, and the Industrial Environments of Postwar Agriculture," 242.

12. Roger Horowitz, "Making the Chicken of Tomorrow: Reworking Poultry as Commodities and as Creatures, 1945–1990," in Schrepfer and Scranton, *Industrializing Organisms*, 215–235.

13. Stephen Pemberton, "Canine Technologies, Model Patients: The Historical Production of Hemophiliac Dogs in American Biomedicine," in ibid., 191–213.

14. Finlay, "Hogs, Antibiotics, and the Industrial Environments of Postwar Agriculture," 246.

15. Barbara Orland, "Turbo-Cows: Producing a Competitive Animal in the Nineteenth and Early Twentieth Centuries," in Schrepfer and Scranton, *Industrializing Organisms*, 167–189.

16. Horowitz, "Making the Chicken of Tomorrow," 215–235.

17. Roderick Nash, *Wilderness and the American Mind* (New Haven, CT: Yale University Press, 1967); William Cronon, *Changes in the Land: Indians, Colonists, and the Ecology of New England* (New York: Hill and Wang, 1983); Carolyn Merchant, *The Death of Nature: Women, Ecology, and the Scientific Revolution* (San Francisco: Harper and Row, 1980); Donald Worster, *Dust Bowl: The Southern Plains in the 1930s* (New York: Oxford University Press, 1979).

18. Merritt Roe Smith and Leo Marx, eds., *Does Technology Drive History? The Dilemma of Technological Determinism* (Cambridge, MA: MIT Press, 1994); Wiebe E. Bijker, Thomas P. Hughes, and Trevor J. Pinch, eds., *The Social*

Construction of Technological Systems: New Directions in the Sociology and History of Technology (Cambridge, MA: MIT Press, 1987).

19. Jared M. Diamond, *Guns, Germs, and Steel: The Fates of Human Societies* (New York: W. W. Norton, 1999); Clay McShane, "The Urban Horse as Cyborg" (unpublished manuscript, 2000); Joel A. Tarr, "A Note on the Horse as an Urban Power Source," *Journal of Urban History* 25 (1999): 434–448; William Boyd, "Making Meat: Science, Technology, and American Poultry Production," *Technology and Culture* 42 (2001): 631–664; Deborah Fitzgerald, *The Business of Breeding: Hybrid Corn in Illinois, 1890–1940* (Ithaca, NY: Cornell University Press, 1990); Jack Ralph Kloppenburg Jr., *First the Seed: The Political Economy of Plant Biotechnology, 1492–2000* (New York: Cambridge University Press, 1988); John H. Perkins, *Geopolitics and the Green Revolution: Wheat, Genes, and the Cold War* (New York: Oxford University Press, 1997); Harriet Ritvo, *The Animal Estate: The English and Other Creatures in the Victorian Age* (Cambridge, MA: Harvard University Press, 1987); Donna Haraway, "Universal Donors in a Vampire Culture: It's All in the Family: Biological Kinship Categories in the Twentieth Century United States," in *Uncommon Ground: Rethinking the Human Place in Nature*, ed. William Cronon (New York: W. W. Norton, 1996), 321–366; Robert E. Kohler, *Lords of the Fly: Drosophila Genetics and the Experimental Life* (Chicago: University of Chicago Press, 1994); Nicholas Russell, *Like Engend'ring Like: Heredity and Animal Breeding in Early Modern England* (New York: Cambridge University Press, 1986).

20. Willard Wesley Cochrane, *The Development of American Agriculture: A Historical Analysis* (Minneapolis: University of Minnesota Press, 1979); Yūjirō Hayami and Vernon W. Ruttan, *Agricultural Development: An International Perspective* (Baltimore: Johns Hopkins Press, 1971); Jeremy Atack, Fred Bateman, and William N. Parker, "The Farm, the Farmer, and the Market," in *The Long Nineteenth Century*, vol. 2 of *The Cambridge Economic History of the United States*, ed. Stanely L. Engerman and Robert E. Gallman (New York: Cambridge University Press, 2000). All cited in Alan L. Olmstead and Paul W. Rhode, "Biological Innovation in American Wheat Production: Science, Policy, and Environmental Adaptation," in Schrepfer and Scranton, *Industrializing Organisms*, 43–83.

21. Ibid.; Alan Olmstead and Paul W. Rhode, *Creating Abundance: Biological Innovation and American Agricultural Development* (New York: Cambridge University Press, 2008).

22. Alan L. Olmstead and Paul W. Rhode, "Biological Innovation and Productivity Growth in American Wheat Production, 1800–1940," *Journal of Economic History* 62 (2002): 581.

23. Schrepfer and Scranton, *Industrializing Organisms*. For applications of evolution and selection to technological development (but not organisms), see George Basalla, *The Evolution of Technology* (Cambridge: Cambridge University Press, 1988).

24. David W. Ow, Keith V. Wood, Marlene DeLuca, Jeffrey R. de Wet, Donald R. Helinski, and Stephen H. Howell, "Transient and Stable Expression of

the Firefly Luciferase Gene in Plant Cells and Transgenic Plants," *Science* 234 (1986): 856–859.

11. Environmental History

1. Cheryl Oakes, librarian and archivist at the Forest History Society in Durham, North Carolina, kindly searched the database (titles and abstracts) for me in September 2002 and again in February 2010. The database contains other works on the history of evolutionary ideas, and works that use *evolution* to mean change in general, but this search focused instead on material (genetic) or **cultural evolution** in action. Authors of the works include popular writers, evolutionary biologists, and a paleoanthropologist. Stephen Budiansky, *The Covenant of the Wild: Why Animals Chose Domestication* (New Haven, CT: Yale University Press, 1999); Niles Eldredge, *Life in the Balance: Humanity and the Biodiversity Crisis* (Princeton, NJ: Princeton University Press, 1998); Dan Flores, "Nature's Children: Environmental History as Human Natural History," in *Human/Nature: Biology, Culture, and Environmental History*, ed. John P. Herron and Andrew G. Kirk (Albuquerque: University of New Mexico Press, 1999), 11–30; Stephen R. Kellert, *Kinship to Mastery: Biophilia in Human Evolution and Development* (Washington, DC: Island Press, 1997); Lynn Margulis, Clifford Matthews, and Aaron Haselton, eds., *Environmental Evolution: Effects of the Origin and Evolution of Life on Planet Earth*, 2nd ed. (Cambridge, MA: MIT Press, 2000); Rick Potts, *Humanity's Descent: The Consequences of Ecological Instability* (New York: Avon Books, 1997); Paul Shepard, *Coming Home to the Pleistocene* (Washington, DC: Island Press, 1998), and Shepard, *The Others: How Animals Made Us Human* (Washington, DC: Island Press, 1996); Michael S. Alvard, "Evolutionary Theory, Conservation, and Human Environmental Impact," in *Wilderness and Political Ecology: Aboriginal Influences and the Original State of Nature*, ed. Charles E. Kay and Randy T. Simmons (Salt Lake City: University of Utah Press, 2002); Edmund Russell, "Evolutionary History: Prospectus for a New Field," *Environmental History* 8 (2003): 204–228; Edmund Russell, "Introduction. The Garden in the Machine: Toward an Evolutionary History of Technology," in *Industrializing Organisms: Introducing Evolutionary History*, ed. Susan R. Schrepfer and Philip Scranton (New York: Routledge, 2004), 1–16; Douglas J. Kennett, *The Island Chumash: Behavioral Ecology of a Maritime Society* (Berkeley: University of California Press, 2005); David P. Mindell, *The Evolving World: Evolution in Everyday Life* (Cambridge, MA: Harvard University Press, 2006); Paul Ehrlich and Anne H. Ehrlich, *The Dominant Animal: Human Evolution and the Environment* (Washington, DC: Island Press, 2008); Franz J. Broswimmer, *Ecocide: A Short History of the Mass Extinction of Species* (London: Pluto Press, 2002); Raphael D. Sagarin and Terence Taylor, *Natural Security: A Darwinian Approach to a Dangerous World* (Berkeley: University of California Press, 2008).

The two citations in the research register were to Anatoly N. Yamsov and Laura Rival. Other entries also use the term *evolution*, but I did not count them if they were using it in a generic or nonbiological sense (e.g., evolution of soils). It is possible I misunderstood entries and over- or under-counted, but the overall pattern of few entries certainly holds. "Documenting Environmental Change," Centre for History and Economics, King's College, Cambridge University, http://www-histecon.kings.cam.ac.uk/envdoc/.

2. Eric C. Stoykovich, "In the National Interest: Improving Domestic Animals and the Making of the United States, 1815–1870" (PhD dissertation, University of Virginia, 2009); Deborah Fitzgerald, *The Business of Breeding: Hybrid Corn in Illinois, 1890–1940* (Ithaca, NY: Cornell University Press, 1990); Deborah Fitzgerald, *Every Farm a Factory: The Industrial Ideal in American Agriculture* (New Haven, CT: Yale University Press, 2003); Joseph E. Taylor III, *Making Salmon: An Environmental History of the Northwest Fisheries Crisis* (Seattle: University of Washington Press, 1999); John H. Perkins, *Insects, Experts, and the Insecticide Crisis: The Quest for New Pest Management Strategies* (New York: Plenum Press, 1982); John H. Perkins, *Geopolitics and the Green Revolution: Wheat, Genes, and the Cold War* (New York: Oxford University Press, 1997); Harriet Ritvo, *The Animal Estate: The English and Other Creatures in the Victorian Age* (Cambridge, MA: Harvard University Press, 1987); Edmund Russell, *War and Nature: Fighting Humans and Insects with Chemicals from World War I to Silent Spring* (New York: Cambridge University Press, 2001).

3. Donald Worster, "Historians and Nature," *American Scholar*, (Spring 2010) http://www.theamericanscholar.org/historians-and-nature/; John R. McNeill, *Something New under the Sun: An Environmental History of the Twentieth-century World* (New York: W. W. Norton, 2000), 192–227; Philip Pomper and David Gary Shaw, eds., *The Return of Science: Evolution, History, and Theory* (Lanham, MD: Rowman and Littlefield, 2002); Daniel Lord Smail, *On Deep History and the Brain* (Berkeley: University of California Press, 2008).

4. Diamond, *Guns, Germs, and Steel: The Fates of Human Societies* (New York: W. W. Norton, 1998); Nicholas Russell, *Like Engend'ring Like: Heredity and Animal Breeding in Early Modern England* (Cambridge: Cambridge University Press, 1986), 216–218; J. Holden, J. Peacock, and T. Williams, eds., *Genes, Crops, and the Environment* (New York: Cambridge University Press, 1993).

5. Eric R. Pianka, *Evolutionary Ecology*, 6th ed. (San Francisco: Addison Wesley Longman, 2000), xiv. Douglas Futuyma's popular, eight-hundred-plus-page introductory textbook on evolutionary biology says little about domestication and omits Darwin's *Variation of Animals and Plants under Domestication* from its forty-one-page bibliography. The single indexed reference to breeding focuses on inbreeding and outbreeding in the wild. Domestication merits two brief mentions in the index to Ernst Mayr's 974-page opus on the growth of biological thought; "breeding" does not appear in the index. See Ernst Mayr, *The Growth of Biological Thought: Diversity, Evolution, and Inheritance* (Cambridge, MA: Belknap Press of Harvard University Press, 1982). (In a later work, Mayr argues that the study of animal breeding was critical for Darwin's theory. See *One Long Argument: Charles Darwin and*

the Genesis of Modern Evolutionary Thought [Cambridge, MA: Harvard University Press, 1991], 81–85) This pattern is not new. In *Origin*, Darwin chided his colleagues for not paying enough attention to domestic species. Charles Darwin, *On the Origin of Species by Means of Natural Selection; or The Preservation of Favoured Races in the Struggle for Life* (London: Odhams Press, [1859] 1872), 31.

Books by agricultural scientists often make a nod to evolution and then drop the topic. Evolution does not appear in the index of F. G. H. Lupton, ed., *Wheat Breeding: Its Scientific Basis* (London: Chapman and Hall, 1987). Evolution appears once, in the context of an "evolutionary breeding method" that relies on the idea that natural selection weeds out weaker individuals, in Oliver Mayo, *The Theory of Plant Breeding*, 2nd ed. (Oxford: Clarendon Press, 1987), 175. Evolution appears on the first page and not thereafter in R. F. E. Axford, S. C. Bishop, F. W. Nicholas, and J. B. Owen, *Breeding for Disease Resistance in Farm Animals*, 2nd ed. (New York: CABI, 2000), ix. Evolution appears in the introduction and not thereafter in Everett James Warwick and James Edwards Legates, *Breeding and Improvement of Farm Animals*, 7th ed. (New Delhi: TATA McGraw-Hill, 1979), 5–7. Evolution appears three times, in each case implying that evolution ended with domestication, in Temple Grandin, ed., *Genetics and the Behavior of Domestic Animals* (London: Academic Press, 1998), 21, 146, 204. In contrast, Lewis Stevens divided the evolution of domestic fowl into three stages: evolution of the genus *Gallus*, emergence of domestic fowl from ancestors in *Gallus*, and development of current varieties and breeds. See Lewis Stevens, *Genetics and Evolution of the Domestic Fowl* (New York: Cambridge University Press, 1991).

6. Pianka, *Evolutionary Ecology*, xiv, 10.
7. The titles of early works in environmental history illustrate the pervasive influence of ecology: William Cronon, *Changes in the Land: Indians, Colonists, and the Ecology of New England* (New York: Hill and Wang, 1983); Donald Worster, *Nature's Economy: A History of Ecological Ideas* (New York: Cambridge University Press, 1977); Carolyn Merchant, *The Death of Nature: Women, Ecology, and the Scientific Revolution* (San Francisco: Harper and Row, 1980), and Merchant, *Ecological Revolutions: Nature, Gender, and Science in New England* (Chapel Hill: University of North Carolina Press, 1989); Alfred Crosby, *Ecological Imperialism: The Biological Expansion of Europe, 900–1900* (New York: Cambridge University Press, 1986); J. Donald Hughes, *Ecology in Ancient Civilizations* (Albuquerque: University of New Mexico Press, 1975); Lester J. Bilsky, ed., *Historical Ecology: Essays on Environment and Social Change* (Port Washington, NY: Kennikat Press, 1980); Arthur F. McEvoy, *The Fisherman's Problem: Ecology and Law in the California Fisheries, 1850–1980* (New York: Cambridge University Press, 1986). In her popular textbook, Carolyn Merchant notes that *ecological history* and *environmental history* often have been used interchangeably; she subsumes the latter under the former. See Merchant, *Major Problems in Environmental History* (Lexington, MA: D. C. Heath, 1993), 1.

Public health histories that contributed to the founding of environmental history do not cluster around a single term, but *pollution* often appears. See, e.g., Martin Melosi, ed., *Pollution and Reform in American Cities, 1870–1930* (Austin: University of Texas Press, 1980). Joel Tarr's pioneering work first appeared largely in journals and is collected in his *The Search for the Ultimate Sink: Urban Pollution in Historical Perspective* (Akron, OH: University of Akron Press, 1996).

8. I thank Cheryl Oakes for conducting a keyword search for "ecolog" (ecology and its variants) and "health" in titles and nonindexed fields (including abstracts) in April 2010. Oakes to Russell, personal correspondence, April 13, 2010. Donald Worster urged environmental history to stay close to environmentalism in his comments at the plenary session, American Society for Environmental History meeting, Durham, NC, March 28, 2001.

9. E. B. Ford, *Ecological Genetics* (London: Methuen, 1964), and Pianka, *Evolutionary Ecology* (New York: Harper and Row, 1974). Both appeared in multiple editions.

10. Ecological ideas useful in analyzing these issues include connectivity among species (often via the ecosystem concept), stability through species diversity, limits to growth (carrying capacity), habitat change, population dynamics, and extinction. Environmental historians often have drawn on the ecologists who emphasized these issues such as Howard Odum, *Environment, Power, and Society* (New York: Wiley-Interscience, 1971), and Odum, *Systems Ecology: An Introduction* (New York: John Wiley, 1983); Eugene P. Odum and Howard Odum, *Fundamentals of Ecology*, 2nd ed. (Philadelphia: Saunders, 1959); Robert H. MacArthur, *Geographical Ecology: Patterns in the Distribution of Species* (New York: Harper and Row, 1972); Robert H. MacArthur and Joseph H. Connell, *The Biology of Populations* (New York: John Wiley, 1966); Charles S. Elton, *The Ecology of Invasions by Animals and Plants* (London: Methuen, 1958); Robert E. Ricklefs, *Ecology* (London: Nelson, 1973), and Elton, *The Economy of Nature: A Textbook in Basic Ecology*, 4th ed. (New York: W. H. Freeman, 1996); Paul R. Ehrlich, Anne H. Ehrlich, and John P. Holdren, *Ecoscience: Population, Resources, Environment* (San Francisco: W. H. Freeman, 1977), and Ehrlich et al., *Human Ecology: Problems and Solutions* (San Francisco: W. H. Freeman, 1973).

11. On sociobiology, see Edward O. Wilson, *Sociobiology: The New Synthesis* (Cambridge, MA: Belknap Press of Harvard University Press, 1975), and Wilson, *Consilience: The Unity of Knowledge* (London: Little, Brown, 1998); David P. Barash, *Sociobiology and Behavior*, 2nd ed. (New York: Elsevier, 1982); Richard Dawkins, *The Selfish Gene* (New York: Oxford University Press, 1976); Peter Koslowski, ed., *Sociobiology and Bioeconomics: The Theory of Evolution in Biological and Economic Theory* (New York: Springer, 1999); Michael S. Gregory, Anita Silvers, and Diane Sutch, eds., *Sociobiology and Human Nature: An Interdisciplinary Critique and Defense* (San Francisco: Jossey-Bass, 1978); Georg Breur, *Sociobiology and the Human Dimension* (New York: Cambridge University Press, 1982); Alexander Rosenberg, *Sociobiology and the Preemption of Social Science* (Baltimore: Johns Hopkins University Press, 1980); Robert W. Bell and Nancy J. Bell, *Sociobiology*

and the Social Sciences (Lubbock: Texas Tech University Press, 1989); Arthur L. Caplan, ed., *The Sociobiology Debate: Readings on Ethical and Scientific Issues* (New York: Harper and Row, 1978); Ashley Montagu, ed., *Sociobiology Examined* (New York: Oxford University Press, 1980); Michael Ruse, *Sociobiology: Sense or Nonsense?* (Boston: D. Reidel, 1984); Matt Ridley, *The Red Queen: Sex and the Evolution of Human Nature* (New York: Viking, 1993).

Some philosophers have treated evolution as a source of new questions or approaches within their fields. Evolutionary ethicists, e.g., have treated Charles Darwin's *Origin of Species* (1859) and Edward O. Wilson's *Sociobiology* (1975) as challenging them to see whether one can develop an ethics based on genetic evolution. See Paul Thompson, ed., *Issues in Evolutionary Ethics* (Albany: State University of New York Press, 1995), back cover; Emmanuel K. Twesigye, *Religion and Ethics for a New Age: Evolutionist Approach* (Lanham, MD: University Press of America, 2001). For supporters of evolution in philosophy, see Michael Ruse, *The Darwinian Paradigm: Essays on Its History, Philosophy, and Religious Implications* (New York: Routledge, 1993); Daniel C. Dennett, *Freedom Evolves* (New York: Viking, 2003), and Ruse, *Darwin's Dangerous Idea: Evolution and the Meanings of Life* (New York: Simon and Schuster, 1995).

On evolutionary psychology, see Henry Plotkin, *Evolution in Mind: An Introduction to Evolutionary Psychology* (London: Penguin, 1997); Susan Blackmore, *The Meme Machine* (New York: Oxford University Press, 1999); Charles Crawford and Dennis L. Krebs, eds., *Handbook of Evolutionary Psychology: Ideas, Issues, and Applications* (Mahwah, NJ: Lawrence Erlbaum Associates, 1998); Louise Barrett, Robin Dunbar, and John Lycett, *Human Evolutionary Psychology* (Princeton, NJ: Princeton University Press, 2002); Steven Pinker, *The Blank Slate: The Modern Denial of Human Nature* (New York: Viking, 2002), and Pinker, *How the Mind Works* (New York: W. W. Norton, 1997); David F. Bjorklund and Anthony D. Pellegrini, *The Origins of Human Nature: Evolutionary Developmental Psychology* (Washington, DC: American Psychological Association, 2002); Alan Clamp, *Evolutionary Psychology* (London: Hodder and Stoughton, 2001); David M. Buss, *Evolutionary Psychology: The New Science of the Mind* (Boston: Allyn and Bacon, 1999); Robert Wright, *The Moral Animal: Evolutionary Psychology and Everyday Life* (New York: Pantheon Books, 1994); Jerome H. Barkow, Leda Cosmides, and John Tooby, eds., *The Adapted Mind: Evolutionary Psychology and the Generation of Culture* (New York: Oxford University Press, 1992). For the case against evolutionary psychology, see Hilary Rose and Steven Rose, eds., *Alas, Poor Darwin: Arguments against Evolutionary Psychology* (London: Jonathan Cape, 2000).

For social studies of science and technology, see Joseph E. Taylor III, *Making Salmon: An Environmental History of the Northwest Fisheries Crisis* (Seattle: University of Washington Press, 1999), 10; Steve W. Fuller, *Philosophy, Rhetoric, and the End of Knowledge: The Coming of Science and Technology Studies* (Madison: University of Wisconsin Press, 1993); Bruno Latour, *Science in Action: How to Follow Scientists and Engineers through*

Society (Cambridge, MA: Harvard University Press, 1987); Bruno Latour and Steve Woolgar, *Laboratory Life: The Social Construction of Scientific Facts* (Beverly Hills, CA: Sage, 1979); Sheila Jasanoff, Gerald E. Markle, James C. Petersen, and Trevor Pinch, eds., *Handbook of Science and Technology Studies* (Thousand Oaks, CA: Sage, 1995); Ruth Schwartz Cowan, *More Work for Mother: The Ironies of Household Technology from the Open Hearth to the Microwave* (New York: Basic Books, 1983); Claude S. Fischer, *America Calling: A Social History of the Telephone to 1940* (Berkeley: University of California Press, 1992); Donna Haraway, *Simians, Cyborgs, and Women: The Reinvention of Nature* (New York: Routledge, 1991); Thomas Parke Hughes, *Networks of Power: Electrification in Western Society, 1880–1930* (Baltimore: Johns Hopkins University Press, 1983); Donald A. Mackenzie, *Inventing Accuracy: An Historical Sociology of Nuclear Missile Guidance* (Cambridge, MA: MIT Press, 1990); Ruth Oldenziel, *Making Technology Masculine: Men, Women, and Modern Machines in America, 1870–1945* (Amsterdam, Netherlands: Amsterdam University Press, 1999); Londa Schiebinger, *Nature's Body: Gender in the Making of Modern Science* (Boston: Beacon Press, 1993); Wiebe E. Bijker, Thomas P. Hughes, and Trevor J. Pinch, eds., *The Social Construction of Technological Systems: New Directions in the Sociology and History of Technology* (Cambridge, MA: MIT Press, 1987).

For sharply critical views of science and technology, see Theodor W. Adorno and Max Horkheimer, *Dialectic of Enlightenment* (1944; repr. London: Verso, 1997), 4, 6; Jacques Ellul, *The Technological Society* (1964; repr. New York: Knopf, 1973); David F. Noble, *America by Design: Science, Technology, and the Rise of Corporate Capitalism* (New York: Knopf, 1977); Langdon Winner, *The Whale and the Reactor: A Search for Limits in an Age of High Technology* (Chicago: University of Chicago Press, 1986).

On biological determinism, see Virginia Scharff, "Man and Nature! Sex Secrets of Environmental History," in Herron and Kirk, *Human/Nature*, 31–48, and Vera Norwood, "Constructing Gender in Nature: Bird Society through the Eyes of John Burroughs and Florence Merriam Bailey," ibid., 49–62; Daniel J. Kevles, *In the Name of Eugenics: Genetics and the Uses of Human Heredity* (New York: Knopf, 1985); Nicholas W. Gillham, *A Life of Sir Francis Galton: From African Exploration to the Birth of Eugenics* (New York: Oxford University Press, 2001); Carl N. Degler, *In Search of Human Nature: The Decline and Revival of Darwinism in American Social Thought* (New York: Oxford University Press, 1991); Alexander Rosenberg, *Darwinism in Philosophy, Social Science, and Policy* (New York: Cambridge University Press, 2000); Ronald L. Numbers and John Stenhouse, eds., *Disseminating Darwinism: The Role of Place, Race, Religion, and Gender* (New York: Cambridge University Press, 1999); Mike Hawkins, *Social Darwinism in European and American Thought, 1860–1945: Nature as Model and Nature as Threat* (New York: Cambridge University Press, 1997).

12. Stephen Jay Gould, *The Mismeasure of Man* (New York: W. W. Norton, 1996); Richard C. Lewontin, *The Triple Helix: Gene, Organism, and Environment* (Cambridge, MA: Harvard University Press, 2000); Richard C.

Lewontin, Steven Rose, and Leon J. Kamin, *Not in Our Genes: Biology, Ideology, and Human Nature* (New York: Pantheon Books, 1984); Luigi Luca Cavalli-Sforza, *Genes, Peoples, and Languages* (Berkeley: University of California Press, 2000); Lynn Margulis, *The Symbiotic Planet: A New Look at Evolution* (London: Weidenfeld and Nicolson, 1998), 3; Paul Ehrlich, *Human Natures: Genes, Cultures, and the Human Prospect* (Washington, DC: Island Press, 2000).

13. Douglas J. Futuyma, *Evolutionary Biology*, 3rd ed. (Sunderland, MA: Sinauer Associates, 1998), 5–6 (emphasis in original).

14. George C. Williams and R. M. Nesse, "The Dawn of Darwinian Medicine," *Quarterly Review of Biology* 66 (1991): 16–18. See also Paul W. Ewald, *Evolution of Infectious Disease* (New York: Oxford University Press, 1994); Randolph M. Nesse and George C. Williams, *Why We Get Sick: The New Science of Darwinian Medicine* (New York: Times Books, 1994). For a wider view, see J. J. Bull and H. A. Wichman, "Applied Evolution," *Annual Review of Ecology and Systematics* 32 (2001): 183–217. On HIV evolution, see Scott Freeman and Jon C. Herron, *Evolutionary Analysis* (Englewood Cliffs, NJ: Prentice Hall, 1998); K. A. Crandall, ed., *HIV Evolution* (Baltimore: Johns Hopkins University Press, 1999).

15. On evolutionary economics, see John Laurent and John Nightingale, *Darwinism and Evolutionary Economics* (Cheltenham, UK: Edward Elgar, 2001); Richard R. Nelson and Sidney G. Winter, *An Evolutionary Theory of Economic Change* (Cambridge, MA: Belknap Press of Harvard University Press, 1982); Jack J. Vromen, *Economic Evolution: An Enquiry into the Foundations of New Institutional Economics* (London: Routledge, 1995). For an application of evolutionary economics to the environment, see John M. Gowdy, *Coevolutionary Economics: The Economy, Society, and the Environment* (Boston: Kluwer, 1994).

On evolutionary approaches to culture, see William H. Durham, *Coevolution: Genes, Culture, and Human Diversity* (Palo Alto, CA: Stanford University Press, 1991); Richard Dawkins, *The Selfish Gene* (New York: Oxford University Press, 1976); Luca Cavalli-Sforza and M. W. Feldman, *Cultural Transmission and Evolution: A Quantitative Approach* (Princeton, NJ: Princeton University Press, 1981); Robert Boyd and Peter J. Richerson, *Culture and the Evolutionary Process* (Chicago: University of Chicago Press, 1985); Charles J. Lumsden and Edward O. Wilson, *Genes, Mind, and Culture* (Cambridge, MA: Harvard University Press, 1981). For an effort to develop a common literature of evolution in social sciences, see Johann Peter Murmann, "Evolutionary Theory in the Social Sciences," http://www.etss.net/.

Some historians have applied selectionist models to the history of ideas. See Walter Vincenti, *What Engineers Know and How They Know It* (Baltimore: Johns Hopkins University Press, 1990); Robert J. Richards, *Darwin and the Emergence of Evolutionary Theories of Mind and Behavior* (Chicago: University of Chicago Press, 1987).

Darwin's theory of evolution through natural selection has inspired three approaches to computer programming now grouped under "evolutionary algorithms." See David E. Clark, ed., *Evolutionary Algorithms in Molecular Design* (New York: Wiley-VCH, 2000); Thomas Back, *Evolutionary Algorithms in Theory and Practice: Evolutionary Strategies, Evolutionary Programming, Genetic Algorithms* (New York: Oxford University Press, 1996); Mukesh Patel, Vasant Honavar, and Karthik Balakrishnan, *Advances in the Evolutionary Synthesis of Intelligent Agents* (Cambridge, MA: MIT Press, 2001).

16. Library of Congress subject headings include evolutionary computation, evolutionary economics, and evolutionary programming. The heading for evolutionary ethics is "ethics, evolutionary." Evolutionary psychology appears under "genetic psychology."

12. Conclusion

1. Jared M. Diamond, *Guns, Germs, and Steel: The Fates of Human Societies* (New York: W. W. Norton, 1999).

Note on Sources

1. Edmund Russell, "Science and Environmental History," *Environmental History* 10 (2005): 80–82.

Index

acclimatizing, 171. *See also* adaptation

adaptability of populations and species, 32, 39–41, 52

adaptation, 76–77, 162, 164, 171. *See also* eradication, selection (*all types*), hunting, fishing, resistance

advertising as evolutionary force, 34, 158

agriculture, 49, 53–56, 66, 136–137, 156. *See also agricultural species by common names*, methodical selection, unconscious selection, domestication

alleles. *See* genetics

Amerindians and Industrial Revolution, 104–105, 108, 110–111, 127, 152

anthropocene, 49

anthropogenic, 171

antibiotics. *See* resistance

Arkwright, Richard, 105, 114–115

art as evolutionary force, 153–154

artificial selection. *See* selection, artificial

Ashton, T. S., 110

Bacillus thuringiensis. *See* cotton, genetic engineering

bacteria, 43–45. *See also* resistance

Baines, Edward, 110–111

Bayer, 79–80

beaver. *See* Yellowstone National Park

beefalo, 78

behavior. *See* culture, coevolution

Belyaev, Dmitri, 61–64

bighorn sheep. *See* sheep, bighorn

biological, 171

biology, evolutionary, 153–165. *See also aspects of evolution such as* selection, inheritance, populations, sampling effects

biotechnologies, 133–134, 152, 171 as factories, 136–137; as products, 138–139; as technological innovation, 139–142; as workers, 137–138

Biotechnology Industry Organization, 134

bison. *See* hunting

bollworm, 81–82

Bosch, Karl, 136

Boyd, William, 140

breed, 171. *See also* varieties

breeding, 171. *See also* selection, methodical

Brinkhous, Kenneth, 137

Budiansky, Stephen, 69

capitalism as evolutionary force, 75. *See also* advertising, corporations, industry, Industrial Revolution

Caribbean, 109, 111–115

Cartwright, Edmund, 105

cattle, 138–139

causation, 100

Cavalli-Sforza, Luca, 89, 148

chance, 15, 172

chicken, 139

class as evolutionary force, 75

climate, 49–52

cloning, 82–83, 165, 172

coal. *See* industry

coca. *See* resistance
cod, 27–28, 97
coevolution, 172
    behavior and multiple traits, 94–95;
    concept, 85; culture and genes,
    95–102; domestication, 69–70; insects
    and insecticides, xviii; lactose
    tolerance and dairying, 91–94; plants
    and human skin color, 3; skin color
    and domestic plants and animals,
    89–90; Red Queen hypothesis, 141
Columbus, Christopher, 111, 113
contingency, 149
convenience as evolutionary force, 160
Coppinger, Raymond P., 69
corporations as evolutionary forces, 39
cotton
    anthropogenic evolution, 108–109;
    carding, 117; data on length and
    strength, 113; domestication, 66–68,
    108–109; Egypt, 119; English imports,
    114–116; genetic engineering, 78–82;
    genetics, 104, 121–124; herbicide
    resistance, 79–80; hybridizing, 76;
    importance of New World fiber for
    machines, 104, 111–121, 152; India,
    119–121, 124–127; insect resistance
    to genetically engineered varieties,
    81–82; Industrial Revolution,
    overview, 103–105; New World and
    Old World species, 104, 108–109,
    111–128; pest control, 78–79; prices,
    117–119; species and varieties, 71–74,
    78. *See also* (New World and Old
    World species *in this entry*); spinning
    and weaving, 104, 107–110, 116;
    transportation of varieties, 76–77;
    United States, 106–107, 109, 111,
    119
cotton gin. *See* Whitney, Eli
cottonwood. *See* Yellowstone National
    Park
Crompton, Samuel, 105, 114–115
culling, 73–74, 77, 163, 172. *See also*
    selection, unconscious
cultivar, 172. *See also* varieties
culture, 95–102, 172. *See also* coevolution

Darwin, Charles, xvii, 6, 10–11, 14–16,
    172
Dawkins, Richard, 96

DDT. *See* resistance
determinism, technological, 139–140
    biological, 140, 148; genetic, 173
Diamond, Jared, 146, 161
disease. *See* resistance
DNA. *See* genetics
dogs, 54, 58, 63, 65, 75, 137–138
domestic plants and animals. *See*
    domestication, *species by common
    names*, varieties
domestication, 3, 16, 69–70, 173
    importance for human history, 54–56,
    162; animals, 56, 61–66; plants, 56,
    66–69; hypotheses, 57–60. *See also*
    coevolution; cotton; selection,
    methodical; selection, unconscious
drift, genetic, 173. *See also* sampling
    effects

ecology. *See* environments
economics, 48. *See also* industry,
    corporations, Industrial Revolution,
    cotton
economics, evolutionary, 150
Egypt, 76–77
Ehrlich, Paul, 148
elephants. *See* hunting
elk. *See* Yellowstone National Park
energy. *See* technology, industry
engineering, genetic, 78–83, 133–134, 160,
    165, 173
England, 103–105, 110. *See also* Industrial
    Revolution, cotton
environments, 40–42ff., 173
    human impact, 2, 49. *See also* bacteria,
    climate, moths, predation,
    Yellowstone National Park
Envirotech, 133
epigenetics, 12, 173
eradication defined, 31
evolution, 6ff., 172–173
    anthropogenic, 14, 55–56, 107, 151;
    cultural, 172; Darwinian, 172. *See
    also human activities that affect
    evolution* (e.g., hunting, fishing,
    eradication, domestication),
    *evolutionary processes that people
    affect* (e.g., selection, sampling effects,
    mutagenesis), *and consequences* (e.g.,
    Industrial Revolution)
evolution rates. *See* adaptability

extinction, 15, 23–24, 49, 52, 76, 83–84, 165, 173

farming. *See* agriculture
fashion as evolutionary force, 155
Finlay, Mark, 138
fish. *See* fishing *and common names of species*
fishing, 25–29, 49, 156
    size selection, 26–29, 97, 162. *See also common names of species*
Fitzgerald, Deborah, 74, 140, 146
Fitzgerald, Gerard, 139
flies, fruit, 51
flies, screwworm, 83
fly shuttle. *See* Kay, John
folate. *See* vitamin B
founder effect, 173. *See also* sampling effects
foxes, domestication, 61–65
fruit flies. *See* flies, fruit
Fu-Tuan, Yi 69
fustian, 114
Futuyma, Douglas, 149

Galapagos Islands, 8
genes, 173. *See also* genetics, epigenetics
genetic engineering. *See* engineering, genetic
genetics, 11–12, 25. *See also* engineering, genetic; inheritance; mutation; recombination; hybridizing; sampling effects; variation
geopolitics as evolutionary force, 75. *See also* states
germs. *See* resistance
Gould, Stephen Jay, 148
government. *See* states
Grant, Peter and Rosemary, 8

Haber, Fritz, 136
habitat. *See* environments
Hargreaves, James, 105, 115–116
Harley, C. Knick, 106
Hartwell, R. M., 106
herbicides. *See* resistance, cotton
heritability, 173
history of art, 153–160
history of medicine, 153–165
history of science, 153–165

history of technology, 132ff., 152–165. *See also* biotechnologies, industry, Industrial Revolution, innovation
history, diplomatic, 153–165
history, economic, 153–165
history, environmental
    use of ecology and public health, 147–148; use of evolution, 152–165; use of evolutionary biology, 145–146
history, evolutionary, defined, 4–5, 173
history, political, 153–160. *See also* states
history, social, 153–165
Hobsbawm, Eric, 106
Hornborg, Alf, 106, 111
Horowitz, Roger, 139
hunting, 4, 156
    bighorn sheep, 19–21; bison, 21–25; elephants, 17–19, 25, 153; size selection, 20
hunting and gathering, 55, 58–60, 65, 89
hybridizing, 74–76, 164, 174

imperialism as evolutionary force, 160
inbreeding 82, 165, 174. *See also* selection, methodical
Indians (Americas). *See* Amerindians
Indians (Asia), 104, 111, 116, 119, 124–127
Industrial Revolution, 3, 47
    anthropogenic evolution as catalyst, 104–105, 108–111; dependence on nature, 130–131; England, 103–105; inventors and inventions, 105–106; reliance on New World, 111–121; role of genomic differences in cotton, 122–128; role of slave trade, 128–130; schools of historians, 105–107; summary of contrasts between current literature and arguments in this book, 130, 151–152. *See also* cotton *and inventors by last name*
industry, 47–48. *See also* cotton, Monsanto, Bayer
inheritance, 8, 10–12, 40, 82–83, 95, 174
innovation, 139–142. *See also* Industrial Revolution
insecticides. *See* resistance; cotton
insects. *See* resistance; cotton

insurgency as evolutionary force, 157
intentionality, of people when shaping
　　evolution, 57–59, 67, 71, 109. *See also*
　　culling; extinction; selection, artificial;
　　selection, methodical; selection,
　　unconscious
inventions. *See* Industrial Revolution
inventors. *See* Industrial Revolution,
　　inventors by last name
Israel, Paul, 134
ivory. *See* hunting

Kay, John, 105, 115
Kloppenburg, Jack, 75, 140

lactase persistence. *See* lactose tolerance
lactose tolerance, 91–94
Lamarckian evolution, 11, 173
Lancashire, 104–105, 114–115
Landes, David, 108, 111
Laughlin, Jimmy, 137
Lewontin, Richard, 148
Line (plant or animal), 174. *See also*
　　varieties
lines. *See* varieties
Liverpool, 114, 129

malaria. *See* resistance
Mann, Julia de Lacy, 128
Mantoux, Paul, 106
Marx, Karl, 106
Marx, Leo, 135
master breeder hypothesis or narrative, 57,
　　174
mating, selective. *See* selection, methodical
McCloskey, Donald, 106
McNeill, John, 107, 146
medicine, evolutionary, 149–150
　　as evolutionary force, 156
Mehta, Makrand, 107
meme, 96, 174
methodical selection. *See* selection,
　　methodical
Mexico, 109
Mokyr, Joel, 105–108, 111,
　　114
Monsanto, 79–82
Mosley, Stephen, 107
mosquitoes, 51. *See also* resistance
moths, peppered, 45–49
　　diamondback, 81

mule (spinning machine). *See* Crompton,
　　Samuel
music as evolutionary force, 155
mustard. *See* climate
mutation, 12, 77–78
　　mutagenesis, 83, 164

Native Americans. *See* Amerindians
natural selection. *See* selection, natural

O'Brien, Patrick, 107, 111
obesity, 43–45
Olmstead, Alan, 107, 110, 141,
　　147
organisms as technology, 135–136. *See*
　　also biotechnologies

passenger pigeon. *See* pigeon, passenger
pathogens. *See* resistance
Paul, Lewis, 105, 115
Pemberton, Stephen, 137
peppered moths. *See* moths, peppered
Perkin, Harold, 107, 130–131
Perkins, John, 69, 75, 140, 146
pesticides. *See* resistance; cotton
Pianka, Eric, 147
pigeon, passenger, 52
pigs, 136, 138
Polanyi, Karl, 106
policy. *See* states as evolutionary forces
Pollan, Michael, 69
pollution. *See* industry
Pomeranz, Kenneth, 106, 111
Pomper, Philip, 146
populations, 8, 10, 12, 15, 40, 174. *See*
　　also names of species
poverty as evolutionary force, 155
predation 46, 49–50
preserves, nature, 52
profit seeking as evolutionary force,
　　157
psychology, evolutionary, 150

Radkau, Joachim, 107
railroad. *See* technology
rainforests, 53
recombination, 78, 174
recreation as evolutionary force,
　　154
Red Queen hypotheses. *See* coevolution
reproduction, 8, 11, 27, 40–41, 174

resistance, 174
 insects to insecticides, xvii–xviii; malaria
  to drugs and mosquitoes to
  insecticides, 35–36, 100; number of
  species resistant to pesticides, 38;
  pathogens to antibiotics, 1–2, 10–11,
  32–36, 35–36, 97–101; plants to
  herbicides, 36–38. *See also* cotton
Rhode, Paul, 107, 110, 141, 147
rickets, 88
rifle. *See* technology
Ritvo, Harriet, 75, 140, 146
Rostow, Walter, 106
Russell, Nicholas, 146–147

salmon. *See* fishing
sampling effects, 15–16, 175
 founder effect, 24–25; genetic drift, 25;
  inbreeding, 82
Schrepfer, Susan, 107, 134
science as evolutionary force, 160
Scranton, Philip, 107, 134
selection, artificial, 12–14, 171
selection, general, 175
selection, methodical, 10, 14, 55, 74–75,
 82, 108, 139–142, 146–147, 163,
 174–175
selection, natural, xvii, 10, 12, 14–15
selection, sexual, 10, 23, 175
selection, size. *See* fishing, hunting
selection, unconscious, 10, 14, 17–18, 55,
 58, 60, 66–70, 108, 175. *See also*
 domestication, eradication, fishing,
 hunting, resistance
selective mating. *See* selection, methodical
sexual selection. *See* selection, sexual
Shaw, David Gary, 146
sheep, bighorn. *See* hunting
silverside (fish), 27–29
Simmons, I. G., 107
skin color, 85–91
slave trade, 104–105, 128–130
Smail, Daniel Lord, 146
smallpox, 84
Smith, Charles K., 69
soap. *See* resistance
sociobiology, 150
speciation, 6, 22, 175
species, 15, 43
spinning jenny. *See* Hargreaves, James
spinning. *See* cotton

squirrels, 52
staphylococcus, 97–99
states as evolutionary forces, 18–20, 28,
 36–39, 44–45, 48–49, 76–77,
 153–160
Steinberg, Theodore, 107
sterility, 83, 175
Stoykovich, Eric, 146
strain, 175. *See also* varieties
Strutt family, 117
suburbs, 45
susceptibility, 175. *See also* resistance
synthesis, modern, of evolutionary biology
 and genetics, 11–12
synthesis, neo-Darwinian. *See* synthesis,
 modern

Taylor, Joseph, 146
technology as evolutionary force
 concept of, 135; energy, 48; insect
  control, 39; railroad, 24; rifle, 24; role
  of nature, 135
textiles. *See* cotton
Thompson, E. P., 106
Thorsheim, Peter, 107
Toynbee, Arnold, 106
trade as evolutionary force, 155–156
traits, 175
 cultural, 172; genetic, 173. *See also*
  evolution *and* selection (all types)
transportation to increase variation, 76
triclosan. *See* resistance
tularemia, 139
tusklessness. *See* hunting, elephants

unconscious selection. *See* selection,
 unconscious
United States government. *See* states

variation, 8, 10, 12, 40, 72–73, 82, 175.
 See also cotton, mutation,
  recombination, varieties
varieties, 14–15, 66, 72–76, 175
vitamin B, 87
vitamin D, 87–90

Wadsworth, Alfred, 128
war as evolutionary force, 39, 76–77, 157
water frame. *See* Arkwright
weaving. *See* cotton
weeds, 51, 80

West Indies. *See* Caribbean
whitefish, 27
Whitney, Eli, 106, 118–119
Williams, Eric, 128
wolves, 58–60, 65. *See also* Yellowstone
National Park

World Health Organization, 84
Worster, Donald, 146
Wrigley, E. A., 106
Wyatt, John, 115

Yellowstone National Park, 49–50